PR

"I thoroughly enjoyed this fast-paced, darkly funny, and compulsively readable novel about unexpected fatherhood, international politics, and finding one's place in the world. With a sharp eye for detail and a great ear for dialogue, Belletto shows us how the personal and political are always— thrillingly, dangerously, and emotionally—connected."
ALIX OHLIN, AUTHOR OF *We Want What We Want*

"An adventure story that subverts the genre's tropes, Belletto's blazingly intelligent and often wildly funny novel explores the possibility that what we never wanted may turn out to be exactly what we need. This marvelously surprising and deeply moving novel fulfills a demanding task: it shows us how, against all odds, buried courage may be uncovered and a human heart may expand."
LEE UPTON, AUTHOR OF *Visitations*

"In *For You I Would Make an Exception*, Steven Belletto takes the reader on adventures from the US to Kenya to Bihar and back as he examines, hilariously and elegantly, the wild ride of any kind of love. An astute chronicler of the complex and changing geopolitics of our time, acclaimed scholar Belletto's first novel is immersive and riveting; I could not put it down."
JENNIFER GILMORE, AUTHOR OF *The Mothers*

"Steven Belletto's *For You I Would Make an Exception* is a Swiss Army knife of a novel: an academic novel that is also a travel novel that is also a novel of manners that is also a coming-of-age novel. Or rather, a coming-of-age novel about a man who is forced to come of age years after he should have come of age. Funny, spot-on, and surprisingly moving, this is a wonderful novel that shows us that it's never too late to leave home and grow up."
BROCK CLARKE, AUTHOR OF *Who Are You- Calvin Bledsoe?*

"Intelligent and laden with surprises. This marvelous and wittily titled novel is full of news of the way we live now."
LORRIE MOORE, AUTHOR OF *I Am Homeless If This Is Not My Home*

ABOUT THE AUTHOR

Steven Belletto is author of two books of literary criticism, *No Accident, Comrade*, and *The Beats: A Literary History*. His short fiction and travel writing have appeared in such venues as *Cimarron Review*, *Los Angeles Review of Books Quarterly Journal*, and *Wisconsin Review*. He lives in Westport with his dog.

stevenbelletto.com

FOR
YOU I
WOULD
MAKE
AN

EXCEPTION

STEVEN
BELLETTO

www.vineleavespress.com

In the five hindrances men and angels
stay caught in the net, in the immense nets
which spread out across each plane of being, the multiple nets
which hamper at each step of the ladders as the angels
and the demons
and men
go up and down

Charles Olson, "As the Dead Prey Upon Us"

1.

ANGIE STAYED OVER a third night in a row and had apparently forgotten to take her birth control before leaving for her breakfast shift. "No big deal," she texted, but wanted to make sure I brought the pills to her show later that day. After the initial message, she clarified the urgency of the situation with a few jokes about fatherhood and a surreal meme involving Octomom, so I finally dragged myself out of bed. "Aren't you supposed to be working?" I texted.

"Multitasker," she wrote back. "And it really is in your best interest not to forget those guys."

I shuffled into the bathroom and found the mauve clamshell in the basket we had designated for her stuff, a move that had been a major development for me, although I had played it off like it wasn't, and I put the pills next to my keys on the kitchen counter. I sent her photographic evidence of the arrangement, and topped it off with a complaint about being awake at 6:30 a.m. Even the cats were still sleeping.

"That's what you get for keeping me up late," she wrote.

The night before, I had been trying to illustrate appellations of California pinots using examples from various wine clubs I belonged to, but Angie was Pennsylvanian through and through, and so hadn't really appreciated the nuances. We still got drunk, though. She enjoyed wine, in fact loved going to local wineries, felt it was a sophisticated date activity, but Pennsylvania produced the worst I had ever tasted— so bad that I hesitated to even call it wine. Angie argued that it wasn't about the wine as such, but the experience of discovering out-of-the way vineyards, which she found "charming" and "picturesque." I thought these places were picturesque in the way an Olive Garden was picturesque, with lots of stonework—or faux-painted stone—muted Tuscan yellows, dusty vines, and unnerving expanses of grape-related paraphernalia for sale. On weekends there were usually smooth jazz quartets and klatches of women bubbling with anticipation about the sugary juices on offer, candy-colored abominations with names like *Strawberry Kiss*. Once during a barrel tasting I had asked the wine maker why they were aging in plastic totes, and he explained that barrels were overrated because he could source oak chips at volume discounts, and since the tote plastic was BPA-free, it never leeched into the product. This method produced much the same results as barrel aging, if not superior results, because he could pass the savings on to his customers.

"Pennsylvania strikes again," I said to Angie as we were walking to the car, and she punched me in the arm for disparaging her native state.

—

With the pills secured, I dozed off for a few more hours but was again awakened, this time by a call from the chair of my department, Mark. We were friends, both veterans of the local dating scene, had spent years going on benders at fern bars and supper clubs until he finally gave up and married someone from the sociology department. Last year he had been appointed department chair and now his days were mainly about fielding neurotic grievances from our colleagues. I knew he had recently been dealing with a parent who was incensed on her daughter's behalf about a grade I had given this daughter in my Psychopathology in Literature course. The daughter had earned a B+, and B+ students (and their parents) were historically the most likely to feel a sense of injustice at being denied an A. I had never of course heard from the student herself, but her mother had been harassing Mark and threatening to take the case to the President and the Board of Trustees. Mark was doing his best to hold the line, but this woman had been so persistent and annoying that he was desperate, was now calling to appeal to our friendship.

"I swear to god this woman is insane," he said. "She's deluging me with emails and cc-ing the Deans about how her daughter *needs* to get into med school, that this course was an elective anyway, and that you're penalizing her for expressing conservative views."

"This is why we went to graduate school?" I said sleepily.

"Can you please just speak with her? I'll buy you a bottle of Glenlivet."

"Isn't it some sort of HIPAA violation to even be communicating with the mother in the first place? A breach of confidentiality? Or is it FERPA?"

"Do me this kindness, please. I'm dying."

I refused, on general principle, citing academic freedom.

"I already gave her your information," Mark said, and at that instant I was getting a new call from an unknown number.

I may have called him an asshole.

"Whatever you want to do," he said quickly, "I've got your back. You're the man!" He hung up before I could say anything else.

The mother began with tense, extravagant civility, asking to please speak with Professor Sorley because she was interested in discussing what she perceived as irregularities regarding how final course grades had been calculated. I was polite back, pretending to be genuinely surprised to hear from her. She made her case, but the more I stonewalled, the more manic and high-pitched she became, and I imagined this woman in her 1.2 million dollar house in Basking Ridge, squeezed into Spandex and leaning against a quartz kitchen island the size of a swimming pool. As she pressed me, she was getting herself really worked up that this lowlife professor wasn't immediately folding to her demands, and I pictured the veins in her temples straining her Botox and fillers. She had several arguments prepared, said she would hate to have me censured (whatever that meant), and I let her talk and talk and talk.

This is what my so-called Dream Job amounted to. Six years prior and against all odds, I had managed to get hired teaching literature at a minor college in Pennsylvania, a job that, weirdly, thousands of my peers would have killed for. How did this happen? Luck. Happenstance. At some point during the interview I must have mentioned a book or TV show one of the search committee members liked. Or I appeared unthreatening. Or drank just enough over dinner to seem potentially companionable. I'm sure this last was how I got Mark's vote; *institutions reproduce themselves*, said Pierre Bourdieu or Robespierre.

That was back in 2007, just before the economy melted down, and once Lehman Brothers imploded, through some intricate web of finance I didn't really understand, higher ed cratered too, and I watched the prospects of my friends and acquaintances from graduate school disappear as if by sinkhole. I did my best to double down so as not to get fired, developing a roster of shameless courses like Psychopathology in Literature, laboring over articles no one would ever read, and volunteering for committees on which my fellow faculty wrestled with issues they truly considered weighty. During this time I saw most of my friends accept teaching posts at high schools or nebulous roles at start-ups where they were paid very little to be "creative." Once I'd been hired, they could barely contain their jealousy that I was technically able to make payments on my student loans while they remained in forbearance limbo, had several degrees but would still qualify for the Earned Income tax credit well into their thirties.

And yet despite my good fortune at landing a legitimate job, I couldn't bring myself to feel as elated as my friends demanded. Instead, I never shook the nagging interior terror that I was probably going to die in Pennsylvania. That's an OK fate for lovers of *Strawberry Kiss*, but I'm a fifth-generation Californian, and never imagined I'd be living out my days in an overpriced "loft-style" apartment in a rusted industrial center well beyond its glory days. The college racket didn't care for anyone's geographical preferences, of course, and the horrible irony was that after you attended graduate school in a city or town that was a hive of stimulation, ideally on a coast, you applied for jobs as widely as possible, even in North Dakota and the Deep South, and then gladly took whatever was dangled. This is how I wound up in Pennsylvania, asphyxiating, more or less, in a valley cordoned from Manhattan by the state of New Jersey.

On my job interview, after the last official event, Mark was excited to take me for a beer and the off-the-record scoop on the area. He was only two or three years in himself, and since we were both single at the time, he felt free to explain how meeting people locally was out of the question, but that we were within "striking distance" of New York City, and that New York women were all some combination of neuropathologist, art history minor, print model, and trust fundee—and that they were almost universally turned on by intellectuals. In hindsight, I never really knew if Mark was deluded or had been deliberately misleading me, but as I discovered after taking the job, local women were indeed undatable, but he himself couldn't stand the stale gasoline smell of commuter buses and so never got into New York at all. I hardly went either, because my general impressions were informed by the *Times* and *New York* magazine, with their frequent explorations of New Yorker "identity," which largely seemed to cohere around indignation regarding tourists and "transplants"—though everyone there was a transplant in one way or another.

So the valley was somehow a world, a cauldron of allergens teeming with warehouses and tractor trailers, refineries and duplexes, cancer clusters, and suspicious Republicans. The weather was cruel and changeable, with approximately three-and-a-half temperate days per year. Once optimistic Main Streets were shuttered and blighted, secondary arteries crowded with hulking row homes with Confederate or Caribbean national flags in place of window treatments, depending on the neighborhood; gas stations and Dollar Generals were the lone outposts of commerce in certain regions. In theory I had an enviable job—but it came at the cost of my baseline mental health.

And I was being forced to entertain this raving woman, who I was now imagining striding around a ten-million-dollar estate in Greenwich and screaming at her liveried servants. She was telling me she didn't believe it was "right" that I had "coerced" my students into reading *Lolita*, which she knew was offensive because she'd started watching the movie version with Jeremy Irons, a good faith effort she had abruptly terminated because it was so offensive, this movie, and didn't I realize that such disgusting material was triggering, that I was negligent in my failure to provide the appropriate trigger warnings to her daughter, who had suffered some unspecified trauma as a preteen?

We were a long way from the B+, she was throwing whatever she could at me, and I finally told her as graciously as possible that I had enjoyed having her daughter in class, but that in order to be equitable to other students I had to maintain standards, that she was paying for the faculty to maintain standards, and I thanked her so much for her valuable feedback.

At that she hacked wetly, as if choking on a bad oyster. "I hope you're proud of yourself with your little power trip," she said, and hung up.

—

By this time the cats were roused and swarming for food. I texted Mark that I would be requiring the Glenlivet stat and went to deal with them.

I had four cats, all rescues, I couldn't help it because they had seemed to me a way to fill up the gray loneliness of Pennsylvania. They yowled and rubbed, and one of them leapt onto an end table, bumping off the sole framed photograph I had in my apartment: my brother, me, and my sister, ages five, nine, and twelve, on a bench at Knott's Berry Farm, the sun in our faces, impossibly young, impossibly happy. I picked up the photograph, wiped dust off the frame with the bottom of my shirt, then studied the frozen smiles of my brother and me, looking for resemblances between us, clues to how we had felt in that moment. For the photo, he had squeezed himself as close as he could to me, beaming, having the time of his life.

As for the cats, my sister had her own take, as she often did, had theorized that they represented too-literal "save-the-cat" moments: she had
read that protagonists in books or screenplays needed an early act like
saving a cat to make them more likeable to readers or audiences.

"But I'm not a character in a book," I countered.

"Sure, but the observation stands. You're so obsessed with presentation, so it's a piece of information you can put out there to make you
seem more attractive, like the time you volunteered for a month and
then would work it into conversations for years after."

My sister was always supremely confident, if not necessarily astute,
in her psychological profiles of me.

"Statistically women view single men with cats as effete," I said.
"That's an established fact, so your observation's shot right there. And
I'm hardly obsessed with 'presentation.'"

"Mmm hmm," she said.

Whatever their symbolic function, in the non-symbolic realm of my
apartment the cats were self-centered and exasperating, and I started
in on the complicated task of feeding them at strategic removes so they
wouldn't resort to attacking one another. I had the procedure down,
but there were always risks.

Once they were appeased, I made some coffee, scrolled around on my
phone, then figured it was time to get ready because I was supposed to
meet Angie at the Democratic Association for her show. She was an
artist, a photographer, but since that didn't pay the bills, was always
also juggling several jobs—waitress at the breakfast place, bartender,
barista, freelance graphic designer, among others—and liked to express
her astonishment that I, in maddening contrast, never seemed to be
doing any discernable labor at all.

I made a mental note to tell her about how my summer was already
being impinged upon by tiger moms calling me on my personal cell.

I showered, then scrubbed my face again with Ultimate Age Defying
Cleanser, patted my skin down with a clean hand towel, fished wispy

cotton balls from their bag to apply Advanced Replenishing Toner, daubed pee yellow *Collagène Liquide* or Liquid Collagen around my cheeks, forehead, and neck, then went over those spots again with Ultimate Age Defying Cream, finally performing a delicate under-eye rub with Rescue Eye Therapy with Caffeine. This is what things had come to, and still the results weren't particularly impressive. Somehow I had been convinced that spending hundreds of dollars a month on skincare—money I didn't really have—was something mature and responsible 21st Century Men were expected to do. I think it was *GQ* that had announced this, and as evidence had spreads of leading men who were much older than me but looked much younger, were robust and cut, with faultless wrinkle-free faces.

After the indignity of cleansing and moisturizing, I had a lengthy debate with myself about what to wear to Angie's show. I settled on black slacks and a black blazer, combining pieces of outfits I had worn at conferences years apart, because I had a vague sense that people at art openings wore black. Or was that caricature? I wasn't quite sure but was covered in cat hair almost immediately and had to find a sticky roller under the sink. I caught a glimpse of myself in the mirror, opted for another quick layer of Rescue Eye Therapy with Caffeine, and went to collect my keys.

To my horror, the birth control was nowhere to be found. After some frantic seconds when I was seriously doubting my sanity, I realized that the culprits were Kick and Lad, my fattest and most impertinent cats, who had been making sport of knocking shit off the counter and onto the floor. There was loose change all over the linoleum, a pen or two, Chapstick, a blue plastic seal from a milk jug, one of Angie's hair ties. But there was no mauve clamshell.

I searched on my hands and knees, discovered that the bottoms of my cabinet doors were a lot dirtier than I would have expected, and finally found the pills nestled in a fluffle of dust bunnies under the refrigerator. I fished them out with a broom handle while Kick and Lad sat on the edge of my bistro table, looking down at me imperiously and twitching their tails.

Once I had retrieved the birth control, I was filthy, doubly covered in cat hair, and so re-rolled myself, then made a big show of giving treats to the other cats, explaining to Kick and Lad that sinners were unworthy of indulgences. Kick looked at me and batted the Chapstick back to the floor.

—

Driving through town on the way to the Democratic Association, I played a game I often played: comparing my current life in the valley to what I had left behind in the Bay Area. Here, I wound through neighborhoods of decaying apartment complexes and tiny, 800-square-foot single families originally built to house factory workers, matchboxes which still had their blocky 1950s landscaping and cracked-plaster Virgin Marys tilted near the front walk; there, I had lived off Washington Square Park, nominally affordable with roommates, and could walk under white church towers imposing shadows on the grass, nod at the tattered poets declaiming to themselves there, grab a pour-over at the hipster spots in North Beach, slip myself among the milling residents of Chinatown, and then window-shop at the glitzy boutiques off Union Square—all in a half hour. There, despite the ever-climbing housing costs and aggressive local politicians, they had light and fog and the Golden Gate; here they had Superfund sites, crummy cemeteries, and corpses of deer who hadn't made it across the highway. The women there were all razor-sharp professionals who'd gone to UC Santa Barbara or Stanford and belonged to the de Young and had personal trainers; here they worked overnight at the Amazon distribution center, had acid reflux and raunchy senses of humor, plans for bigger and better things, were chipping away at associate's degrees, talking always of solvent days ahead, were interested in trucks and high school sports rivalries and who would or wouldn't be a positive influence in their children's lives.

Thank god for Angie, the exception to Mark's rule that no datable women existed in the area. We had met in a rom-com scenario, at the coffee place where she worked: I had approached the counter to explain that my espresso hadn't come out at the proper temperature.

"Did you pull a blank shot through the portafilter?" I asked. "Because that can be the issue."

She was in the middle of steaming a latte and turned to give me a frankly incredulous look. I hadn't actually noticed her before, had assumed from a distance she was a teenager, but when looking then I saw her anew: chunky glasses and gull-wing lips and the minutest of gaps between her two front teeth, which she later pointed out was the mark of a lusty woman, either because the Wife of Bath had had a tooth gap, or because the association was already widespread in Chaucer's time. In any case I regretted complaining.

She stopped what she was doing and turned to face me full on, which had the effect of disarming or disquieting me. "You for real?"

"It's not a big deal," I said, flushed. "I just thought—"

"—you're welcome to come back here and show me how to do it," she said, gesturing around to the space at the edge of the counter.

Now I was shamed, the woman waiting for the latte was shaking her head and giving me a sour sneer, and I said to forget the whole thing and took the lukewarm espresso back to my table with my head down.

Over the next weeks, we kept things professional when I would come in, but Angie would call out "extra hot" when handing me a drink, even if it wasn't an espresso, and I would smile ambiguously.

Then one day business was slow and she was straightening up the tables. After working her way to my vicinity, she leaned over with a rag, glanced at my set-up, and remarked that the cover of some critical book in my hand was a Barbara Kruger rip-off.

"And don't express your amazement that I know who Barbara Kruger is," she said.

"It's not very good anyway," I said. "No wonder the publisher couldn't afford the genuine article."

That exchange was the tip of détante. She inquired as to what I was doing in the coffee place with my laptop and legal pads, I asked her about the tattoo on her forearm, what looked to be three stylized fish pointing at each other like spokes in a wheel, and sharing one eye, and we began to chat a little more each time I came in, developing a jokey flirtation that seemed to me on the edge of friendly customer service and real romantic interest.

Eventually I asked her for a drink.

She seemed mildly surprised, amused, balling up the rag in her hand and placing her fist at her hip.

"Hmm," she said, "my mother always warned me against men who read Mark Danielewski in coffee shops."

"It's for work," I said.

"Even worse."

That wasn't a hard no, and ultimately, she did relent. I brought her to what passed for a beer garden in the valley: sparse gravel, splintery benches, and planters made from galvanized horse troughs.

We presented our abridged autobiographies: she was only a couple years younger than me, had been away for college, had never been married. And she didn't have any kids—a miracle, as far as I was concerned, for a woman born and bred in the area. In my experience, the locals paired off in high school and were knocked up not too long after.

On that date, as we got further into our histories, Angie turned serious after a tasting flight, saying she had something to tell me, to confess, because certain information was essential to know before moving forward. A preface like that was a brilliant rhetorical move because it had me imagining Worst Case Scenarios, that she was a Scientologist, was allergic to sex or riddled with syphilis, and so I was softened up for what she actually did confess.

"Remember how I told you I went to RISD ..." she began, letting the sentence trail off like the punch line was something too terrible to utter.

"Sure," I said, stomach immediately knotted.

She went on to say quietly that the school was her dream reach, and when she unexpectedly got in, she learned it was crazily expensive, and her family made just enough to be ineligible for financial aid. Her parents urged her to attend the regional public, with its practical cost structures, but Angie had cried and pleaded, and her father finally caved, said it was her life, but was going on record as opposing such a decision, and she signed on for loans she didn't fully understand.

"My parents, they helped me out as best they could," she said. "But I was eighteen and stubborn. What did I know? Fast forward and I'm thirty-four with $63,000 in student loans." She made a face like she had just sucked a lemon, squinting her eyes down to pinpoints. "I started out with sixty."

I knew that sixty grand was about double the national average of student loan debt because I myself was right on target at 30k, right on trend. Angie looked at me expectantly, holding the puckered face until she could tell whether the revelation had scared me off.

"That's only one question on the *$64,000 Question*," I said. "Not even."

I later found out that RISD had returned on her investment with cachet among certain artistic types, bursts of graphic design work, but that the money was never enough to live on or make a dent in her loans, hence her rotating cast of part-time jobs and a total balance that somehow inched up, not down. In addition to her waitressing and bartending jobs, she did wedding photography in the summers and some website design for the city's Water & Sewer Resources Department, where her father had worked for two decades. But in general she felt that her creative talents were being eclipsed by the mundane labor she did to survive.

"Well, adulting," I had said, and ordered another flight.

Given these struggles with monetizing her artistic skills, the show at the Democratic Association was a real opportunity for Angie. She was anxious but hopeful, had been talking about it for weeks, and I was trying to make a conscious effort to be obviously supportive, showily supportive, thinking always of my sister, who claimed that I was too self-involved and had suffered for years from Resting Bitch Face.

Offering unsolicited advice for my moral improvement was my sister's specialty, and as soon as she had heard tell of Angie, she declared her "a keeper," and would subsequently side with her even when there was no cause to choose sides.

"Will!" my sister would say. "Don't be a lovable fuck-up"—by which she meant I shouldn't embody too fully a certain strain of male privilege book reviewers had been pointing out recently. My sister's version of literary analysis was to read the season's blogged-about novels and then apply their gender critiques to me, and so after Angie had impressed with her sense of humor and no-nonsense maturity, my sister informed me that I fit the profile of over-educated, thirty-something white dudes who were droll and "intellectual"—always in air quotes—but tediously adolescent, in certain ways. Lovable fuck-ups, some novelist called them, and my sister was concerned that in my dotage I was edging into one.

"Don't ruin this relationship, too," she had said.

I had defended myself at the time, citing all the quirks and hang-ups of the various women I had dated over the years, but I don't think my sister was really listening.

I made it to the Democratic Association on the grittier South Side of town; my rattling, oil-leaking Tercel fit right in on the littered street packed with similarly corroding embarrassments. The place was behind a peeling door between the Iglesia Pentecostal Arca de Refugio and a soaped-over glass storefront that had once been an IBEW field office. On the slightly tonier North Side, the town did have what were, in a strict sense, "art galleries," but from what I could tell they catered exclusively to those interested in Thomas Kincaid-type paintings of cottages and meadows. Which is to say there were no established venues to host a real art show. But since Angie seemed to know or was related to everyone in town, she had managed to borrow the meeting room at the Democratic Association, usually occupied only in presidential election years, when it was adorned with bunting and cardboard cut-outs of Obama or whoever.

I found the door unmonitored and unlocked, and pushed inside, down a yellowed, smoke-smelling hall crowded with crooked mono-chrome portraits of local Democrats of yore, white men with handlebar mustaches and slick hair parted down the middle. There were framed newspaper clippings reporting what I assumed were negligible munic-ipal victories, the print now faded and the paper brittle.

The meeting room was in the back. All the chairs had been stacked in a corner and Angie's photographs had been hung around the room at eye level, and I wondered briefly when she had done that. There was a wobbly-looking green vinyl card table in another corner laden with wine of the *Strawberry Kiss* variety, as well as round plastic trays with carrots and celery fanned out. I had brought two bottles of mid-range California pinot and dropped them off at the table just as Angie was coming in through another door.

"You made it!" she cried. She must have had time to go home and change because she wasn't wearing her uniform from the diner, but a flouncy peasant dress with sandals and a loose ponytail held together in a leather cuff. She had a kind of contagious positive energy that I couldn't really relate to personally, but I had come to rely on her opti-mism whenever I would get down about the backstabbing ways of my colleagues or the general lack of culture in Pennsylvania. She would encourage me to look on the bright side, would invariably identify and annotate a bright side that had been invisible to me. Now she was upbeat but harried, rushed to hug me and repeat that I had made it, as though she hadn't been totally confident I would.

I produced the birth control from my jacket pocket like a conjurer materializing a vanished coin.

"Oh, right," she said absently. "Good." I went to hand her the pills, but she was looking puzzled, scrutinizing me, and I assured her I had brought the wine as promised, pointing to the table. "But why are you dressed like that?" she said, picking at my lapels. "You look like you're going to a funeral. And your ass is like matted with cat hair." She tried to swat the fur off me as best she could.

"Don't you need to take a pill?" I said.

"Well, what do you think?" she said, indicating the room.

Because Angie was perpetually on the hustle, she had noticed that the valley's moneyed class liked to hang reminders of their smog-filled past in their foyers. Based on this realization, she had worked backward to produce objects she could sell, and zeroed-in on the defunct steel facility hunkered along the banks of the river. Stalking around the plant, she did a series of photographs that were what I would classify as Deindustrialization Art, if that's a school: close-ups of rusting cracks, oxidized metals, the cleaves in slate, pits in brick, long neglected and degraded things. There were lots of shocking blues and layered oranges, eddies of turquoise, aqua, burnt sienna, all zoomed in so closely that they appeared to be abstractions. These were the pieces positioned around the space.

"Love it," I said.

"I know it's kind of pathetic," she said. "The show. But it was zero dollars, and my family's getting people to come who might actually buy stuff. So fingers crossed."

She looked at me eagerly, and I noticed that she'd applied lip gloss and dark eyeliner, unusual as she was typically a sly minimalist when it came to makeup.

"You look great by the way," I said. "A real brooding artist."

"I need provocative piercings," she said. "Or more tattoos. And a side-shave—or I could just shave my whole head, for effect."

"Let's not go crazy. But this is nice. Like a proper gallery show."

"Ha!" she said.

I went over to the refreshments table, poured some sparkling water into a flimsy plastic cup, then held it up with the mauve clamshell, raising my eyebrows up and down.

"You psychopath," she said, taking the clamshell and snapping it open.

—

Sooner than expected, people began materializing, all of whom seemed to be Angie's family and friends. I didn't care for situations in which you are obliged to make small talk while balancing plates with twisted napkins still on them, but I had already broken into one of the pinots and so was content to blend into a bare part of the wall. Angie, though, was like a bride at her own reception, circulating through the room, greeting people with a shriek, thanking them for coming, hugging, shaking hands, demurring when they praised her work, offering breezy backstories on particular photographs, or else inventing such stories on the spot.

I watched her for a while, then started scrolling around my phone, trying to look absorbed enough that nobody would approach me. The Wi-Fi belonged to the church next door and was crawling, so I jumped from news sites to my webmail program. That student's mother had already written a "follow-up" email which I deleted without reading, along with a bunch of solicitations from credit card companies and debt consolidation services. I had offers for discounted pizza and inter-minable bureaucratic notices from the college, but nothing of personal interest. There was, however, one anomalous email, from an address I didn't recognize, with a subject line in lowercase: "don't delete me please!!!" I tapped it open:

> You don't know me but my name is Petra. I'm a teenager living in Kenya at the present moment.
>
> Apologies for writing "out of the blue" but I'm reasonably assured you are my biological father. In actuality, I am posi-tive you are. William Sorley, PhD. D.O.B. 10/22/1976. 6 foot, brown hair, brown eyes, and I don't know what you weigh. Your email address is prominently accessible on the internet. If you are him (he?) I am hereby informing you that you have a daughter. Would it be possible for you to reply at your earliest convenience because I could greatly benefit from fatherly assis-tance. Thank you.

At first, I didn't register what I had read.

How could such a life-changing thing happen in such a throwaway, in-between moment, when I was slouching against a nicotine-stained wall, trying to kill time and not be too conspicuous?

I drained the wine in my cup and read the note again. I understood the words, but they didn't seem to pertain to me specifically, didn't seem to me immediately or materially meaningful. But they were still chilling, the words, the tiny, pixilated letters, because they were accurate with the vitals, and the mention of Kenya made me think of 419 scams and other nefarious extortion schemes. Probably my personal information was available for a price on the Dark Web. I started to wonder what else about me was floating around in cyberspace, and this question became muddled with the remote possibility that the email might be for real.

Though unmoving, I was sweating profusely, blinking over the words again and then turning my attention to the refreshments table. The room was now congested, I couldn't even see Angie. I clutched the phone in a slick palm, put my chin down, and threaded my way toward the wine. Mercifully but unsurprisingly, the *Strawberry Kiss* had been ravaged but my pinots were largely intact, and I emptied one into my glass. That particular pinot was from the Russian River Valley, the coolest of the AVAs in the region, and unbeknownst to anyone in the room but me, was a product of wine makers who were carrying on the Burgundian tradition of vineyard-designated bottlings, even though their fruit was far less structured than what they would have done in the Côte d'Or. In any case, I chugged it.

I was levelheaded enough to tell myself that the email was most likely a con or hoax of some sort, and thought of my friend Cubby, a legendary practical joker. I worked my way back to the wall, realizing that Cubby and I hadn't spoken for weeks, a month maybe, and this was just the sort of stunt he might pull to get my attention. For instance he knew I didn't want kids, knew that we'd had an ongoing disagreement about procreation for twenty years, and whenever I went to his place, he took real glee in unleashing his own brood, riling them up so they would launch themselves to hang over me and he'd laugh as I clomped around like Gulliver being toppled by grubby Lilliputians.

I tried to melt into the wall and texted Cubby some frat boy humor he'd find funny, letting him know without saying it directly that he hadn't rattled me. I had snagged a can of sparkling water after downing the pinot, and I cracked that for some hydration, watching my phone, waiting.

I texted Cubby again and wiped my forehead with the crook of my arm. The room was close and unventilated and I was regretting the black blazer. Either this was a Nigerian Prince deal or Cubby's handiwork, I assured myself, but certainly not a real email from a real daughter because that would be too absurd and hackneyed.

Even so, I would defy anyone not to find such an email unsettling, especially after a glass or two of wine, and I couldn't exactly focus my attention on the present moment. Cubby wasn't responding, the not-knowing was the worst of it, and I let loose a flood of texts letting him know what a dick he was, that comedy had lines you didn't cross, and so on.

After some minutes, I was starting to feel the effects of the pinot, was willing the alcohol to work harder and trying to peer through the crowd to determine what was left of the other bottle, I was doing all this and still dripping down my back when Angie stepped into my line of sight, cheery and flanked by an older couple who had softer echoes of her own facial features.

"Will," she said. "The wait is over: you finally get to meet the parents!"

Before I knew what was happening, they were coming at me, the mother all smiles, saying that she had been dying to meet me, the father stout and beleaguered, giving me a vice grip handshake and wincing like doing so was a terrible inconvenience.

Apparently, Angie had told them about me because they already knew basic details. Her mother peppered me with questions about how

I was liking the area, and I had to collect myself just to give noncommittal answers, and to smile. Of course my mind was on the email, I'm not insane, but I was trying to focus on the gray-haired lady in front of me, her husband standing just off to the side, hands stuffed in his pockets so they framed his gut.

Angie's mother was wearing a white vest with a tee shirt underneath that read "I Dream of Shiplap," and again I was feeling overdressed. Luckily all the sweat sheeting down my back would be hidden by the blazer. I edged closer to the wall. Angie's mother was fascinated by the fact that I was from California, had evidently only seen Californians on television and kept asking me, in a friendly sort of way, how I dealt with how "weird" it was "out there."

"What do you mean, weird?" I said.

"Oh, maybe not *weird*," she said. "But you always hear about these homeless camps taking over the cities, all your taxes going to pay for surgeries for illegal aliens—"

"—undocumented," said Angie.

"Illegal aliens or whatever you call them," her mother went on. "I'm all for immigration, but come here legally, like my grandparents did, and don't accept handouts. And then they tax you to death, they make you subsidize them."

Angie was looking embarrassed and then challenged her mother for me, saying that was undigested Fox News and asking who it was she meant by "they."

Her mother floundered a bit, as though surprised that anyone could find fault with what seemed to her crystalline fact, and her father frowned and jerked his hands out of his pockets to cross his arms over top of his belly.

I had learned from my time in the valley that it was best to avoid political entanglements, so I said it was true that California was getting prohibitively expensive, a silver lining of taking a job "Back East," as Californians said of anyplace beyond Havasu.

Finally Angie's father broke in. "My buddy's son thought about being an English major," he said. "But then realized that you had to be a woman or a minority to get ahead." He said this as though it were a self-evident data point.

"It's a good thing I'm both a woman *and* a minority," I said. "Which is how I got ahead."

He didn't find that funny, and Angie interrupted to say that we would all get a chance to get to know one another over dinner, but that now she wanted to introduce me to some other people. I nodded dumbly as she yanked me by the arm and pulled me through the crowd to relative safety.

"For fuck's sake," she said when we were out of her parents' earshot. "I'm so sorry. It was a chore just to convince them to come to the *Democratic* Association. They didn't want to 'support' it, but I explained that I hadn't paid them a dime, so they gave in. And I *told* them not to offend you."

"I'm not offended," I said loosely, my mind on the email. "But what's this about dinner?"

"Remember we talked about it? We said we would all have dinner tonight because it's important for you to get to know my family. If we're going to get more serious."

I didn't have much of a memory of that conversation, but that wasn't saying much as I was feeling fuzzy from the wine, and gut-punched by the email. Plus the lack of air conditioning was really starting to overwhelm. I checked my phone quickly, but nothing from Cubby.

"Are you OK?" Angie asked. "You look pale."

"I'm just hot," I said. "It's a lot more packed in here than I expected."

"They're really not that bad. They just listen to talk radio all day. You should take off your blazer."

"It's fine," I said, woozy. "They're great. I'm looking forward to getting to know them." I smiled as widely as I could and told her I just needed some air. She looked concerned for a second, but a purple-haired woman buttonholed her, and Angie yelped, introduced us briefly, then spun off with this woman into another crush of people. I was near the refreshment table, so I opened the second bottle of pinot, filled a new glass, and focused on not spilling it as I made my way to the door.

It was slightly cooler outside, there was an alley with some shaded Dumpsters, and I stole back behind them for privacy. I hit Cubby with a few more texts and noticed that my hands were shaking. The air was doing me good, but there was something rotting in one of the Dumpsters. My shirt was now completely soaked through with sweat. I closed my eyes and breathed, trying to place myself back on that bench at Knott's Berry Farm.

Then I opened the email and studied it again, imagining what it would mean if it wasn't a scam or a joke: I had never been to Kenya nor had sex, to my recollection, with a Kenyan woman—and yet the writer had specified "at the present moment," implying that she wasn't necessarily half Kenyan. But why live there? And what an odd name, Petra, at least in the States. I knew it had something to do with stone, was probably a feminine version of Peter, but it didn't ring any specific ethnic bells, nor did it sound especially African. I started doing some math: "teenager" equaled a range from thirteen to nineteen, so I was looking at a 1994 to 2000 span, square in my San Francisco years. I texted Cubby again, reminding him that he was a pretty much a dick.

I attempted to conserve the wine because I didn't want to go back inside too soon. I was man enough to admit that it was hypothetically possible I had impregnated someone, though unlikely that I would have never been told. I had kept in occasional contact with some of the women I'd known in that window, was familiar with the broad contours of their lives, so I crossed them off my mental list. But there were a few I never spoke to—and one or two others who were bona fide one-nighters—and so I did my best to recall what I could. I'd met one of the one-nighters, Emily Something, at a house party, where she was in the kitchen doing shots and talking about architecture or urban planning. Not knowing her last name, I couldn't find anything on her with a Google search on my phone, but I remembered running into her a few months later at Trader Joe's. We'd had an awkward conversation, and she definitely wasn't pregnant.

The other one, whose name I think was also Emily, was a result of a weekend symposium on the fetish. Emily Two had come in from

Madison or Ann Arbor to present a paper, a grad student herself, and afterward a group of us had worked our way through six or seven bars, and wound up playing old George Harrison records at my pal Chris' place, where this Emily and I stomped merrily to an itchy sub-attic for a fumbling tête-à-tête. I never saw her again, but I've always been clinical about protection, especially with someone I'd known for less than twenty-four hours. So I was reasonably sure she was fine. Plus I seemed to remember her being a big Kate Millet fan.

By the time the cup was empty I had convinced myself that the email could not be real, that it must have been Cubby, and then went inside, one foot in front of the other, mainly for the wine. The crowd was already thinning out, but Angie caught me to say that she had sold three photographs. "Probably just pity sales," she said. "But hey, I'll take it!"

I said that it was awesome, exclaimed that it was awesome, apparently too loudly, because several people glanced over disapprovingly, and Angie suggested I get some water. I thought that was a wonderful idea, found a bottle of regular water on the refreshments table, and gulped it down.

"I'm getting hungry," I said to her. "When is this much vaunted dinner?"

She looked skeptical again, said soon, said that I needed to take it easy, and I said I was merely going with the flow. I smiled toothily. She handed me another bottle of water, said there were some folding chairs on the other side of the room, and went off to answer someone's question about a photograph.

—

When the time for the show was up, Angie fell into prolonged good-byes as people filed out while her parents remained, looking morti-fied by some citation from Bill Clinton hanging near the bathroom door. I was feeling marginally better and made small talk with Angie's father, who was asking me what I thought about John Steinbeck's *Sweet Thursday*, because that was a novel he had once read about California.

After Angie had ushered out the lingerers, it surfaced that a plan had been forged without my knowledge to walk over to a Mexican restaurant a couple of blocks away. I didn't care one way or another at that point, but Angie's parents clearly weren't thrilled about moving through that part of town without the safety of their vehicles. The area had "transitioned" over the last decades, and her parents had no occasion to frequent it as there was a Chipotle off the freeway on the North Side.

But Angie liked that particular restaurant, it was her night, and so her parents went along, arguing over whether the car had been locked. On the walk over, Angie's mother bemoaned the wrappers she'd spotted in the gutter, observed that some people just weren't attuned to deferred maintenance, and her father kept declaring that this restaurant of hers better have ground beef, because otherwise he wouldn't be eating there.

I plodded along, mindful of the cracked sidewalks heaved up by tree roots.

I hadn't been to the restaurant before, either, but it was a bare bones taqueria so I could see why Angie picked it. People were hunched on plastic chairs eating tortas and open-faced street tacos for $1.75 apiece. There was a big glass cooler stocked with Jarritos and Cokes, and a calendar illustrated with anthropomorphic cacti. Nobody paid any attention to us, but Angie's parents were openly uncomfortable.

"Let's go to the steakhouse," her father said. "After all, we're celebrating."

"This is what I want," said Angie. "And it's good, so come on."

It was a seat-yourself place, and we settled into a table with utensils already stuffed upright into a glass, communal style, and Angie's mother pulled out a disinfecting wipe and started going over everything. The menu had *adobada* and *lengua* and *cabeza*, but no ground beef. I was loving it. Angie's parents were frowning at the menu like it was the Rosetta Stone and Angie had to decode it for them even though it was in both Spanish and English.

"I don't mind Mexican food," Angie's father was saying. "But is this even Mexican? They don't have enchiladas *or* nachos. What is '*menudo domingos*?'"

"You don't want to know," said Angie. "And it's only on Sundays."

Angie ordered them some plain chicken tacos. I was excited to get *horchata* with my food, grateful for the sugar and hydration. It was a drink I missed from California and seldom saw in Pennsylvania. Angie's mother was rapt when the milky glass was served, and when I explained what was in it, she seemed even more intrigued, but refused to try some or order one for herself because it was homemade and therefore untrustworthy. The tacos were among the best I'd had since leaving California, or maybe I was famished, but either way I was amused to see Angie's parents poking around on their own tacos and wondering why in the world anyone would put raw onions on anything. I ate ravenously while they ignored the hot sauces and kept folding their tacos over too tightly, causing the tortillas to break and Angie's mother squirted hand sanitizer, at a loss as to why this food seemed designed to make a mess everywhere.

I was just trying to get through the meal when my phone started buzzing. Angie's father was in the middle of explaining how the valley's water supply came from 23,000 acres of protected watershed in the mountains, how it had been named the best water in the region. "In numerous taste tests," he kept saying, filling up on chips and salsa.

It's hard to say whether, back in 2013, it was bad manners to check your phone when you were at your first dinner with your girlfriend's parents. Later, of course, it would be remiss not to. But that was then and the phone kept buzzing, message after message, and I thought it had to be Cubby, especially since I'd lost count of how many texts I'd sent him over the last hours.

As Angie's father went on and on, I rubbed the phone through my pocket, trying to calculate precisely how rude it would be to pull it out, but I must have looked distracted because Angie's mother suddenly wanted to know if my food was maybe causing some intestinal problems, and I said I was perfect, but then almost involuntarily followed that up by informing the table that I was going to check my phone because someone was trying to get in touch with me and I wanted to make sure it wasn't an emergency. Everyone looked confused or concerned, but I was already deep in the phone: a barrage of texts from Cubby, what looked to be quotations from David Brent, a photo of me passed out at a party in college, a string of poetic phrases I couldn't quite decipher. I knew I was starting to sweat again, Angie was alarmed, and I excused myself, saying I was really sorry but that I needed a moment to deal with a personal matter.

I pushed off from the table and trudged outside without looking back. Under the green, white, and red awning, I took a deep breath and called Cubby.

He picked up straightaway and asked me what kind of methamphetamine I was on, what with the manic onslaught of nonsensical texts and all. I told him it was fucked up, what he did, hoping that he would admit to the whole thing, and I could get on with my life.

But it developed that he was utterly mystified, and he maintained that he had been baffled by the texts, noting that a lesser man would have been affronted by being called a dick for no good reason.

I explained, in a long breathless tumble, what I had read in the email, and my theories about it being a joke.

After a pause he said: "Uh, well, these days I don't really have time to concoct hoaxes, so no. But it does sound legit, from what you're saying." He quoted a line from *The Untouchables* about people only claiming to be certain things, not treasury agents, not daughters.

Something fiery, bile or half-digested hot sauce, was starting to claw its way up my esophagus, and I accused him of not taking this seriously, that quoting Sean Connery was evidence of his unseriousness, and he told me to calm down and relax, that I wasn't exactly talking about the doomsday apocalypse here. He even had the nerve to say it might be "cool," having a new connection, and we got into an argument about how cool existential upheavals were, and finally I said I had to go because I was in the middle of dinner with Angie's family and he said wait a sec, is that official, and I said I'd catch up with him later.

Given the implications of that conversation, I had to make a stop in the bathroom to splash water on my face and hyperventilate. I stared at myself in the mirror, not quite recognizing the person blinking back, then mustered whatever reserves of fortitude I had and went back to the table.

When I sat down, Angie and her mom expressed concern while her dad was picking onions off his taco with showy annoyance and I made up an excuse about my sister getting into a car accident, a move I instantly regretted as disproportionate to the circumstances.

The women gasped and wanted assurance she was all right, and when I kept going, saying it was nothing, a fender-bender that had just rattled her a bit, Angie's father looked even more annoyed and made a remark about how my sister'd probably get screwed on her premiums now.

Angie took my hand, but I said it was nothing to worry about, really, that the cops were there and the car was drivable, and Angie's father launched into a story about the time he had been side-swiped by an Iranian, had been forced to take the guy to court, not because he was Arab but because he had no insurance, and I was relieved to have attention back off me for the time being.

—

After dinner, once everyone had said their goodbyes, Angie and I walked her parents to their car, which I think they had expected would be stolen or at least fouled with graffiti. Her father crushed my hand in his and her mother insisted we were coming over for dinner soon, and once they had rounded the corner, Angie turned to me fiercely.

"The fuck is going on with you?" she said.

I shrugged in a stupor, didn't want to have that conversation on the sidewalk, and so suggested we stop in at a bar nearby, an Irish one we went to sometimes.

She was confounded. "Don't you want to call your sister?"

"It's a non-issue," I said. "She's fine. I could just use a drink."

"I'll bet," she said, and flung her arms out in the general direction of the bar.

We walked to the bar in silence, but by the time we got there, she had calmed down, or at least seemed not to be blaming me exclusively for the evening, and in fact apologized again for her parents. "They have good hearts," she said.

"I could tell," I said as we went into the bar. It was one of those places that had wall holes from sloppy scuffles patched with unpainted MDF and St. Patrick's Day streamers implying all Irish people were drunks, still limply hanging even though it was June. Monday at 6:56 p.m. meant that only the most dedicated alcoholics were yet at the bar, and the bartender called out my name and asked if I wanted the usual, which was a 7&7.

"Absolutely," I said. "And a lemon drop for the lady."

"And waters!" Angie called.

We found a tottering table and I sucked down half the 7&7. Angie sipped her lemon drop and toyed with the sugary rim of her glass.

"I still can't believe it about your sister," she said. "You sure you don't want to call her? She must be shook." She blinked at me with the purest affection and concern, and I knew I couldn't hold it in anymore, and so took another gulp of the 7&7 and told her everything.

"Funny story," I began, then told her about the email from my supposed long-lost daughter, about the phone call with Cubby, about my acute, layered feelings of dread. I had an inkling that springing the email on Angie was unfair, since we were supposed to be celebrating her successful show, but there are limits to what a person can keep behind a mask.

She didn't respond at all, except to frown and stare into her drink. I knew it was a lot to absorb, and so went to get another round.

When I returned to the table with my 7&7 and another lemon drop she hadn't ordered, she was still quiet, uncharacteristically quiet.

I waited a few beats. "So …" I said finally, trying to balance on my stool. "Any advice?"

"Just to be clear on something," she said somberly. "Your sister *wasn't* in a car accident?"

That was her take away? I had to tread carefully.

I exhaled and admitted that I'd been misleading, but insisted it was a spur of the moment decision, that I didn't feel, in that instant, it was appropriate to drag her parents into my personal torment. The new 7&7 was tastier than the last.

"I just don't understand why you would lie. I mean, you've met my parents once and now you've already lied to them. You know that honesty is the most important thing for me. Not a good look moving forward, Will."

It was a little exasperating that she kept using the word *lie* when I viewed it as a skippable footnote to the main narrative thread, but I realized that in order to placate her we would have to do a whole mini-argument about my behavior. I explained that it was a highly unusual circumstance, an emergency even, that I was caught off guard and blurted out something dumb. She said what you might expect, how concerning it was that my knee-jerk reaction was a lie about my sister's wellbeing, which aside from everything else was horrible karma, and after she said her piece I gently directed her back to the fact that a person had contacted me claiming to be my daughter, an immediate, clear and present crisis.

Two rounds later, Angie seemed willing to move past my sister's fictional calamity, even as we didn't exactly resolve the issue (she was fanatical about truth telling). I guess she thought it was shady, or maybe that it indicated some deeper constitutional shadiness on my part, and I couldn't help but wonder if she was regretting introducing me to her parents in the first place.

But I really wanted her perspective on the email, so even as I knew we were papering over some things that were worrying her, I circled back to it to see what intuitions may have been tingling in her.

"You're seriously asking me what I would do," she said. "As a woman?"

I nodded and sucked on my drink.

"As a human being," she said, "I would email the person back. Isn't that the first step, the obvious step?"

"Obvious-not obvious," I said. "Because it might be a scam."

But ultimately, I admitted I did need to respond, because that's what human beings did, and the bar was suddenly claustrophobic and broiling. I pushed myself off the table, emphatic but unsteady, saying we had to get to my laptop right away, that this had to be done forth-with, and Angie shook her head, curled two arms around my own, and we went swaying into the night.

2.

FOR THE SECOND day running, I'd been awakened earlier than I would have liked, this time by Kick and Lad, who were completing floor exercises, and my chest was the floor. They were assisted in their efforts by a clanging emanating from somewhere, and as the cats pummeled me, I realized that the noises were coming from Angie, from my own kitchenette.

The descriptor "loft-style" sounds attractive in the abstract, and had seemed to me a small saving grace of the valley when I had first arrived. The reality, it turned out, was much creakier and had a mold problem. My damp and bowing place had exposed brick and one big rectangle to live in: faded yellow oak cabinets strung along one corner, dirty-grout tile countertops installed just before hard stone surfaces had become standard; my bed in another corner, a plain mattress over box spring, no headboard, only partly secluded by a folding divider from St. Vincent de Paul; my trusty couch flanked by pressboard bookshelves spilling over onto vertical piles on the floor; and a final corner built out to create a cramped bathroom with a stacked washer/dryer where a linen closet might have been. I had one enormous, unopenable window overlooking a gravelly expanse of train tracks that bore rumbling, unhurried freighters at inconvenient times. At that moment, still puzzling out whether recent events had happened or been dreamt, I understood that Angie was making breakfast, and not being especially subtle about it.

Smelling eggs and toast and coffee, I was drawn to my tiny bistro table, only to discover she had made food only for herself. This didn't compute, I started to ask about eggs for me, but she glowered and dropped the frying pan into the sink, setting a sizzling jet of water over it.

I decided to pivot from the egg conversation and went to feed the cats, eyeing Angie to see if she'd say that she'd already done so. She didn't. They pounced and pawed one another, and I moved in silence, shuddering against the icy energy in the room. When the cats were taken care of, I found a box of cereal and scooted up next to Angie as she finished her hot meal. I flooded my cereal with milk that may or may not have been slightly rancid and tested buoyancy with my spoon. She was ignoring me in an elaborate sort of way, and so we ate in continued silence for a few minutes until I finally said I hoped she wasn't still upset about the night before.

"There's no point in bringing it up again," she said flatly, poking at the last of her eggs. She seemed to consider something, took a sip of orange juice. "But just know," she said after a moment, "that if you ever pull shit like that again, we're done."

I rubbed her arm and repeated a few things I'd said the night before.

"I just told you we don't need to get into it all again. Everybody's under a lot of stress, it's the new human condition. But you choose how you respond to that stress."

Definitely she was still pissed, but I could tell she was willing herself to let it go. Her nature was not to hold grudges. I thought it might be a good idea to change the subject so I brought up the weather and cowardly politicians she hated and how proud I was that her show had been a hit.

"Mmm hmm," she said vaguely, the exact way my sister did, and went to dump her plate in the sink. I noted that she didn't rinse it, her small way of sticking it to me, which I deserved. But then she stopped at the coffee maker, paused for an almost-imperceptible second, and asked over her shoulder if I wanted a cup.

Rapprochement to offset the dirty dishes, and she returned with two steaming mugs. "Extra hot," she said under her breath, then at normal volume: "So how are you doing with the email situation?"

"I wasn't sure you wanted to talk about it."

"Clearly it's spooking you, so yeah."

As she said that, I recalled isolated moments from the night before—that, for instance, once we'd made it back from the bar, I had insisted on responding to the email, per her advice. But details were fuzzy. I dimly recalled my laptop, which was still at that moment opened on the coffee table. I recalled making reasoned arguments about agency and autonomy while eating pretzels. I recalled mixing my own 7&7s.

I sipped the coffee and tried to visualize the caffeine rocketing its way around my brain.

"Well, I did write her back," I said finally, half statement, half question.

"Yes I know that. I was there."

"And we're feeling good about the response? That we'll root out any would-be scammers?" I couldn't remember the content of the email, just the fact of its composition, and was hoping Angie might fill in the blanks without my having to ask her explicitly.

"I told you last night," she said. "I don't necessarily think it's a scam."

"In that case," I said, "I might have to kill myself."

It was a joke, but she took it the wrong way and said I was really starting to "concern" her. I said I wasn't actually going to kill myself, of course, but that the whole thing was a lot to take. She appraised me for a moment, seemed about to say something but thought better of it, then considered the door to the bathroom.

"I'm gonna grab a shower," she announced, taking her coffee with her.

Given the lingering tensions, I decided to do the dishes so everything would be clean when she emerged, and busied myself scrubbing her semi-dried yolks off the plate and frying pan, getting those yolks entangled in my green scrubbing pad, and then wondering for the millionth time why somebody didn't invent a scrubber that wouldn't become a cottage cheese mess after scouring eggy film from skillets and plates. The harder I scrubbed, the deeper and more hopelessly inextricable the skeins of eggs became, and finally I threw the pad in the garbage in a rage, faintly aware that I was displacing that rage, and likely confusing fear with anger directed at an inanimate object.

I made a sweep of the room, tripping over cats who hurled themselves in my path with abandon, stepping around them as I collected the wine and old-fashioned glasses from the coffee table, a wooden bowl with pretzel remnants, bunched tissues that had either been Angie's or mine, I wasn't sure. Morning light from the window threw intense white trapezoids and triangles over things, illuminating the paw-printed dust on the wood surfaces and reminding me, again, that the place could use a deeper cleaning.

As I neatened up a pile of books stacked around my lone framed photograph, I saw something Angie had been reading, Issa's *The Spring of My Life*, bookmarked with a pamphlet declaring "Your Pets are Counting on You to Learn About LASER SURGERY." The pamphlet was one my vet had tucked into a prescription bag at some point, but I had no idea where Angie had found it. At first I looked closer just in appreciation of the incongruity there, but since the pamphlet was sticking out the top of the book, I could see some of Angie's distinctive spiky writing on the back, blank except for a website you could visit to learn more about laser surgery for your pets.

I looked guiltily toward the bathroom: the shower appeared to be operating at full blast, steam curling under the door. I contorted to thumb open the book, careful not to lose her place, and quickly scanned what she had written, noting at once that it was rife with "W." for Will:

5/29

Finished talking to Gabby and I feel kind of awful because I unloaded all this negativity and complaints on her. She says it's normal not to feel like yourself sometimes. But what does it mean to feel like yourself? Why don't I have a real career? Should I suck it up and move to the city? Who do I want to be with? Can I really see myself with W. long term? <u>Nothing</u> is ever perfect!

June

1. My parents can be a lot no doubt but that performance was borderline deal breaking.

2. Is it selfish to wonder how a child in W.'s life would affect <u>me</u>? Not that he asked me about that, which is understandable I guess, but how am I supposed to factor this? It's a little scary, this reaction like he's eighteen and a senior in high school. And who is this woman? What kind of woman does this? It seems to me

The writing narrowed down at the bottom of the pamphlet, grew cramped and microscopic as it pushed towards the corners and edges and I had a hard time deciphering the sense as it switched into more abbreviations, so the "Ws" were run together with "mmature," "fun," "smrt," "arch," "rideordie" and I couldn't quite tell what was meant even by squinting.

The LASER SURGERY pamphlet was marking a page with a poem Angie had starred:

The world of dew
is the world of dew.
And yet, and yet—

I knew that was one of Issa's most famous poems, written after the death of his daughter. In the headnote leading up to the poem Issa had wondered, "How can I, her father, stand by and watch her fade away each day like a perfect flower suddenly ravaged by rain and mud?" The haiku in response to that question begins with the Buddhist recognition that the world is fleeting, mere dew, and so everything, even a father's grief over his dead daughter, is illusion. A self-evident tautology that the poet understands intellectually. And yet, and yet—

So Angie was concerned about my "scary" reaction—as though I were supposed to manfully claim a bond with some figment I didn't even know to be real? As though it were "immature" (?) to be a person who didn't want children, and to be disturbed by the prospect of one's sudden materialization in my life. Was this a fair assessment?

In the light-hearted early stages of our relationship, Angie and I had sort of jokingly danced around the topic of kids, pretending it was a thing so far off as to be theoretical. The Kid Question had torpedoed a couple of previous relationships of mine, since at the end of the day, most people did want them, eventually, and in the back of my mind I told myself that if Angie wasn't pressing it, it wasn't a real issue—I was thirty-seven about to be thirty-eight, Angie was thirty-five, and my sister had said that if a woman was thirty-five and didn't press the issue of kids, she didn't want kids. But I didn't know that to be necessarily true in Angie's case.

Contrary to what Angie was wondering, I liked to believe that my reactions to the email were complexly motivated, "mature" even, if only legible to me in pieces. For instance I believed that these reasons had to do with my parents' divorce, with my wanting to protect abstract children I would never have from that sort of suffering. And of course the divorce was inseparable from an incident that occurred when I was nine, The Incident that had led, tortuously, to fusty visitations, backhanded remarks about gambling or alcoholism from one parent to another, cars idling in front of townhouses, cold pizza, my sister and I caught always in the middle, literally and figuratively.

This all had to do with my brother Benj. It was summer, the day of my sister's long-awaited orthodontia appointment, the one where they finally put the braces on; my parents had been saving a year for this, and were fond of reminding us kids how expensive we were. That morning my mother informed Benj and me that we'd be coming along to the appointment, to witness life and what it cost. I begged her to let us stay home, argued that I was old enough to watch him. She was skeptical, but it was only for a couple hours in the middle of the day, and finally she conceded, leaving with my sister, who went out with her chin up and a sideways comment about not burning the house down.

Benj and I flew into the backyard, just a small fenced square between countless others on our street of ticky-tacky stucco boxes. But to us it seemed endless. The one distinguishing feature was a camphor tree near the back fence, ringed with rocks my dad had dug up when planting or installing sprinklers.

We played hide-and-seek a while, but Benj wasn't an especially good hider, partly because he had blond hair and was wearing a bright yellow shirt that day. And cord cut-offs, and filthy white sneakers, and socks with red and blue stripes at the ankles. I remember one of his front baby teeth was missing and the nub of a new one was coming in. I remember his freckles and his giant plastic watch that our grandfather had given him, one that spun around loose on his wrist.

Retreating to the shade of the tree, I showed Benj how to rub mulch on his skin to create dark marks. He smudged some black under his eyes for war paint, which led to my describing how one climbed a tree stealthily, like a ninja or a cat burglar, and I slunk up the fat trunk to one of the lower branches. Benj marveled, so to show off my prowess, I shimmied further up the branch, and on to a higher one, scaring myself a little because I'd never been that high, but putting on a brave face for my brother. He believed I could have been a cat burglar, and I carefully got myself back down to the lowest branch, then leapt to the ground with a flourish.

Benj was so impressed he wanted to try, and I did hesitate at first, but he was forever complaining about not being able to do what I did, what the bigger kids did. I had to give him a boost because he was too short to reach even the first branch, and I remember pushing him up the trunk as he struggled.

Finally he pressed himself unsteadily into the crotch of that first branch.

"It's not even scary," he said.

"See if you can get higher," I said, and I don't know why. I think I was annoyed that he wasn't more afraid, or that he was pretending to not be afraid, but was also telling myself that I was encouraging him, helping him to be confident and grow. Or it's possible I told myself that later.

He did make the next branch, then the next, always glancing back down to see if I was watching him. The higher he got, the more I became afraid for him. I don't know how high he was, but I remember thinking that, from my vantage, it was too dangerous, and I called for him to climb back, cautiously, and as he looked down, his uneven smile changed in a moment to an expression of panic, but a brief one, because still he didn't want to seem afraid in front of me, and he said it was no problem, that it was the easiest thing in the world to come down. But then he slipped.

I heard the shower shut off and quickly replaced the copy of *The Spring of My Life* back onto the book pile, positioning the LASER SURGERY pamphlet exactly as I had found it, and jumped back into the kitchen.

Angie nudged open the bathroom door, all rosy and steamed.

I had the kitchen completely clean, and pointed out as much as she dressed behind the room divider. I did feel remorseful about reading her diaristic notes on the pamphlet, but glad that I had gathered more information, because of course she was right that I hadn't considered her perspective, that in all my self-involvement, I hadn't wondered about how things might affect her.

As I was mulling how to handle this, she stepped from around the room divider, dried and suddenly chipper, saying it was time to deliver the photographs.

She looked hopeful or excited for the first time that morning, smiling at me expectantly, even as her mention of "deliveries" made me feel again that whole chunks of the night before were lost to me.

"To the people who bought stuff last night?" she said probingly, sensing my confusion. "We discussed this at length. You were going to help me deliver them, then drop me off at work."

"Oh *that*," I said. "Yeah, duh, of course. I'm ready."

—

We spent the rest of the morning driving around town delivering photographs. There was the friend of Angie's dad, who explained to me at great length about all the nefarious things the college was doing to the city council, and I was forced to admit that real estate and zoning weren't my departments; there was the friend of Angie's mom, an ancient lady with beaded eyeglass chains and stacks of moldy books; there was the acquaintance of Angie's cousin, an endocrinologist who had just moved from out of state and was setting up an office because morbidity rates in the valley were off the charts, thanks in part to the unusually high incidence of diabetes.

The virtue of offering next day delivery on those photographs, Angie had explained, was immediate payment, and she needed the money. By lunchtime she had about $600.

"This is going right to Visa," she said.

The coffeehouse where she worked afternoons required an all-black ensemble, plus a green apron, which she had stuffed in a backpack. "Feel free to change in the back seat," I said, but she groaned and said she'd do so in the bathroom at work. We weren't supposed to see each other that night because she was working close at the restaurant after her barista shift, and as I pulled up to the coffeehouse, she said she hoped I was making progress on my "research"—a word she often used teasingly, in quotes.

"Remind me to tell you about the irate parent I had to deal with," I said. "Over the *summer*."

"Can't wait to hear all about it," she said, hopping out of the car. "And try not to get yourself too worked up."

—

As it happened, I did get worked up later that afternoon.

I had run a few errands and was planning to swing by the grocery store when I glanced at my phone at a stoplight, and my stomach lurched at another email from Kenya.

I managed to pull off into a parking lot before reading it, a feat since I was already quaking. I cracked a window for ventilation, and under the buzz of a neon fast food sign, read:

Hiya Dad.

I guess you're right, there's no way of knowing for sure I'm not catfishing you. Except I'm not. I swear on my mortal soul. (to get this out of the way: I am not asking you for money. I will never ask you for money. My mom is rich!)

Basically the entire reason I wrote in the first place is because I need you here in person. No Skyping, no texting. I need you "in the flesh." Mom never wanted me to know who you were btw so don't blame her. But I'm highly intelligent so I found out.

You wouldn't understand what it's like to be a girl here in this environment. Where I'm living now in Lamu it's all Muslim and super clicky and I'm an outsider even though we've been here pretty much for forever. Being a girl here with no people just basically sucks (understatement). I'm technically boarded at this school but it's like a convent bc I can't really leave or even interact with anybody. I'm not even supposed to have access to the internet. You could say I'm basically a prisoner. So the way it works is if my father presents himself here they will release me to him. If not I'm pretty much stuck and needless to say some of these people... aren't like friendly to Americans. I won't say anymore about that right now. My dearest mother has gone AWOL on me again. I'm not asking that you take me home or anything! I'm not asking anything but that you come out here for the sake of your daughter, not that I'm guilting you :)

Maybe it would even be fun? Ever been to Kenya? It's gotta be pretty soon if you do come. Some of the guys here are what you might call "crude." It's just different than what you're probably used to. Once you get to a certain age, they notice you. Like overnight. Ever seen the Big Five? They are: elephants, lions, rhinos, leopards, cape buffalo. We have giraffes too, my favorite. Please come…

Expectantly,

Petra

PS: Audra Wester

The postscript was the part that sliced me most ruthlessly through the viscera.

How could I have forgotten about Audra Wester?

—

I started driving to Cubby's.

For what? Counsel? Sympathy?

I was keyed up, speeding, jittery.

Actually, I hadn't forgotten about Audra. That's not fair to say. But I must have subconsciously discounted her out of hand. It's true that while we'd had a brief, intense relationship during the period in question, Audra had an edge to her, attached in my mind to how coldly she had broken things off. So I must have disassociated her from whatever I imagined "maternal" meant—and she never crossed my mind as I racked it for possible candidates.

I had met her at—or, really, near—a wedding in San Francisco. I was in my pal Tam's at the Westin St. Francis and Audra happened to be staying there at the same time. Tam was a fellow broke grad student, but was marrying Mik, who had grown up in a Pacific Heights mansion near Danielle Steel and her preposterous hedge, so their union was a gilded, cut-crystal affair. I was sharing a room with three other friends because even with the special rate we plebs could only afford a room collectively, and there was no thought of missing any after-parties by heading home that night. It was late enough that the wedding guests had long since been kicked out of the banquet space and had been a little too rowdy at the lobby bar, and so some of us were making arrangements for a party in two rooms that communicated by a shared door.

I was on my way to the front desk to ask about the nearest liquor store when I saw Audra standing there with her hands spread out on the counter, imposing as she could sometimes be, complaining about the disturbances the wedding guests were causing. She had called down twice, she was saying measuredly, as though speaking to a child, and yet no resolution. She wanted to know what the clerk, personally, was going to do to rectify the situation.

Gossip held that Mik's father had spent something like 200k on the wedding, which probably explained why the Westin staff were reluctant to openly chastise some of the more inconsiderate guests. Whether the person working reception knew this I couldn't say, but he was certainly flustered, assuring this intimidating woman that he would send someone up there right away, proposing that she be moved, upgraded even, that he had vouchers and Starwood Points.

At that moment I realized I was still wearing my man-of-honor tux, not to mention holding a champagne flute half-filled with scotch, and so I took a step back, intending to slink away unseen.

But something caught her eye, and she turned, looked me over, and tucked a strand of straight black hair, razor-cut just above the shoulder, behind one ear, a move I later discovered was one of her signatures. She was striking, immediately calling to mind all the adjectives they use in shampoo ads because she had this obsidian hair that stood out against milky white skin. Even though it was after midnight, she still wore the standard corporate costume of that era: gray slacks, white collared shirt with knife-sharp lapels, and matching gray blazer, tailored more narrowly than a man's, subtly accentuating her curves. I recall also her heels because they made her seem almost six feet tall, deadly pointed at the toe, surely costing more than I made in two or three months. She drummed her fingers on the counter for a couple of beats, I remember distinctly, evaluating the fool in the disheveled monkey suit.

"You," she said finally, and my heart stopped.

The desk clerk, seeing his opening, started to say something about keeping it down, but I didn't really hear him; in fact, all the ambient noises in that surprisingly bustling lobby were completely swept away as I noticed her gray-green eyes with a slight crinkle around them as she broke into a skeptical smile. I was a little bit drunk, but it was like existing at absolute zero if you could survive at that temperature, the universe ground to a halt and buckled to a single moment in time and space as she approached me, wagging a finger as she would to a naughty child, still in slow motion, stepping to within inches of my face so I could suddenly smell her and see the diamond studs in her lobes and the graceful curve of her philtrum, the out-turned groove between her nose and upper lip, the precise word for which I had later learned in order to describe it in poems to her, and she took the champagne flute from me and shot back the two fingers of scotch sloshing in it.

She said it was obvious that she wouldn't be getting any sleep that night, and suggested I buy her a drink.

I forgot all about the party brewing in the adjoining rooms upstairs and guided her lightly by the lower back to the lobby bar, called the Clock Bar, which I knew was sparsely populated and had a leather booth in an appropriately shadowed corner. She wanted something with vodka and ginger beer, and I decided to stick with scotch, a high roller, although I abandoned the champagne flute at the bar. After ribbing me about how my animal friends and I saw fit to disrupt the hotel, where some people were actually working, we settled into conversation that seemed to me both natural and new, energizing.

It turned out she was eight years older than me, which would have made her thirty-one. She had gone to Dartmouth and then Harvard Business School, one of those people who are astoundingly articulate, distinctly pronouncing every syllable, especially hard final consonants such as *d* and *t*. She worked for a consultancy, she said, and although she lived in a condo in Georgetown, she had been flying across the entire continent twice a week for the past three months, working on a project for some bank in the financial district. She wasn't even supposed to be there on weekends, she explained, but orders came from on high so there she was.

Understand that I was in my early twenties, barely surviving my second year of graduate school, malnourished, begging any job I could—telemarketer, security guard, even a swing-shift at a salsa packaging facility—all while trying to keep up appearances, to maintain the frenetic social schedule of grad students everywhere, who must above all else never be perceived as working too hard while inwardly panicking and tortured by profound self-doubt and feelings of academic fraudulence, outwardly implying that they had read all of Benjamin in the original German.

Audra was like a being from another planet: unpretentious though in absolute control, accomplished, polished, flush with cash. She was an adult getting on with her life. I was fascinated that this woman was even speaking with little me and had the passing thought that maybe she just wanted to get laid, which is sort of what I wanted in that moment, too, so I tried not to overthink it.

That night we talked until the bar closed after two, and I didn't make it to the party as we went to her room instead, where she never thought twice about breaking into the exorbitantly-priced bottles in the mini-bar. After indeterminate time in muted light she said finally that she was a sucker for a man in a tux, I simply following her lead, she took it off as we kissed and I was turned on by the faint odor of executive-level labor that clung to her body, trapped by those tailored layers of cotton and wool.

———

After that night, we spent most of her free time together. She worked very long hours, from seven in the morning to nine or ten at night, sometimes later, sometimes on Saturdays, but I made myself available at times she appointed at the St. Francis, where I realized all the doormen and lobby staff knew who she was, had speculated about her personal life behind her back, and once I was in the picture they had decided I was her boy toy, and shot me knowing smirks as I walked through the doors, which I interpreted then as vicarious respect, thinking little did they know I'd had like $78 in my credit union checking account.

She would return from the financial district and slip into casual-seeming jeans and plain tees with extravagant accessories I hadn't even known existed like YSL handbags with gold padlocks and a Blackberry 850, brand-new that year and like something from *Star Trek*, a magical device which gave her the ability to access email from anywhere. We dined in the best restaurants in town and she would always say not to worry, that she was expensing it, and I got to know all the martini bars, in fashion then, and she had a rented M3 that she rocketed around town, grinding the clutch on the hills, perversely blasé, and sometimes she would stay for the weekend and we would head up to Napa or Sonoma and she would show me her favorite homespun restaurants in Guerneville. Audra—fun aristocrat, one of my grad school friends had dubbed her.

Once in Guerneville, under an arbor of trailing roses, she said that on the Monday before she met me, on the redeye from Dulles to SFO, she awoke with a twitch and couldn't remember whether she was flying home or to work and felt a sense of despair so overpowering that she sobbed in the darkened plane. I never could picture her sobbing, but realized then that despite her accomplishments and success, her hyper-lucid manner of speaking, she was inside a profoundly lonely person whose life had been given over to a career at the expense of cultivating personal relationships.

It was then she said she loved me, and I unblinkingly reciprocated.

Our relationship entered a new plane of bliss, and I really did think we would get married. I began looking into what it would take to transfer to Hopkins or even Maryland; and she, for her part, seemed to have a renewed sense of happiness as the more time we spent together, the more she became convinced that I loved her for her, and not for the sanitized version of glamour her lifestyle afforded a graduate student. I wrote her poetry, which I haven't done for any woman before or since, and she read it with wry appreciation.

Once I confessed to her that since high school I had been secretly waiting for a woman to quote my favorite line from Leonard Cohen, the one where the woman in the song explains that she prefers handsome men, but that for him she would make an exception.

"The woman was Janis Joplin," said Audra. "From what I understand."

I flew out to DC on several occasions, as she had more frequent flyer miles than she could ever possibly hope to use, and I tried to imagine myself inserted into her life there. Her sleek condo was furnished with the kind of angular modernist pieces I'd really only seen in catalogues, and I would have flashes of my own sunken mattress, dragged in tow to college and then graduate school, as I sat on the edges of her Philippe Starck chairs, which were designed to look like classic Louis XV baroque armchairs (she explained), but were made from solid pieces of transparent polycarbonate; or else gingerly used her George Nakashima coffee table, which she had commissioned from his daughter, who had sketched out a design to meet Audra's particular specifications.

Her East Coast friends were all lawyers or finance guys with places in Dupont Circle and Tribeca who had low opinions of California and wanted to know what I thought about Gray Davis and Ernesto Zedillo and Prop 187. Back in San Francisco there was a diaspora of her HBS classmates; they had moved there out of anywhere else in the country, married one another, and were renovating two or three million dollar Victorians in Noe Valley. They were wickedly smart, these people, brutally athletic, often gracious, entertaining, good-looking, and their skepticism about why I would want to analyze novels for a living ironically united this one percent with the ninety-niners I later met in the carcinogenic bars of Pennsylvania.

But Audra, she respected scholastic endeavors of any kind, said to me all the time that she envied my freedom to pursue things that weren't dictated solely by "exchange value," and I could tell she was genuinely proud when I would venture to tell her about some article I was working on or a presentation I had given. She considered having read difficult literary novels badges of intellectual prowess, and had books like William Gass' *The Tunnel* on her shelves, and would ask me incisive questions about them and even work them in to conversations about other things.

So it came as a shock when she called me one afternoon at the house—cell phones existed, but I certainly didn't have one—as I was packing a bag to come see her.

She was sorry, she said, but she had just admitted to herself that the thing between us was "irrational," that besides she was being sent on an extended assignment out of California. She said, again, that she was sorry or so sorry, and hung up, and I ripped the grimed-over push button phone from the wall and threw it across the kitchen because I hated it, in fact hated every object and person in our uncaring void of a universe.

That was Audra Wester.

—

Pushing the vibratory limits of my Tercel, I made Cubby's in record time. I felt he would have guidance, would know what to do about this email. As I shot through the countryside of lush, ten-acre estates, I thought how far he had come while still retaining his basic sense of Cubby-ness. Had we met as adults, it's unlikely we would have been friends—but I'd known him since the age of twelve.

My best memory of Cubby was from senior year in high school, when I had discovered those Leonard Cohen songs I would later quote back to Audra. I became a closet aficionado because we both seemed to have trouble with women, 1967 Leonard and I, and I convinced myself that all those great-looking athletes who listened to Top 40 and drove 300 Zs were in reality slack-jawed lemmings in letter jackets, and who wanted to go to prom anyway?

But good old Cubby, still searing from his success with some *Baywatch* extra look-alike, never castigated me for being introverted, for having Resting Bitch Face. Far from it. When I read a report that Cohen had renounced worldly things and taken vows at the Mount Baldy Zen Center, incredible because located in the very mountains that were the backdrop to our entire suburban childhood, not even an hour away, he insisted that we go check it out, that maybe we could spot him. I said what about your trip to Huntington with the baseball team, but he swore this was more important and we drove up into the mountains to find the Zen Center with no plan but to gawk at Leonard Cohen.

Tending the grounds was a gruff cartoon monk who told us to scram but Cubby was undaunted and we snuck around to a wooded area where there were gaps between the fence slats and he peered through with pure enthusiasm saying holy shit I see him, look, he's there on a bench, and I pressed my eye to the gap, making out a blurry figure beyond, surely not Leonard Cohen, but Cubby believed, wanting to cheer me up, and I said oh yeah, you're right, it *is* him, and he pounded me on the back, saying see, there you go.

Now, twenty years later, after Cubby had gone to Wharton while I'd opted for an English degree ("recklessly," he said), he lived in a sprawling, colonial manse in the northern suburbs of Philadelphia, and would declare, counter-intuitively, that I was "lucky" with my prehistoric car and rotten apartment in the way a villager in an Amazonian jungle was lucky, because for both of us, the villager and me, things were "simpler." He had a wife and three kids and investment accounts and a lengthy driveway that wound through endless over-fertilized lawns and rare, ornamental evergreens to reveal his massive white-shingled house, stately and infuriating. He even had out buildings.

When I pulled in, suddenly realizing that I hadn't called ahead, I saw him standing at the mouth of one of those out buildings, a carriage house, polishing the hood ornament of a Mercedes Benz so black it seemed imaginary, a mirrory symbol of something or other distorting the sun and clouds in its reflection.

He looked up at the sound of my car, recognized it, then acted like it was the most natural thing in the world that I was showing up unannounced on a weekday. He was wearing khaki shorts and a striped rugby shirt, which is what he almost always wore, and was looking, as he had over the last ten years or so, a little bit rounder and more padded than the last time I'd seen him. He had glasses with bright purple frames, a statement of youth or sophistication—or possibly desperation, I could never quite tell.

When I got out of my car, made all the more humiliating by the glistening Mercedes, I must have looked incredulous or disgusted, because he batted his eyes innocently and indicated the car with the chamois in his hand.

"Didn't I mention this?" he said.

"Nice," I said. "And sorry for dropping in. But I need to talk."

He beckoned me over, then massaged the car as he might a race horse while going into an involved story about how he had had every intention of getting some sort of electric vehicle, that he had even gone down to the lot, but found to his dismay that everything was back-ordered, and that he literally had no choice but to buy the Benz given that it was a top safety pick and he knew that I knew he would never compromise on safety.

As he was saying all this, I was momentarily distracted from the email and my supposed child, thinking about how Daimler-Benz hadn't exactly shied away from working with the Nazis once they came to power. In fact, they had been pretty enthusiastic about it, taking out these obnoxious ads in the *Volkischer Beobachter* linking their cars to the rightness of a certain vision of national destiny. Plus they were happy to retool their factories to build tanks, airplane engines, rocket components, you name it, and as the war dragged on, the company ramped up its armaments manufacturing on the backs of something like 60,000 forced laborers, prisoners of war, and camp detainees. A modern, technologically driven company "literally" reliant on slave labor.

This was the sort of thing I knew, but Cubby was smiling in that expansive way of his, raising his eyebrows up and down, so I let it go.

"A man of your stature can't really expect to be seen in a Prius," I said.

"Shoulda gone to business school, dude." He admired the car for another long minute, giving the hood ornament a few more passes with the chamois, then turned to me. "So how's the crisis?"

Just as he said that, from a side door burst his many kids, his three kids which seemed to me like a dozen or more, yelling and squealing and flinging themselves at him.

"Watch the car, watch the car, watch the car," he was saying over and over as one of the kids threw himself unbidden into Cubby's arms, and Cubby wrenched his back, or probably did, as he heaved the kid up, kid then dangling monkey-like and babbling drool. The elder daughter was gravely explaining that dinner was ready.

I was somewhat jumpy and had to pee. "Is this a bad time?" I said. "Because remember, you've always said that I can come by whenever, that I could just show up, because that's the kind of relationship we have."

"It's never a bad time," he insisted, groaning under the weight of the kid now hanging off his neck. He dislodged the kid, who then got perilously close to smearing sticky fingers across the Benz before Cubby yanked him by the back of his pants and deposited him out on the driveway. "Hungry?"

I looked at my phone and noted that it was barely five.

Inside, I stole into the powder room and relieved myself. When I was finished, I saw that my eyes were sunken, that I looked even pastier than usual. I splashed some water on my face, made a mental note to double up on the Age Rescue Eye Therapy with Caffeine, and tried to pat down and manipulate my sweat-plastered hair, but not to any real avail.

Finally, I wandered into the central part of the house. Unlike my loft-style apartment, Cubby's dominion was truly spacious, free of mildew, assertively air conditioned. The remodeled and expanded kitchen was anchored by an island onto which Cubby himself had poured a concrete countertop that was intended to lend a contemporary dimension to the colonial architecture. Yoon-Ju had it all done up in shabby-chic, so there were lots of artificially-weathered pieces of furniture, white-washed, rough-cut maps of the United States, distinctive farm implements. This careful décor had of course been overtaken utterly by ankle-busting toys strewn everywhere: plastic cars, yellow and pink tricycles, dinosaurs. Their $12,000 Sub-Zero fridge was encrusted with magnets and splotchy watercolors, a fact I took petty pleasure in.

The kids were now brimming around the island, Yoon-Ju was stirring something, and did a comical double take when I appeared and waved lamely.

She smiled, not altogether brightly, I mumbled some sad sack line, and she yelled at one of the kids for rattling a cabinet door. Cubby found some beers.

We made it through an unseasoned meal of chicken fingers and cardboard mac and cheese, during which the kids monopolized the time by trying to outdo one another for attention and being generally more rowdy and rangy with the geography around their blunt color-blocked plates than the dinner table normally allowed. They play-fought, flung macaroni elbows, and picked with their fingers, which didn't look to me particularly clean, even after their cursory pre-dinner rinse. None of this fazed Cubby or Yoon-Ju, who carried right on above the nonsensical murmuring. Yoon-Ju was ramrod straight in her chair, not even touching the back, and barely concealed her irritation regarding my unannounced presence. Cubby winced and smiled and tried to make conversation about Angie, whom we both knew Yoon-Ju liked.

Cubby could tell that I was antsy, and he and Yoon-Ju were exchanging what are called meaningful glances, punctuated by Yoon-Ju occasionally asking me again if I wanted some ice water, because I looked "peaked." Once the kids had picked through what they were going to pick through, Yoon-Ju collected their plates, hooked Cubby by the collar (figuratively), and they had a clipped debate by the degraded Sub Z.

I sat watching the kids argue over a fire truck, thinking about the real ones that day Benj and I were in the yard. Some images flash back when you least expect them: a gurney, a fogging oxygen mask, a can of Coke a cop had given me, shaken all over my knuckles.

Cubby snapped me out of my reverie, pushing my shoulder and indicating I should follow him.

We disappeared to his office, a different world, mahogany paneled and leather clad, a parody of what a rich person's study is supposed to look like. He had his Wharton diploma displayed in an ostentatious frame, and I had no idea the fate of my physical diplomas.

He actually had one of those hinged globes that open to reveal liquor and glasses, the kind of sepia-washed prop you see in a soap opera titan's den, and he noisily poured us a couple of drinks. I had planted myself in a huge club chair and he handed me one. He stood over me for a moment, torn between annoyance and apprehension, waited until I sipped, then asked me what the hell was going on.

Exhale, the bourbon was pretty good, and I summarized the new email, which suggested it wasn't a scam after all. He demanded to read it, so I brought it up on my phone and turned it over.

He read slowly, saying holy shit, holy shit, holy shit.

After some time I grunted a Neanderthal plea for recognition and he starting laughing. "To be fair," he began, "you *are* a slut. And sooner or later, this is what happens to sluts."

I wanted to punch him in the mouth, but instead I just sat there and took it, feeling my face growing hot.

"Relax," he said. "Everything's so serious with you. But this is good news, no?"

"You're missing the point," I said, nestling the drink in my folded arms. "Audra Wester is the point."

He spun around, bewildered, hurt almost, no longer laughing. I was slumped in the chair and he came over and sat sidesaddle on the arm and put his hands on my shoulders, like an older brother about to deliver a heart-to-heart.

"Audra?" he said. "The one with the tits and the BMW? How is *she* the point?"

Is that how I had described her? I felt physically beaten by the truth of the email, a sensation compounded by the fact that Cubby knew very well my totally reasoned arguments against having kids—and yet there he was, a dumb fucker who had failed, in a general way, to entice me with the charms of his own children, leaning in, suggesting that a woman who had broken my heart and kept a pregnancy from me was irrelevant to the new facts of my life. It was patronizing, vaguely insulting, and he kept going on about how it was time I changed my point of view and adapted to the reality at hand.

I waved him off, so he took a different tack, appealing to what he took to be my professorial inquisitiveness.

"Aren't you curious though, a little? Cuz ... the details in the email are pretty disturbing." He still had my phone, and read off the parts about this girl not being able to leave, or this girl being cat-called by men, pausing over and rereading the lines that implied some clash of cultures, a conflict between what he was no doubt imagining as a kid not unlike his own daughter, and the darkest and most retrograde vision of Islam we can muster in the West. Pretty soon he had lathered himself up into a scenario in which al Qaeda was mentioned, child brides were mentioned, sex trafficking was mentioned, and I finally said to dial it back, but it was too late, he'd wormed his way into my head and had me feeling like a dirtbag.

"If it's some horror show over there," I said weakly, "where is her mother? Why is this my problem?"

Now he was disappointed. He read from the part of the email about Audra being AWOL, said it was time for me to man up, to act like a father.

"How can I possibly be a 'father' when I wasn't even aware of this person two days ago?"

I know Cubby very well, and I could tell in that moment he was resisting the urge to mock explain the birds-and-the-bees, if only to lighten the tension. Instead, he said something about life itself being out of my comfort zone, that this was an example of "life" and that sometimes you just had to take "life" as it comes.

"No offense," he was saying, "but maybe now is the time to put on your big boy pants and think about someone besides yourself. I say this with affection, but maybe this is the moment to deal with reality, this reality, which is a girl distressed enough to write some guy she's never met, probably not knowing if you flaked out on them, if you didn't want her, this girl asks you out of how many billion people in the world for a little understanding, and you're a grown man, so what exactly is the problem?"

It's possible he was right, but I was in no mood to acknowledge it. It was moot anyway because I couldn't afford to fly to Kenya, which I said, and then regretted it instantly because now I'd introduced a problem he could solve. He was on his laptop like a retriever on a rabbit, attacking it almost, typing and clicking and saying well let's just see what tickets are going for these days.

I made some feeble gesture to the effect that I couldn't allow him to pay for the ticket and he said nonsense, a dynamic that had played out many times over the years, especially as his net worth marched north-ward while mine remained mired in the margins of poetry books.

He absorbed himself in a booking website as I stared into space, and then he started wondering aloud what Audra was doing in Kenya in the first place. "She worked at Accenture or Deloitte or someplace?"

"Yeah," I said, refilling my drink. "But remember, I haven't spoken to her in fourteen years, so who knows, really."

He was a master at working online, and as he was searching flights, he plugged Audra's name into the usual search engines and social networking sites, but was coming up short, like totally short, as in there was nothing about her online, a discovery Cubby found deeply unnerving.

"She's living off the grid in Kenya, apparently," I said.

"Kenya has a grid, you racist!" He was zipping around the internet, and still couldn't find anything about her, and as he was emphasizing how strange this was, especially if she did still work for a major consultancy, he emerged with what he claimed was the ideal flight according to some metrics he didn't share. I didn't hear the details but it was JFK to Nairobi by way of London, and was soon, and he was circling with his mouse like should I book it?

I needed to back things up a second. Cubby was talking as if I were just going to wing it over to Africa with no plan whatsoever, but naturally I had questions. Did I need a visa? How to get to Lamu, a place I had never even heard of? What, anyway, would I do when I got there? Who would watch the cats?

"Listen to this," said Cubby, peering into his screen. "From the State Department website: 'Some schools and other facilities acting as cultural rehabilitation centers are operating in Kenya with inadequate or nonexistent licensing and oversight. Reports of minors and young adults being held in these facilities against their wills and physically abused are common.' Whoa. This is *evidence*. But what the fuck?"

That snippet from the State Department clinched the deal in Cubby's mind, and he took it to mean that everything in the emails was true, that I had yielded to his plan, neither of which I knew to be the case.

The conversation snowballed, though, and in a wash of more bourbon and dexterous searching, we learned that Lamu was on the coast near Somalia, far from Nairobi but a vacation spot with duney beaches, that I could get a Kenyan visa for fifty bucks upon arrival, that there were flights from Nairobi to Lamu that departed from a smaller airport elsewhere in the city. Cubby was making it all sound like a snap, but I was now doubly uneasy as my going there started to look like a tangible possibility. Probably I would need shots—for all I knew it was a region where certain fungal infections were common.

"What if it's a region where certain fungal infections are common?" I said, aloud, and he snorted.

I had done my share of traveling, but it was almost all to Europe—Western Europe, at that. My most exotic excursion had been to South Korea for a conference. It was in Seoul, and I went mainly because the costs had been covered by a diversity grant fallen in the college's lap, plus I wanted to say I'd been to Korea, but the whole experience was so expertly managed that I hardly felt in a foreign country at all. I had been met at the airport, driven by chromed town car to the chromed hotel, which also housed the convention center, was spoken to in passable English by the hotel and conference staff, given meal vouchers for kimchi and noodle breakfasts, kimchi and grilled meat dinners, all served in the banquet halls of the hotel, and was taken on tours of the Ville outside Camp Casey and the Namdaemun, or Great Southern Gate, then being restored after a fire. Otherwise, I only left the hotel complex to bar hop around Seoul with some old friends from graduate school. I had once described this trip to impress Yoon-Ju, asking her if it were true that certain bridges and overpasses were wired with explosives in case of invasion from the north, but she said not to believe everything you hear, and by the way Itaewon wasn't like that anymore. I had never been to a place like what I imagined Kenya to be.

Cubby was Googling and urging me not to get too wrapped up in shots.

"Are you going to be handling any livestock," he said, mostly to himself. "Doubtful. No. I'm saying 'no.'"

Don't think I was yielding easily, because I certainly did articulate my objections, repeatedly, but was no match for Cubby's zealous problem-solving skills and formidable bank accounts. Finally I was defeated when, all at once, he was gripped by a flash of insight, and cited some guy Deuce, who had briefly roomed with Cubby in Philly the year before he met Yoon-Ju. This Deuce loved to drink, Cubby was saying, surely I remembered him and the night we finished what was intended to be an unfinishable fishbowl concoction at a college bar. I did recall this, but only dimly. When Cubby knew him, Deuce was doing an anthropology postdoc at Penn but had been at Chicago and had specialized, Cubby was pretty sure, in Uganda or Ghana or one of those places.

"What you need," he was saying, "is a fixer. And Deuce is like Mr. Africa. He'll hook you up, smooth the waters, pave the way."

"This is all metaphorical!" I yelled, spilling my drink a little. What would happen, in the non-metaphorical realm?

Cubby had homed-in on some informational site, was making notes and cross-references, said not to worry, and I told him I *was* worried, that I needed a minute, was starved for air.

I tipped a few more drops of bourbon in my glass and noticed a tabletop humidor near the globe and gestured at it like you mind if I have one of those cigars? Cubby glanced over and said sure, that they were Cohiba Robustos, the genuine article from the Viñales Valley that he had procured via a guy he knew at "the club." Because embargoes don't really apply to Captains of Industry. He started telling me about the leaves, the veins in the leaves, but I just said where's the cutter thing and lighter, and when I had them I took everything out to the deck, leaving him to the internet.

It was immense, the deck, overlooking the property and constructed not of regular lumber but of a space-age engineered composite that would never crack or require painting. I found a secluded corner, clipped the cigar, then got it going with Cubby's ridiculous plasma torch, a light saber for a Jedi gnome. I'm not really a cigar smoker, but I figured it might calm me down, so I experimented with tentative slow drags and couldn't remember if you were supposed to inhale completely or hold the smoke in your mouth.

I tried different techniques for a while, but my thoughts weren't exactly focused: What did this girl have to do with me? Why is fire in your throat desirable? Why were claims being made on me? How much did that deck cost? What are the early signs of esophageal cancer? Why should I disrupt my life? I posed these questions to myself, but had no real answers to them, and started speculating about what my sister would do in this situation, because like Cubby, she was more instinctively fluent in the language of others than I.

The minute she had graduated high school, my sister fled for a cheap college north of Boston, leaving me with my dad and his girlfriend Valerie while I saw less and less of my mother, who became enmeshed with Ted the Truck Driver, as my dad always referred to him, and started taking trips to Vegas with surprising frequency. Meanwhile, my sister was in a Sleater-Kinney type band as she studied psychology, slowly becoming fed up with the whiney granola men and women who judged her if she used lipstick. She moved back to Southern California, purportedly to be closer to our mother, who may or may not have developed a gambling problem. She had arrived back on the West Coast with debts and a degree she didn't use, instead working a string of crappy jobs until finding a decent one in the offices of a real estate developer. By then, I had gone off to college myself, and since she'd become relatively settled in her own life, with an apartment, a boyfriend, and a graduated student loan repayment plan, she started calling me twice a week to harangue me good-naturedly and dispense wisdom.

By the time I had moved to Pennsylvania, she'd gotten married to a guy she had met through work. He had tattoo sleeves and a raised truck and his own drywall business that subbed for the real estate developer when they rehabbed houses out in Echo Park or Silverlake. They wound up having a kid, nicknamed Chico because of some inside joke with his family, and I visited them only once for the holidays and they were a photogenic but quietly strained family. Within a year she discovered something on his computer that led, after months of negotiation and broken dishes, to their divorce. Of course I was a continent away for all of that, and so heard about it third-hand, from my sister's point of view, and would console her to the best of my abilities as life as she knew it unraveled—and then again, as she faced the terrifying prospect of dating in her later thirties, shuttling a child half-time.

A few years after her divorce, my sister got hung up on visiting me for Thanksgiving, said she didn't want me to be alone even though I kept assuring her that I truly didn't care, that it was just another day to me, but she insisted because Chico was at his dad's and she had like five days off in a row and I agreed and had to buy a bunch of new cookware so she could make an unnecessarily complicated turkey dinner.

As we tucked into the meal, she smiled and said wasn't it better than forlornly watching Mr. Carlson drop live turkeys from a helicopter on *WKRP in Cincinnati*, and though I was serious about not caring about Thanksgiving, I told her that it was.

But that didn't last long because she had poured a lot of wine with dinner, and in the course of fielding her highly-specific questions about my love life, I had mentioned that I was no longer interested in dating single mothers—I should have known better—and outrage ensued. She accused me of being anti-feminist, and I countered by saying how is being up front and honest anti-feminist, and she said that a blanket policy of discrimination was anti-feminist, and we went round and round until she finally said to leave it alone.

Later, after more wine, she had her promised phone call with Chico, who was at a huge feast at his grandparents' house. There was nowhere to go in my loft-style apartment so I watched as my sister did such an impressive job of being extra high-voiced and enthusiastic as her son ticked off all the people who were there and all the fun he was having, and when she hung up after only a few minutes, as Chico was wanted by some cousins, she cupped her phone under her chin and looked up at me with a special kind of heartbroken desolation I hadn't seen on her before, and I realized, stupidly, embarrassingly late, that the visit wasn't really about rescuing me from a holiday alone, that it wasn't really about me at all.

Out on Cubby's architectural deck, I thought that when it came to understanding how my sister triangulated her opinions about dating and Thanksgiving and feminism, I was often missing the point. I decided to call her. She answered immediately.

"What a treat," she said. "What's the emergency?"

"Funny you should mention emergencies," I said.

I told her the story, said in a manic breath that Cubby was encouraging me to go to Africa but I couldn't tell if he was doing so because he thought it would be hilarious to put me in such an uncomfortable situation or if he sincerely believed it was a good, workable idea.

"Slow down," she said. "Are you drunk?"

"Hardly. I just need a little of your famous sisterly advice."

The line was silent for too long a time after I got all this out, the cigar was making me feel not calmed but queasy, and after many seconds, because it seemed awkward, the silence, I said that we'd used birth control, been responsible.

"Bup bup bup," she said. "Don't want to hear about your sex life."

"I wasn't being stupid is all I'm saying."

Another silence, another sigh, and I was trying to figure out if she was disappointed or skeptical about the whole sequence of events or what. My stomach was turning, though for some reason I kept on smoking the cigar.

"Will," she said finally. "I think you know what the right thing to do is. I think you're calling me merely to confirm that you're doing the right thing."

"But I have no idea what I'm doing. That's why I'm calling."

"Don't be like our parents," she said flatly. "Now say hello to your nephew."

Our parents. It was only ten months after Benj had fallen that they were done, and my mother didn't have the emotional wherewithal to fight for custody of my sister and me. For years she only saw us one weekend a month, and even then could be remote and hostile.

"You may be interested to know," she said to me once when she'd had too much to drink, "that it's your fault your father and I split up. No one can withstand that kind of tragedy, no one."

A lifetime later, my therapist said to take that with a grain of salt, assuring me that everyone processes grief differently.

I pushed myself off Cubby's Design Within Reach rattan barrel chairs, which were $2100 a piece, he'd noted, and aimed for the railing with the intention of admiring the rolling property in the golden twilight. But the instant I got to my feet, I realized simultaneously that I was unsteady and was going to Kenya, that I was sick from the unholy combination of bourbon, mac and cheese, and the cigar, and barely made it to the railing before I vomited over the side onto a bed of hydrangeas, which Cubby had said flowered in different colors depending on soil acidity.

I heaved and heaved and wondered later if the acrid contents of my body would one day manifest in otherworldly blooms.

3.

WELL BEFORE ANY of this had happened, I had read an essay in *Granta* by Binyavanga Wainaina called "How to Write About Africa." The best-minded people had found it to be a deliciously spot-on catalogue of all the beats non-African writers put in their portraits of Africa: the AK-47s, the child soldiers, the loyal servants, the obsession with sky and open spaces, etc. Now it's famous, this essay, handy when teaching nineteen-year-olds about the image of Africa in the West, and I had discovered a slickly-produced video of Djimon Hounsou reading excerpts to a blank-faced white girl who flickered in and out of the jump cuts, and rather than see themselves in this girl, my students, the white ones, would twist in their chairs and point out how ironic it was that a year after Wainaina's essay appeared, Hounsou starred in *Blood Diamond*, a Doomed Africa flick that uncritically reproduced virtually every device Wainaina mocks. My students were defiant in this observation; but everybody has to eat, I thought, even Hounsou, who in his spare time was an underwear model.

I remembered Wainaina later, on the flight to Kenya, but not in the moment at Cubby's. Scarcely in my right mind, I had wandered back inside in a state of clammy post-vomit euphoria and announced that I would, magnanimously, undertake a journey to Africa.

"My man," said Cubby. He turned the computer screen to face me and pushed the mouse over in my direction. "The arrow's right on the purchase button, it couldn't be easier. All you have to do is click."

He had a knack for making even pipe dreams seem reasonable, and I looked back and forth at the mouse and the hovering arrow, looked at Cubby with his white-capped grin and purple glasses, shot my hand down and clicked before I could back out.

"My maaaan," he exclaimed again.

I sipped some Seven-Up and tapped out a trembling message to this girl, giving her my flight information, pressing for more details about Audra, about their situation, but the only reply the next day was an address of sorts, just Orchid Club, Lamu.

This was only the first of the red flags.

After the email about Orchid Club, for instance, I heard nothing further. Since the ticket was nonrefundable, and she had said her internet access was difficult, Cubby said spotty communication was to be expected, and though I wasn't so sure, I just sort of allowed myself to be carried on the raft he had set in motion.

He had negotiated everything over email with Deuce, who was in turn negotiating over Skype with a friend who knew a fixer in Kenya, and when I expressed my discomfort with this nebulous chain of links, Cubby once again brushed it aside, telling me that's how it's done there, "informal economies," he kept saying, and so I'd better get used to it. I relented, because Deuce had apparently insisted that although he had never met this fixer in person, he was cousin of one of his best friends in Kampala and was therefore to be trusted implicitly.

—

Cubby invited me to crash in his guest suite that night, and I could feel the cold front emanating from Yoon-Ju's general direction, so the next morning I quietly slipped out a side door and made my way back home, somehow both parched and bloated.

The cats were furious and had destroyed a door mat and throw pillow Angie had bought me.

I saw her later that evening, when she showed up following a double shift, smelling like aerated fryer grease and bearing cartons of Chinese food. As usual, she was laden with bags: plastic bags stretched out with the food cartons, a floppy canvas Strand Bookstore bag she used for daily transport, and an overstuffed olive drab duffel filled with clothes and other necessities. As she extricated herself from these bags, distributing them across the kitchen counter and flopping the duffel on the bed, I told her about the latest emails, about my decision to go to Kenya. I did mention Cubby, but only as a peripheral player, because I wanted to give the impression that I had arrived at this ethical decision all on my own.

Unburdened from the bags, she listened and nodded, opening up the cartons and sticking spoons into them. It was only when we had pulled up to the food at my bistro table, only after she had taken off her shoes, curled her swollen toes, and hunched over some noodles with a pair of freshly separated chopsticks—it was only then that she acknowledged what I had told her.

"Sounds like an adventure," she said in an open-ended way that suggested she wanted me to invite her along.

"It's far from a vacation," I said.

"That's somewhere I've always wanted to go."

"I'm trying to mentally prepare myself for how stressful it will be."

"To see animals in the wild like that."

"Apparently you need drivers, guides. You can't just turn up with a backpack like in Europe."

"I have personal days saved up."

"Apparently I need shots, malaria medication. The whole nine."

"Elephants."

"Apparently there are State Department warnings for certain regions."

"The buddy system is tried and true."

We went around like that for the duration of the meal, eggrolls to fortune cookies, and it became clear not only that she expected to be invited, but also that she thought, in a visceral or intuitive sort of way, that I was out of my depth attempting Kenya alone. She had lived in Cambodia for a year in college, during which time she had witnessed a failed political assassination, and she used this experience as a kind of credential, proof that she was worldly and experienced. The truth was, I didn't mind if she came with me because I was anxious and conflicted about the whole undertaking. Neither of us really had the money, but over my objections, Cubby had paid for my plane tickets ("$5000 is nothing to me, and this isn't even half that").

Angie cracked open a fortune cookie, pulled out the ribbon languidly, but then nearly fell off her chair when she read it.

"Um, OK," she said, handing it to me. "This is fucking eerie."

I took the fortune and read: "Better to see something once than hear about it a thousand times."

I knew about the origins of fortune cookies, about the tangle of Japanese and Chinese immigrants from San Francisco to New York City, about the connections to the Chinese Exclusion Act and Executive Order 9066—this was also the sort of thing I knew, but knowing it didn't necessarily negate the eeriness of this particular fortune.

"What the hell?" I said.

"It's our karma to go together."

"I don't believe in fortune cookies."

"Just admit it's a sign," she said, tugging on my arm playfully. "And how about this? I'll kick in the six hundred bucks from the photographs? I'll come up with some more cash and get a week off. All my managers love me. An airtight plan if there ever was one, hey?"

Karmic resonances of the fortune aside, the idea of having Angie along was in fact a relief, a safety net, and I heard myself too readily telling her that if she contributed the six hundred, we'd figure out the rest, meaning that I'd likely be loading up my own credit cards, providing she could get the time off without consequences. I kept thinking about what she had written on the LASER SURGERY pamphlet, that she felt "awful," and though I wasn't privy to what precisely was making her feel awful, she seemed momentarily transformed at the prospect of going to Kenya, was like her old upbeat self before I had poisoned her with all my negativity. Even as I was hesitant about the wheels now in motion, I thought this could be a bright side to the proceedings, a gift I could give to Angie, who tended to support me unequivocally.

"Let's do it," I said, and she smacked me on the lips melodramatically, realizing aloud and with urgency that she'd need to draw up a packing list immediately.

Predictably, her parents were openly skeptical when she told them we were going to Kenya, even as we omitted the real reason for the trip. Her father was mainly confused as to why we weren't going "some-place nice" like Dublin or Paris, while her mother was hysterically concerned for her safety. She "just didn't know" what sort of "facilities" they had over there in Africa, whether there were any trustworthy cops mixed in with all the corrupt ones, nor if the people there could "help themselves"—and we didn't know what exactly she meant by that. "They have safaris in *South* Africa you know," she said. Angie calmed them not with facts and rationality, which would never have worked, but with an emotional appeal that she was their only daughter and this had been a dream of hers since she was a little girl, and so on, and they finally softened and even agreed to float her some walking around money.

I didn't bother mentioning the trip to my own parents, but I did email my sister, if just to let her know that I was doing what she considered the right thing.

—

A neighbor agreed to check in on the cats, thus relieving slightly a major source of stress, and after minimal other planning on my part, three days later Angie and I disembarked at Jomo Kenyatta International Airport in Nairobi.

If I was apprehensive, Angie was the picture of confidence, the kind of person who could take new countries and new situations in stride. She had bought a guidebook to Kenya, had gone out and sourced a bucket hat, hiking boots, and nylon pants you could zip the legs off to convert into shorts—that's how excited she was. What Swahili she knew came from *The Lion King* but she had also bought a phrase-book, though I pointed out that English was an official language, too. "People feel seen if you learn a little of their language" she said. We both had these ungainly metal-framed hippie backpacks we picked up at the Army Surplus store. I had an ill-considered money belt that was already causing a rash at my navel and proved totally impractical when I attempted to change some dollars to shillings at the airport, something Angie kept warning me against because her guidebook cautioned that the rates there would be unfavorable.

After I received my wad of shillings, I could tell Angie was looking to me for our next move, so I steeled myself and led her out the international arrivals door, striding past everyone penned behind the stanchion, ignoring the touts and pushy taxi drivers there because I was trying to look like I knew what I was doing. That tactic worked in the short term, but it only got us as far as the curb, and I was stymied there, so pretended to scrutinize the line of cars creeping forward, as though I were looking for a close friend who was picking us up.

In fact, we were supposed to have been met by the acquaintance of Cubby's buddy Deuce, who had emailed Cubby back right away, within the hour, saying that he knew of a guy in Nairobi who was the greatest fixer in all of East Africa. He soon wrote again saying that since time was of the essence this person, Simeon Karanja, was available in the coming week, and for a trivial fee for time and expenses, would meet us at the airport and accompany us by plane to Lamu, where he would help us locate the exact address the girl had given me.

I guess I had expected that Simeon would have greeted us at the airport, with sunglasses and a sign, but instead we were left lingering on the freshly painted curb, inundated with steamy macadam heat, sooty exhaust, and a smoky grill smell wafting from a restaurant that seemed attached to the arrivals area.

"Look at this," Angie was saying. She had a long-snouted camera hanging from her neck, she didn't care, and uncapped the lens. She was talking about the chaos of people getting in and out of cars, maneuvering between vans and buses, and was instantly absorbed in taking shots while I was left to plot our next move, hungry from the smell of whatever was being grilled.

I was already sweating, though the weather itself was surprisingly temperate, and was beginning to second guess my judgment on the whole matter. We had no hotel booked, nor did I even know which airport hosted the domestic flights. We had our anti-malaria pills, sunscreen, and Angie's guidebook, but I didn't even have this Simeon's number, which was irrelevant since I had convinced Angie to leave our phones at home for fear of theft. Patting my empty pocket and my wrist, I realized also that I didn't even have a watch.

Angie, though, was utterly in the moment, was waving and chatting with people, asking permission to take their photo as she laughed and crouched for better angles, good-naturedly scolding the men who were flirting with her and taking her picture with their phones as I stood off to the side, studying the crush of vehicles.

Just then, a battered 4x4 utility vehicle, a mud-caked Nissan Patrol, appeared from the smog, convulsed at the curb before me, and someone inside called my name.

I bent down to peer in: the driver was alone, wearing a corn-colored polo shirt and jean shorts, a gold watch on one wrist and a silver bracelet on the other.

I asked if he was Simeon and he was already impatient. "No, Denzel Washington. Get in."

Angie snapped a few more shots, said goodbye to her new friends, tossed her gear into the backseat, and hopped in. I started to follow her into the back, but Simeon twisted around incredulously.

"Yo, my guy," he said. "Up here. I'm not a chauffeur."

Angie flashed me a smile, shrugged, and I climbed in front, onto the springy and sticky vinyl seat. I reached across to shake his hand, unsure, still, of how he knew it was us.

"A wild guess," he said, jamming into gear and taking off without checking his mirrors.

He had these seventies style glasses fitted with transition lenses that would darken or not depending on the ambient light. Once out of the truck I discovered he was on the short side, but was one of those men who just assumed the bearing of someone much larger and more physically fit. He didn't ask how the flight was, didn't in fact say anything else before pulling into traffic.

Angie was marveling aloud at the differences between Nairobi and New York City, was again taking seemingly indiscriminate shots of everything she was seeing, pointing out whatever was unusual from her perspective, the arc of the streetlights, the number of people balanced on a single scooter, the ramshackle M-Pesa stalls crooked in the shadows of glimmering glass buildings.

Simeon was silent, driving as though we weren't even there, so finally after an uncomfortable interval I asked him if he lived in Nairobi, having to shout slightly as the windows were all rolled down for air circulation.

But his phone rang, and he answered, weaving around vehicles in the dense city traffic. He spoke quickly, annoyed, in a mixture of English and a local language I didn't understand. Mainly in the other language. The phone caught my eye because I had owned the exact model maybe five years before, a silver LG clamshell, still marked with the orange Cingular logo, and I turned around to point this out to Angie.

"Look at all these Barclays," she said. "Rubis. Petro. What is M-Pesa?"

Up front, Simeon snapped his phone shut and turned to me for the first time. "Apologies but there's a trifling issue at home, and we need to make a detour."

Angie popped her head up between the two front seats. "Nothing serious, I hope."

"It will be fine soon enough," Simeon said. We'd stay at his place outside Kajiado that night, he explained, then find a flight to Lamu the next day. "This is the best way. The only way."

"So we're *not* going to Lamu," said Angie.

I saw two paths forking into alternative futures: on the one hand, we could trust him; after all, I was a man of the world, an academic with all the negative opinions about colonialism and global capitalism that labeled implied, Angie had lived in Cambodia for a year, so why should we racistly assume this man was going to kidnap us? Maybe Angie didn't assume this, she in fact seemed up for anything, was leaning forward between the seats with an elbow propped up on each one, saying to Simeon that she was excited to see where he lived.

On the other hand, we were in a rattletrap at the mercy of some character we had just met, vouched for by an acquaintance of a friend of a guy best remembered by Cubby for his legendary drinking abilities. We were also in a region where we had no experience whatsoever, on an errand about which I, personally, was ambivalent—to put it mildly.

Simeon was assuring Angie that he lived in a beautiful part of the country, but asked again if the "detour" was all right, directing the question at me, the man, even though I had the feeling he was merely asking for decorum's sake, that the detour was happening no matter how I responded.

I did my best to play it cool when I said fine, fine, that would be fine, and Angie sank back to her seat.

He turned to me again, probably just then registering my discomfort. "I hope you brought some other clothes."

I looked down. I was wearing a long-sleeved khaki shirt, non-breathable, rolled to the elbows, khaki pants with lots of pockets, and, following Angie, hiking boots. All I needed was a pith helmet and luxurious mustache.

"Your wife looks good," Simeon said suggestively—or not. "But we'll have to find you some better clothes."

Then, without warning, he swung off the highway, grinding down with afternoon traffic, and onto a dirt bypass.

"Shortcut," he said. "Gridlock is a real bitch through town."

"Ooooo," said Angie.

Simeon explained that a couple of weeks before, his friends had been driving this shortcut and had been held up by a group of guys who'd hidden by the road as it passed Kibera, the city-within-Nairobi endlessly studied and documented because it was either the first or second largest urban slum in Africa.

"AK-47s," he said, and I couldn't tell if he was fucking with us. Maybe he knew Binyavanga Wainaina.

But as we approached Kibera, spread out in a wide valley just below the road, he locked his door and instructed Angie to roll up her window.

"This place will be gone in ten years," he said. "The land is too valuable for slums."

He slowed as we drove by so Angie and I could soak it in: Kibera was a cityscape of low-built houses made from brick, cast-off materials, corrugated metal, fabricated absent foundations on subtly shifting hills of garbage. There you had to watch out for Flying Toilets, Simeon explained. "They don't even have plumbing, so they shit in plastic bags and fling it out their front doors. Fooorrre!"

As we rolled by, Angie was clicking away, and I wondered briefly how this kind of ruin porn would compare in her mind with what she shot around the steel mill in Pennsylvania. When we hit a crest overlooking Kibera, we came upon a crew of surveyors preparing to construct a major highway over the dirt bypass—according to Plan 2030, Simeon was saying, there was supposed to be high-speed rail along that corridor. Earth movers and jeeps were parked among massive mounds of gravel. "When talking about exploitation by foreigners," wrote Wainaina, "mention the Chinese and Indian traders." The surveyors did indeed appear Chinese, wore mesh neon vests and hardhats, and I questioned if what I was seeing were pieces of a postmodern burlesque. We inched past the crew, Angie shot them and waved, and they shook their heads like it was a DMZ and cameras were verboten. Simeon said neutrally that China was now the go-to financier for infrastructure projects in the country, harbingers, he thought, of a new and perhaps even more transformative Scramble for Africa.

"Where will all these people go?" asked Angie, but he didn't answer.

Back on the highway and suddenly talkative, Simeon drove with a level of fanaticism not totally commensurate with the under-regulated road system, passing in the shoulder and cursing those with too-slow reaction times, excoriating vehicles with especially noxious exhaust. As he did so he carried on a series of loosely related monologues: about those Chinese builders who ate all the stray dogs in the area, even being so audacious as to take out newspaper ads offering thousands of shillings regardless of breed, more if they were already skinned, and did we think that was "civilized"; about the bloviating Nicholas Biwott, the self-described "Total Man" of Kenyan politics who dated back to the time of the first Kenyatta; about Simeon's own decades-long battles with shifty tax officials, who in the eighties had appropriated a farm his family had leased, so they had been obliged to raze every last structure the day before the new owners took possession; about the asshole tycoons who had erected acres upon acres of greenhouses along the highway, diverting water from an already water-deprived region in order to grow flowers for export. When something reminded him of his neighbors, the people with whom the crisis was brewing, he would allude to his issues with them, but never went into detail. Each time we passed a cement factory, he would point it out, even though there were a lot of them, and they all looked identical to me.

—

In this way we made it to Kajiado, I feeling that odd mixture of exhaustion and exhilaration that comes from traveling halfway around the world, so was at once bone-tired and stimulated by the barrage of sights, sounds, and smells coming at me through the open windows.

Angie, endearingly, seemed like she'd just snorted a couple Adderall, was focused and lit up and buoyant the whole drive, peppering Simeon with questions about those cement factories or the shopping malls surrounded with razor wire, and he answered everything with meandering stories and she expressed her boundless fascination while snapping all the shots she could, wanting to capture everything.

Kajiado looked to be an unexceptional outpost of block buildings and shops specializing in gritty necessities like carburetor repair or bending metal conduit. We drove right through, then off the highway again, along a system of dirt roads up into the Milepo Hills, which Simeon explained meant "unmilkable" in one of the local languages.

"Nobody wanted to live here in the old days," he was saying, "because wisdom was you could not raise cattle here. But I came and found a way." Occasionally we passed herds of scraggly cows, tended by boys ⁚

shorts and blankets and monochrome baseball caps, and Simeon would describe the fine distinctions among the various breeds of cattle grazing in the area, and why his were superior. I had a hard time following him because every grouping we passed looked the same to me, but Angie seemed genuinely interested, asking what cattle ate, specifically, and where they slept at night.

After a long time traversing these roads, we bumped up to an unscalable zinc fence with dried acacia branches stacked around it for added measure. The gate opened for us as if by magic, and inside I saw a modest yard, maybe half an acre, in the center of which stood a cinder block house, painted stark blue, antennae and satellite dishes and swamp coolers jutting from the roof at oblique angles. Simeon welcomed us to his home.

"Wow!" said Angie. "Nzuri sana"—which she claimed meant "very nice" in Swahili.

Red compacted dirt, beige clumps of crab grass, an ancient rusting Land Rover with the inverted T grille, still plated KLC 746, benches arrayed with plastic geranium pots and bleached white animal skulls, speckled black-and-gray chickens ranging freely. This was Simeon's domain. A lone tree struggled to shade the droopy hound dog tethered to it; he barely registered our arrival. The person who had opened the gate for us, a gangly teenager, trotted over, and Simeon introduced him as his son, Theophilus, which meant, he said, "lover of God." I shook Theophilus' hand but when Angie tried, he demurred, cast his eyes down, and loped away.

Simeon invited us inside. The front room was roughly the size of my loft-style apartment, had mismatched chairs arranged around the walls, as well as a ratty velour couch in light ochre, and an old-fashioned console television paneled in fake wood grain. There were two men in the chairs, and as soon as we arrived, one more came in from the room. They were all dressed in patterned waist-wraps that skirts made from blankets—later Simeon explained these were called kikoi—and either in another wrap around their torsos, or else a tee shirt or button-down. Everybody wore rubber sandals and had showy wrist watches and hip holsters for their phones. Simeon introduced us perfunctorily—me as Professor, Angie as my wife, and they as Mister this and that—and invited us to sit. They resumed a conversation, which Simeon quickly dominated, and Angie and I exchanged confused glances. Simeon and the three others ignored us, continuing their conference, animated and declarative. Angie and I looked around the room, trying to smile.

As wired as Angie seemed, I was nearly crashing in my chair. The thirty-six hours of travel had no discernable effect on her, but I was barely staying awake.

Thankfully, after a minute, an aproned woman appeared from another room, bearing a tray with mugs and an aluminum percolator. Simeon paused for a moment to introduce his wife, Mrs. Karanja. She welcomed us elaborately, offering coffee. Straining to smile and grateful for the caffeine, I poured Angie and myself brimming mugs, finding that the coffee had already been heavily mixed with milk and sugar. Mrs. Karanja said nothing after the first welcome and went around pouring coffee for the men holding their spirited summit, none of whom really acknowledged her—or Angie or me, after our introductions.

So intense did their conversation become that I began to feel our outsiderness even more acutely as I sipped the coffee, scalding despite the milk. Mrs. Karanja disappeared after serving everyone, and as the conversation was becoming more heated, borderline argumentative, I was suddenly taken by the urge to pee, and mouthed as much to Angie. She shrugged and pointed down the hall. We mimed a debate as to the potential location of a bathroom, and finally Simeon noticed what we were doing.

"Toilet?" he said, and I nodded. "Outside. Hurry up please because we are leaving soon. Mrs. Professor, you stay here."

Angie didn't like being called Mrs. Professor, and bristled. "Where are we going?"

Simeon waved at the front door while his friends looked on, confused. "Hurry up to the toilet." Then, addressing Angie: "It's better if you stay here with Mrs. Karanja. We have to deal with a small matter, so you remain here, then we will eat together. Yes?"

"Sure," said Angie, though not enthusiastically.

I had yet to budge, so an exasperated Simeon hustled me out the front door as he shouted something to his wife in a language I didn't understand. Angie shot me an uncertain glance but as I was being marched outside, Mrs. Karanja reappeared, wiping her hands on her apron and urging Angie back toward the kitchen, so I had the feeling she would be fine.

Outside, Simeon pointed to an asymmetrical shack of an outhouse. A few more men had materialized, seemingly out of nowhere, and I rushed over to the outhouse, did my business, and when I emerged, saw that even more men had shown up. What was going on?

Simeon yelled for me to come over, then introduced me to even more brothers, cousins, friends, neighbors, business associates. I must have looked surprised that all these men were casually holding guns—not refurbished AK-47s, but rickety hunting rifles.

"Not to worry," he kept saying. "We're just going to take care of a little business before dinner. Ever handle a gun before?" He called to one of his brothers or cousins, who moseyed over and thrust a lightweight, greasy-barreled gun in my hands, a low-power .22. "Leave the safety on," Simeon said.

I can't say that I knew with any degree of certainty exactly what was happening as the front gate was again thrown open, another utility vehicle driven in, and Simeon was signaling for me to climb in, simultaneously shouting into his phone. I was amongst a tiny mob of excitement and testosterone as everybody found places in the vehicles, and I was swept up, someone declaring that I could have a front seat, which I took, holding the rifle upright between my knees. The driver told me in halting English that we only had a short drive and that it would "all be over too soon."

We jerked and tilted out of Simeon's compound and up a road that wound around the low hills, and after a few minutes we came upon a confrontation between two teenaged boys, one of whom was on the phone, I then realized, with Simeon. The boys were arguing along an acacia barrier, but this fence had a hole in it large enough for cattle to wander through, and there were consequently a half dozen grazing on our side. I was in the second vehicle, and when the first one got on the scene, Simeon leapt out and started dressing down the teenager who wasn't on the phone. As we pulled up, two other 4x4s, also loaded with men, crested the hill on the far side of the fence. My driver advised me to stand behind him, and reminded me again not to unsafety my rifle.

By the time I got myself out of the truck, everybody else had formed two armies around the hole, both sides flaunting their guns and scowling. A white-haired man from the other side interrupted Simeon's harangue of the teenager and got in Simeon's face. They argued hotly as everyone, including myself, stood around trying to look tough.

I started to imagine being shot, wounded, treated in local clinics I couldn't fully round out in detail. Gangrene. Sepsis. Questionable blood transfusions. I swallowed and gripped my rifle.

But after several tense minutes, the white-haired man spat in the dirt, shook his head, and then directed his teenager to herd the cattle back through the hole. The teenager beat them with a gnarled branch and they trotted back obediently.

At this, the air seemed cleared. Simeon's demeanor instantly changed, and he patted the white-haired man's hand, began pointing out some minute features of the fence I couldn't quite discern. The older man didn't look especially happy about backing off, but he did so, at his orders his men climbed into their vehicles, and the original boy began to dreamily drive the cattle somewhere else. Meanwhile, the younger men with us began to repair the fence under Simeon's direction, filling in the hole with more branches, which had thorns three inches long. When this was done to his satisfaction, Simeon found me, took the .22 and handed it off to a cousin or brother.

"Apologies," he said, "but this matter needed to be nipped in the bud." He invited me to get into the Patrol with him, while some in his little mercenary army squeezed in the other vehicles, and the rest simply wandered off.

As we made our way back to his place, Simeon explained that the white-haired man owned the property next to his, and had been causing friction because he had repeatedly allowed his cattle to graze on Simeon's land, through the holes his boys had made in the fencing. It was common practice, he said, to reserve twenty percent of your grass during the rainy season, that way when summer came around, you still had places to graze your cattle. But the white-haired man had elected not to do this, and Simeon had observed this with consternation all season, the older man having dismissed him until in recent weeks his cattle had been found on Simeon's property and Simeon seemed pretty pissed that this guy was stealing his grass. There are certain things that simply cannot stand, he went on, and even being neighborly has its limits. The show of force had worked for the time being, but now he was going to have to schedule a sit down with the local chief or the whole dispute would never be properly resolved.

"What's to resolve?" I said. "Your private property is your private property."

"Yes, but there are differing definitions of *private*," he said. "And property."

We had arrived back at his house, and Mrs. Karanja and Angie met us at the door. Angie was wearing a wax apron flared at the thighs that matched Mrs. Karanja's, and seemed to be having a good time.

"We made Kachumbari," Angie said, and Mrs. Karanja looked amused.

"I brandished a gun!" I said. "What's Kachumbari?"

At my mention of the gun, Angie seemed to visibly shudder, though I remembered her saying that her dad had taken her hunting when she was small, and I pictured tiny ten-year-old Angie in a blaze orange vest and cartoon Elmer Fudd hat with flaps.

"It's a salad," she said, choosing not to follow up on the gun remark.

"Come," said Simeon. "Time to eat!" He conferred with his wife, who bustled back into the kitchen and returned with cardboard boxes and plastic containers. Simeon instructed Theophilus to load everything into the Patrol, and Mrs. Karanja began untying Angie's apron.

Simeon started to usher us outside, and it was clear Mrs. Karanja wasn't coming. Angie questioned this, but Mrs. Karanja only smiled and shook her head, and Simeon said that she had already eaten. "Come, come," he said.

Angie was annoyed by this injustice, by what she perceived as an injustice, and I whispered in her ear: "Walking on water wasn't built in a day." She turned and loudly thanked Mrs. Karanja for preparing the meal she would not eat with us. Simeon didn't seem to get the message.

So it was just the three of us in the Patrol, heading up a switchback in another direction, to the crest of the hill. By the time we got there it was nearly dusk, and chilly, with wind whipping up and I was glad for the heavy shirt Simeon had earlier ridiculed. Seemingly over the slight to Mrs. Karanja, Angie kept commenting on the color streaked in the sky—the Sheltering Sky, I thought, though that was the Sahara and we were nowhere near the Sahara. Simeon had an even better view in mind for us and dragged some camp chairs over to a natural patio of sorts, flat stones flanked with scrub cacti. This spot was perched on the very edge of a bluff overlooking an expansive valley that disappeared far far into the distance.

"What you are seeing," said Simeon with a perfect sense of drama, "is the Great Rift Valley."

Angie wrapped her arms around mine and we took in the view. Simeon busied himself cracking bottles of Tusker, passed them around, and we sipped for a while then settled into the chairs. We had boxed dinners of fried chicken, hard-boiled eggs, torn hunks of bread, and the Kachumbari spooned from a bowl.

As we ate, Simeon began another impromptu lecture, explaining that the Great Rift Valley was a series of immense linked depressions stretching from Syria to Mozambique that, he said, was the super-highway of history, so easy had it been for nomadic peoples to follow animal migrations in search of sustenance.

Now *that* was a valley—a far cry from the tick-crawling, radon-choked one Angie and I called home. Simeon had a lot to say about deep ecology and human development: since the eighties he had been meticulously collecting data on the ecological systems formed by the interactions of humans, livestock, and wild animals, and he had friends all over the valley who sent him information every single day. To be a success at raising cattle here, he was saying, you had to understand these relationships. Angie and I had yet to see a single exciting animal, but as Simeon talked, he pointed out the gazelle and eland going about their evening business, hardly discernable as they navigated the acacia on the remote floor below.

—

After dark we returned to his house, lit by a few bare low-watt bulbs wired to a solar generator. He offered us what I think was some kind of palm wine from a repurposed water bottle—it tasted like sugary, brackish hairspray—and we chatted in the main room. Angie kept asking for Mrs. Karanja and Theophilus, but they were nowhere to be found.

Simeon really liked talking about his cattle and was still doing so. As he sipped the wine he went on and on about these cattle and all the work that went into raising them, about the old ways and new ways, about the fact that he and his buddies were capitalists, that they just wanted to scratch out a modest living.

"I'm Kikuyu," he said, slightly drunk. "You probably noticed the Samburu guys in the jitney. I don't really spend too much time on tribal differences when it comes to business—as long as you know the person, of course." He went on to explain the complicated ownership stakes of a particular segment of his cattle, and Angie and I looked at each other, confused and exhausted and affected by the wine.

Maybe to wake us up, Simeon finally asked about how we met, and how long we had been married. Since he had already introduced us as a wedded couple, and since we weren't sure of the local rules regarding unmarried people staying in a room together, I said we'd met at a coffeehouse, that we'd been married two years, and Angie looked over at me, enjoying the game and gripping my thumb like we were in an Updike story. I had been waiting for Simeon to ask us about what we were doing in Kenya in the first place, since I didn't know whether Cubby had passed any of that information on to Deuce. He didn't ask, and I chalked it up to a kind of reserved politeness we didn't have in the States.

But he did ask: "And where were you born?"

Angie said Pennsylvania and I said California, and Simeon perked up, saying "Ah, yes, Hollywood."

"Have you been to the States?" Angie asked.

Simeon found this question unbearably funny and didn't bother to answer. "Where are your people from?" he asked her. "Great Britain? Because I have people from Great Britain."

Angie had her family genealogy memorized and jumped into a convoluted yarn about Poland and Lithuania and Ellis Island and how a grandfather had gone from Wladyslaw to Walter and how hard it had been working at the steel mill: soot, broken unions, mesothelioma.

I, of course, amounted to what they called an unmarked subject, advantaged just enough that my dad could shrug and drink a beer and say his great-grandparents were from someplace in the UK, he didn't know where exactly, maybe a "Mc" got dropped from their surname at some point, maybe there was a distant connection to doomed Sawley Abbey. My mom only traced her ancestry as far back as Fort Macleod, outside Calgary, and all she knew was that they had a rodeo there.

When Angie was finished detailing her people, I said my relatives were from Great Britain. "So it could be we're related," I said.

"And why is it you are going to Lamu?" he asked suddenly, down to the dregs of the palm wine.

I told him the story, such as it was.

As I did so I realized that it must have sounded ridiculous, that an able-bodied professor and his hale and hopeful wife couldn't find their way to a place serviced by air traffic without having their hands held, so I tried to make the journey sound more arduous or ominous than it probably would be, saying that the girl was likely being held by those who wouldn't want her found, and so we would require an insider's knowledge to navigate a potentially hostile situation.

Although I felt sort of dumb framing everything like this, the story actually seemed to resonate with Simeon.

"It's true that Lamu is different from the rest of Kenya," he said thoughtfully. "The coast is different. They are of Arab extraction, some of them." He tipped the last of the wine into his tin cup, shook his head, and said it was an all-right place to visit, Lamu, but living there was a different story.

He didn't elaborate on this comment, and in fact started making it clear that it was time for bed, so Angie and I downed the rest of our wine, and followed him to a spartan room furnished only with a single twin bed and a dresser. He explained that there was bottled water on the bed, that he would wake us when we needed waking, and then he disappeared into the hall.

A spider with high-arched, thread-like legs was making its way down the wall over the dresser.

Angie quoted Issa: "Don't worry, spiders," she said, peering at the one on the wall, "I keep house casually."

"I'm beat," I said.

The water was making an indentation on the bed, tightly tucked with a blanket featuring an image of Pegasus flying through a solar system. Angie brushed her teeth in a corner basin and watched the spider work down the wall. I heaved on the bed and we both groaned.

"So what was with the gun?" she said, but I was already fading out.

—

Despite my exhaustion, I had a fitful sleep on the narrow, board-like mattress, plagued by dreams in which I had murdered someone, had gotten away with murdering someone and was living out my life among regular people, seemingly a regular person myself but for the nagging knowledge that I had destroyed a life, and though no one else knew of my secret, I could never shake the fact of its happening. I jerked awake several times, sweating in the close, un-air conditioned room, unsure of where I was, momentarily terrified. It was profoundly quiet in the room, in the compound, and as my eyes adjusted to the darkness, I could see Angie curled on her side, peacefully sleeping, the thin synthetic covers twisted up to her body, a corner bunched under her chin in a fist.

There in the darkness I lay imagining what it would be like to meet this girl. I couldn't quite picture her circumstances, still hadn't parsed the details of the email that had nonetheless pulled Angie and me around the world. Instead I visualized a fictional girl, an amalgam of my sister and brother when we were young, saw the girl and I together at a sun-drenched theme park, breathless from a ride, thinking this is what grown-up men might do to bond with their distant daughters.

As light was beginning to filter in through the open brickwork near the ceiling, designed for ventilation but not especially effective, I lost the image, was slipping in and out of consciousness until I heard a rooster crowing, dogs barking, and other sounds of life stirring. Something mechanical throbbed on and droned from out in the yard. A dappled gecko darted in through a hole to see what was going on, then watched us warily with slow-blinking eyes.

Angie seemed to wake spontaneously, pulling out the mouth guard she wore to mitigate her teeth grinding, inspected it briefly, and then pointed out that it was our first full day in Africa.

"Check out the wildlife," I yawned, gesturing toward the gecko.

She rolled out of bed, stretched her long limbs, and turned to me. "So today's the day, huh?"

"I can't believe it," I said, watching the gecko, who was frozen in place.

"So..." she said, adopting her Stuart Smalley voice. "How are we *feeling* today?"

"Sick to my stomach. Underwater. Jet-lagged? Dunno."

"Did you take the melatonin?" she asked, dropping the voice.

"I forgot. I was so exhausted. I'm still exhausted. You sleep OK?"

She bent over the side of the bed, easing lower until she could touch her ankles, then held the stretch for a few seconds until I heard a light pop.

"Ah," she sighed, straightening. "That bed's a killer."

She examined my face, my affect, looking momentarily unlike herself because one eyebrow was smashed from the pillow, and appeared as though she had brushed the hairs up with a tiny comb, giving her a slightly deranged air.

"I don't know either," she said. "I'm excited, I guess. Excited to be in Africa for sure, excited for you. Or curious. The anticipation is what's eating me, like I just want to know what's what. You must be freaking."

"I'm holding it in," I said. "I just hope this wasn't ill considered."

"Don't you feel good about doing the right thing?"

"Not really."

She punched me in the arm, rubbed that spot affectionately, stretched again, then said she was off to locate the shower, which Simeon had explained was down the hall.

I lay admiring the gecko (who never budged), trying to make my mind blank.

When Angie returned in her plastic flip-flops, shorts, and a faded RISD tee shirt that read "Go Nads," she seemed highly amused, was a little too enthused about my impending turn in the shower.

"Better get to stepping," she said, smiling.

I gathered my travel bottle of shampoo and my bar soap in its own plastic case, then discovered down the hall a closet-like wet room with a comedy show of a shower, a lead pipe jutting diagonally from the wall, mounted on the end with a plastic, bell-shaped shower head, streams of wires snaking from it into the wall and up through the ceiling, some parts bare and exposed, patched with duct tape, the whole rig secured with what looked like upcycled coat hangers.

I appreciated Angie's amusement, and hunched under the too-low shower head, adjusting a plastic valve so that water issued at an optimal pressure—as I quickly discovered, too much pressure meant there wasn't enough time for the contraption to heat the water, and so I ended up with a lukewarm trickle, and struggled to work the shampoo out of my hair, twice shocking myself when my hand grazed exposed wires.

Back in the room, Angie wanted to know all about my strategy for surviving the shower, which she called a "suicide shower" and had known about from Cambodia, and we shared a shudder as Simeon began shouting from the hallway that we had to get going.

In the mirror over the wash basin, I performed my skincare routine as quickly as I could while Angie made the bed, mocking me since she only moisturized with some high SPF cream from Target. I had brought my arsenal in a second Dopp kit that I had refused to check on the plane for fear of breakage, and when I completed the final steps, I wrapped the whole kit in a tee shirt and carefully packed it into its own zippered pouch at the top of my backpack.

Angie observed me like an anthropologist, concluding: "You. Are. Ridiculous."

We heaved our packs out to the main room, where Simeon was waiting, seemingly agitated, saying that we needed to leave right away or we might not make our flight. I didn't even know we had a flight. Angie shot me a guilty frown and I wondered why Simeon hadn't communicated his plans to us.

"I've budgeted a stop for coffee on the way," he said, nodding for me to bring my pack as he swept Angie's from her side and marched it though the door.

We left his place with zero ceremony, without saying goodbye to anyone, as Theophilus was absent, the members of Simeon's ragtag security forces were absent, and ghostly Mrs. Karanja was nowhere to be found. Angie was concerned that she wasn't able to thank Mrs.

Karanja, wanted to express gratitude for the hospitality and for teaching her how to make Kachumbari, but impatient Simeon said she was off at the market, that he would "relay the message," that we really needed to get a move on or we'd have to cut the coffee stop from the itinerary.

In the suburb of Kitengala, we made our coffee stop at Naivas, an endless fluorescent supermarket, where Simeon advised us to load up on anything we might need because he wasn't sure about the stores in Lamu. Angie found all sorts of unusual snacks she wanted to try, and took zoomed-in label photos of the varieties of bottled water available, arousing the suspicions of store security.

I wandered and took in the products on offer: Blue Band margarine, canola oil, peanut butter, and something called "Spread"; Sunlight dish soap; Royco Mchuzi Mix; Closeup Red Hot Deep Action toothpaste; Rexona deodorant; Vim scouring powder; Oxo, a detergent that looked like Persil but wasn't—all brightly packaged echoes of what I could buy in my similarly fluorescent supermarket in Pennsylvania, except faintly keyed to the local markets (Geisha soap was "African Strength Black Soap") and something in me was wary about these neatly-arrayed markers of consumer capitalism, though I didn't know why.

The aisles were replete, buzzing, and I remained lost in thought for several minutes until Simeon found me and suggested we take advantage of what he called the "first-rate bakery" on the premises.

We had mystery meat pastries with our coffee, said goodbye to Naivas and its bounties, and were off to Nairobi. Once again, he opted for the bypass, and once again we passed Kibera and the construction crews that seemed to have metastasized overnight.

Simeon whipped back onto the highway, took a few twists and turns, and we arrived at Wilson Airport, the smaller one that serviced Kenya's outer reaches. It looked like an office park. There were high fences and a guard, but there were high fences and guards around most everything in greater Nairobi, including the supermarket we had just left, and so it didn't lend the place an especially secure air. Simeon said something to the lanky guy on duty, who peered in over his dark glasses, noted Angie and me, and I guess because we were white, motioned everyone through without further interrogation. Simeon seemed to know exactly where he was going: we drove partway around the tree-shaded parking lot until we came to a glassed wall, again like what you would see in an office park in the States, and he announced that we were there.

"There" turned out to be the ticket counter, waiting room, and sad café for a local airline, 540 Air. Inside, a couple of people were listlessly watching a TV mounted from the ceiling, but otherwise the place was empty. A woman in a neon vest identical to the ones worn by the Chinese construction workers leaned on a chipped counter, arguing with a walkie-talkie.

Simeon let me order the tickets for Lamu, reminding me that we were on my dime from here on out. I paid with my credit card, over $450 plus fees, and the woman wrote our names on paper tickets, handed them to me curtly, then disappeared through a door with our bags.

"Now we hurry up and wait," Simeon said.

We did indeed wait, for hours, even though the flight was scheduled to have left much earlier. Angie was interested in the equipment at the café—there was no espresso machine proper, but they did have an impressive selection of what she called "boutique" blends, smudged carafes filled with coffees from Cameroon, Burundi, and the Democratic Republic of Congo. She bent over the counter to peer at the bags displayed on a shelf above the carafes, quizzing the clerk, who knew nothing about them.

"Burundi Ngozi," she said, handing me one. "See if you get fruit and caramel. Don't worry, it's piping hot."

"Never gets old," I said. It was my second coffee of the morning, but much needed since still I was flagging.

Simeon wanted some kind of special South African tea, went back to the café counter to explain this to the clerk and to educate Angie, but I remained in my hard plastic chair, sipping the blistering Burundian coffee, wondered where Burundi was exactly, and tried not to catastrophize about how my life might change once we landed in Lamu.

By the time they announced our flight, I had finished the coffee, peed twice, and was trying to regulate my racing heart. Ten or fifteen other passengers had wandered in, and we all filed behind the counter woman through a hallway to the tarmac, Angie bobbing and weaving to try to glimpse the plane through the crush of bodies ahead of us in the hall. The orange-vested counter woman collected tickets and tore them in half as at a movie theater, alarmingly low-tech, in my view, then a guard passed a wand around people's torsos and pointed on toward the tarmac. We bumped along in the hot hallway, and only after we'd been waved on by a final guard could we actually see the plane, what looked to me like a World War II-era evacuation craft, an improperly-maintained one at that, with worn propellers and visible repairs, a dented BOAC staircase leading ominously up into its depths.

"Vintage!" said Angie, and popped out of line to frame some shots.

Simeon could see me swallowing nervously, and thought it was hilarious. "Get ready for the vomit comet!" he said.

We ascended into the plane, having to stoop once inside because the fuselage was so tightly designed. The flight was only scheduled to be an hour, but I was already sweating, partly due to my mounting anxiety, but mainly because the air con was broken, and sitting on the tarmac was like baking in an oven.

As usual, Angie was puzzled by my apprehension. Her position was that whatever people were doing before we arrived was working, and would continue to work after we left, so there was no point in fretting over it.

"You are not the factor that changes everything," she said.

Simeon slapped me on the back, scooted past us down the aisle, and immediately started chatting up the person beside him. Angie and I were next to each other, and I pointed out the absence of those laminated cards illustrating crash positions.

"You could look at it as a net positive," she said. "As in, there's no need for them because planes here never crash."

"They don't even have barf bags," I said, pulling out the cracked seat pocket as far as I could.

Once in the air, the ride was more or less fine, except only a ragged bolt of cloth separated the cockpit from the cabin, and it flapped open for most of the trip, so everyone could see the pilot leaning back, feet kicked up, reading *Fortune* magazine until it was time to land. Because of this direct view to the front of the plane, I didn't have to imagine how we came in nearly perpendicular to the airstrip, compensating for the livid winds that kept bouncing us back and forth. But we landed without shattering into a million pieces, and I was the only one who seemed to think this was a big deal.

Stepping off the plane, the heat and humidity enveloped me and nearly took my breath away, unbelievably wet and close, far worse than in Nairobi. I could hardly walk down the stairs because my legs, stupidly encased in heavy pants, were slick and dank, and I knew I would need to change as soon as possible. Angie was in shorts, sandals, and a tank top, having heeded Simeon's advice about conditions on the coast.

I waddled across the potholey tarmac to the main building, which was a kind of open-air waiting room, and kept a look out for the bags. Finally a handler rattled up in a cart hitched to a luggage-filled trailer, and I hauled my pack out, then hurried into a bathroom to change into a pair of shorts and a lighter shirt. They had flip-flops for sale in a gift shop, and I bought a pair.

"Told you so," said Simeon when I emerged.

The airport was spread across Manda Island, and the only way to get to Lamu was by boat, so we walked to the docks to hire a water taxi.

Immediately we were swarmed by barefoot men who politely asked if they could carry our bags. Angie started talking to the youngest porter, but Simeon said to ignore them, hissing something which caused them to scatter. Angie's guy fled, but another persistent one focused all his energy on me, and when I ignored him at Simeon's direction, he suddenly turned dark, saying that tourists came there and didn't even part with a little coin for a normal man, that he was a normal man, and I surrendered and let him take my pack.

Simeon shook his head and said that they were not getting so many tourists as they once were, due to the recent troubles. Not too long ago, he explained, some Europeans had been kidnapped from the beaches by marauders in speedboats and taken back to Somalia, first a British woman, whose husband had been killed in the sand, and then a French one, both of whom had been ransomed. Things have fallen apart in Somalia, he was saying. Times were desperate there, Mogadishu was run by gangsters and these al-Shabaab assholes were causing terrorism problems after the African Union went up there. Al-Shabaab got orphans to throw hand grenades into crowds in Nairobi and Mombasa, but things were worse in the north, in Garissa.

This was all news to me. "Are you saying it's dangerous?" I asked.

"I'm saying it's Muslim," he said.

We had made it to the docks, where the guy held his hand out, then hung on for a bit to gape at Angie as Simeon negotiated with a skipper for a trip over the water to Lamu Town. Angie wanted to make a portrait of the skipper in his boat, but he kept refusing. Once Simeon had settled on a price, we picked our way down onto the wooden-slat benches, and the skipper whipped us around too quickly, past the mangroves bleeding out into the water, and over to Lamu Island. Coming around there by boat you saw the flattish buildings in cream and off-white, minarets here and there, a newish hospital built, Simeon somehow knew, with Saudi money, beached dhows made in the old style, without a single nail.

"Like a postcard!" Angie kept saying. "A postcard!"

We pulled up near a crew building a new jetty, rebar and concrete pilings baking in the sun, the opposite of a postcard, but there were charming donkeys loaded down with material, plodding along the wharf like model citizens.

I paid the skipper from my wad of inscrutable bills, and we walked the short pier onto what I took to be the main drag of Lamu Town: a cobbled strip along the water fronted with rundown hotels, tiny four-tabled restaurants with plaid vinyl tablecloths, a small bank or two with bored youths standing permanent guard. Flat cones of debris, bricks and gravel, were everywhere. The men were all in kikoi and tee shirts, the women all in hijab, some in full abaya, walking briskly, pulling children behind them by the wrist. There was an unusual amount of donkey traffic: bearded men rode them sidesaddle, and shirtless guys with stringy back muscles had them laden with ballooning cargo, tugging them along by braided-rope bridles. Arrayed before most permanent buildings was a second row of makeshift storefronts, stalls from which people sold bottled water, pirated DVDs, and cigarettes; others would press you a glass of sugarcane for about twenty cents. Angie and I followed Simeon's lead, and he strode over to the porch of what turned out to be the Lamu Museum to get out of the sun and strategize.

Angie was saying it all seemed like a movie, like a dream, and I was feeling energized, self-congratulatory that I'd made it so far, noting to myself that a week ago I hadn't even known about this girl, but now mere days later, I was pushing the button on some human obligation, had really done it, not only theorized or thought, but acted, coming over 8,000 miles by plane, truck, and boat, here to this very spot. I was almost eager for what was to come.

But as energized as Angie and I were, Simeon was now suddenly deflated, tired or distracted, and was staring into the multi-colored windows of a narrow Catholic church that stood near the museum. He excused himself and disappeared inside.

Angie and I remained in the shade, unsure of what to do next. "Probably he's asking where to find Orchid Club," I said.

"Probably," said Angie, scrolling through the photos she had recently shot and clucking in approval.

Simeon was in the church for some time, and I was hopeful he would return with actionable intelligence, but he came out even more dejected, and I was about to ask him what he had found out when looked at his feet and said that he had something to admit.

Angie stopped her scrolling with concern. I wiped my forehead and waited.

The preamble was a solid minute of throat-clearing and sighing, and I knew that whatever was coming likely wasn't good.

"You know I'm not really a guide," Simeon began, and Angie and I were both confused. "I *was* a guide, in the past, but that was a decade ago. I'm a businessman now and I don't need the aggravation."

We stared at him, I'm sure dumbly, and he said he had only returned to the island because he'd made a promise to himself, to his family. He inhaled through his nose, loudly.

"My brother Ollie died here," he said, and a hotness prickled on my face.

A story tumbled out: his brother was a couple years younger, was what he described as a free spirit, the cause of many headaches for their parents. When Ollie came of age, he had inexplicably refused to drive a matatu for the mob as their father had done. Nor was he particularly scholastic, or interested in women or money, but was artistic, musical. And restless, so one day he just walked away from home, went to play Benga in the parks in Nairobi, fell in with certain crowds, then wandered on from there, and Simeon couldn't really say what he did to support himself. Then one spring they had word Ollie was in Lamu, was rumored to be living with another man in a carnal capacity and Simeon's father insisted it was nonsense, it was nause-ating, and Simeon never believed such tales anyway even as his father ordered the family to cut off contact. But just as stories about Ollie and his behavior had reached them all the way in Kajiado, they also heard he had died, passed on, heard these things in quick succession, like one-two, no time to process the information. Officials were looking for the family, his father was broken but didn't let on, had dispatched Simeon, the eldest, to claim the body in their family name.

"But remember not to worry," he said rapidly, looking at us, "things were different then, that was a different time, and certainly everything would be different for a white."

When Simeon went to claim his brother, he faced an interminable bus journey because in those days plane fare was out of the question, and when he had at long last arrived on the island, his first and last time, he picked his way through the confusing, closed-in alleys, asking anyone if they knew about the body of the Christian boy who had been there. In a kind of foggy shock, staggering from shrug to head shake he eventually gathered there was something about a slaughterhouse, that he should go down the wharf, past the donkey pens on the way to where the furniture makers were. There he found the open-air place where they slaughtered goats and sheep, and discovered that his brother had been put in a coffin in an ice room. Because he was not Muslim, someone said, they left him alone, unsure of the rites, and waited.

Simeon managed to recruit a few people to help him with the coffin, impossible to manage on his own, and they walked in a procession along the water, turning finally up one of the alleys searching for the island's lone Christian cemetery. Slowly they ascended the hill, plodding in the humidity of mid-day, the worst time to be out, the coffin getting heavier and heavier, and they squeezed through narrow passages behind houses until they found little-used steps leading to a tiny Methodist mission at the top of the hill. Some groundskeeper handed him a spade, and there he dug, the others having bowed out, and he felt absolutely alone in the universe, working down through the sandy soil, almost angry with God. Finally, after hours, he managed to bury his brother on a sloping hillside overhung with vegetation, having no marker but a cross he had made by binding some thin branches together with string.

That day, standing in our own mid-day heat, Simeon said again that he had promised his family that he would find the gravesite and see about getting a permanent headstone, as he didn't have enough money in 1983 for the masons to cut one. When Deuce's friend had contacted him about a paid trip to Lamu, Simeon thought it was a sign from God that now was the time to lay the situation to rest. "You must understand," he said.

Angie was crying, and tried to hug him, but he brushed her off.

Little did Simeon know that I understood perfectly, and his story raked up a host of complicated emotions. I had never, as an adult, visited my own brother's grave. It was not something possible for me to bear.

On the other hand, if I'm being honest, I couldn't help but feel used, misled—a shitty and offensive reaction I could hardly articulate to myself, let alone utter aloud, especially in front of Angie, given the evident moral authority of what Simeon had said.

For some reason I asked how his brother had died, and Simeon said drug overdose officially, but he had his suspicions that someone had killed him, that maybe it was a bad deal gone down, but that it really didn't matter because the heroin had come from Afghanistan and they used the money to fund their jihads, and I began to understand all his disparaging remarks about Muslims, even as the material connection between a major world religion and his brother's death was, to me, opaque.

"So unless you object," he said, "we will find the grave, and then your address, OK?"

"Of course," said Angie, wiping her eyes. "Of course."

Simeon looked at me, and I shrugged. "That's fine," I said, and he was relieved.

Just as we were plotting our next move, a tiny graybeard in a kofia strolled up, sporting a cane and wanting to shake hands. "Greetings!" he called. "My name is Ali Ecstasy. Perhaps you have read all about me in the famous guidebooks!"

It was jarring, being drawn back to the touristic world after being told the story of Simeon's brother, after conjuring the ghost of my own in this unfamiliar place.

Rotund Ali Ecstasy, a little over five feet tall, muttonchops, missing tooth, shook our hands in turn and wanted to know if we cared for a tour of Lamu Fort, wanted to know if we cared to dine in his home that night, where he would make traditional Swahili food and sing traditional Swahili songs. It was plain in his friendly desperation that what Simeon had dubbed al-Shabaab's War on Tourism had devastated Ali Ecstasy as well, and so he had marched up to the only white people on the waterfront that day.

Simeon's glasses were darkened in the afternoon sun, and he said yes, Ali, there was something he could do for us.

It turned out that Ali Ecstasy did indeed know of a Methodist church. Although he never had occasion to go there personally, he thought it was tucked on the outskirts of town, up the hill, sure enough, by way of the place where the slaughterhouse used to be. He agreed to take us there, and led us down an alley that gave way to sand after a few turns. Simeon moved in silence as though stalking something, a marked contrast to his usual disquisitions on a thousand linked topics. His hands were almost fists as he walked, looking meditative as if recalling this or that detail creeping up through time, remembering a particular set of stairs or markings on a door, or the way we opened suddenly onto a littered courtyard with a gantried well and donkey tethers. Angie was letting her camera hang around her neck, unused. I was all knotted up.

In this way we proceeded up the hill, Ali Ecstasy making only a couple of false turns, until we came upon a final set of stairs leading to a walled area with a flaking sign: "Methodist Church in Kenya Singwaya Synod."

Beyond the gates, we found uniformed school children at play, and a man in a kikoi and starched white shirt kicking a soccer ball with a little kid. He was, we discovered, the minister in residence at the decaying church with school attached. Simeon explained the situation and the minister nodded, saying he hadn't heard about Simeon's brother, but that he had only taken over a few years prior. There was indeed, he said, a place where people were buried. Simeon wanted to be taken there right away. As the minister led us off the soccer field into unkempt foliage, pointing out particularly thorny branches that might cut our legs, I could see Simeon was slightly winded, sweating and hitching up the ends of his kikoi as he stepped over brambles and ducked low-hanging branches with hopeful fixation.

Finally we were dispersed in a broken single file along a hillside, Angie and I behind Simeon and the minister, with Ali Ecstasy lagging. There was no open space, no gated and tended cemetery as I had envisioned—just a slope thick with underbrush and almost completely shaded by huge out-fanning trees, a dusty, insect-prone sphere. The minister hadn't been through there himself in some time, and crashed around busily, pulling aside branches to reveal sunken stone or concrete markers. These markers were hidden among ankle-high bushes spun with wide cottony webs.

Once on the slope, Simeon looked around, trying to conjure a particular tree, or to recall what the landscape looked like thirty years before. The minister seemed undaunted as he moved leaves and pulled branches, blowing on the shallow, scarcely-legible lettering, Simeon shaking his head no, no, it would not be stone.

By that time it was clear to everyone that the specific location of the grave would elude us, that the cross would have rotted away in a matter of months, that the vegetation would have encroached, topography would have changed. Simeon leaned against a tree, breathing hard and thanking the minister—imploring him, in fact, to get up.

This hillside, Simeon decided, this general spot, was surely where he had buried his brother, he remembered it, and so it therefore had a symbolic particularity distinct from any other place in the world. If one wanted a pilgrimage site, he thought, one could do no better than this thorny, spider-infested hillside. He declared as much, and asked the minister who he should see in town about having a headstone made.

All this happened in the several minutes it took Ali Ecstasy to catch up with us. Wheezing and hobbled, warned by his doctor about his high cholesterol, ordered, he had said on the walk up, to slim down with regular swimming, he huffed and wiped his forehead at the brim of his kofia, using his cane to push aside a branch while Simeon nodded, and looked and looked. Ali Ecstasy looked at Simeon looking, drained of tour pitches and local lore, not knowing what to say. Simeon rested against the tree, an occasional sun shaft pushing through the canopy, so motes transformed to pinpoints of light floating around his face.

A few minutes passed as we all took everything in, then Simeon thanked the minister, flushed and dewy, not entirely from the heat, and he turned to shake Ali Ecstasy's hand, then mine in turn, holding it in both of his, cradling it tenderly and saying that he very deeply appreciated the opportunity, and I was unsure how to respond as he kept on holding my hand while Angie brushed away tears.

After, we walked back down the hill, again through the maze of alleys and tiny courtyards, and stopped again on the wharf, where Simeon had a brief and intense conversation with Ali Ecstasy; when they finished, Simeon instructed me to give Ali Ecstasy some money.

I handed him a wad, I don't even know, and Ali Ecstasy bowed elaborately, reiterated how nice it was to meet my wife and me, and that his home was open if we cared for authentic cuisine. Then he toddled off through an open doorway.

Simeon patted his forehead with a handkerchief and looked at us.

"So I found out how to get to this address of yours," he said.

4.

ORCHID CLUB WAS in Shela, an even more remote village on the far side of the island, and so the best way to get there was again via water taxi. As we motored out on the greenish water, I could see extravagant mansions or resorts with their own private beaches on another island across the channel, beyond which was the open kingdom of the Indian Ocean. I was doubled over and clammy, and Angie was concerned for me, having slowed the picture-taking the closer we got to the girl. Simeon, though, seemed serenely at peace, leaning back on his elbows and enjoying the wind on his face. Angie said she hoped that he'd found what he was looking for, that a headstone would form some closure for him and his family, and he thrust out his lower lip. We hugged the coast close enough to see people walking along a waterfront path, a woman struggling to corral her kids, who kept breaking free to lunge on pieces of driftwood or remnants of fishing nets.

The far side of the island had no pier or jetty, so the boat slid right up onto the shallow beach, and the skipper leapt out and tugged it closer. But we still had to step in the water, holding our flip-flops and wading onto shore.

Shela was even sleepier than Lamu Town, with a flat beach overrun with kelp or algae and littered with stones. Edging up to the beach were homes of a vaguely Arab type, like what I imagined seeing in Muscat or Samarkand, compounds with walls made of coral, salmon-colored and rough to the touch. On that part of the island, no paths were paved, and because people had built walls to the very limits of their property lines, nor were there open spaces, at least for the first several hundred yards past the beach, so in order to enter the village you had to hike into a warren of sandy alleys with no discernable signage—you just had to know the way.

A couple of teenagers in board shorts and soccer jerseys were loafing in a shaded spot near a wall, and I detected the faint odor of hash, or thought I did. I paid the skipper as Simeon hailed the teenagers, who were openly eyeing Angie. After a quick conference, one of them slapped the hand of the other, snapped his fingers, and sauntered over to the mouth of an alley, waiting. Angie and I hitched up our packs and followed the Rasta youth. Although the path was probably twenty degrees cooler than the beach, for me it was slow-going and difficult to negotiate, especially because the sand hid not only bits of plastic wrapper and flints of cardboard, but also shards of coral and possibly glass. Still barefoot, I tried to pick my way with care, but Angie was fearless, and kept pace with Simeon and the teenager, who had forged ahead, chatting companionably. As they disappeared around corners, I knew I would never be able to retrace the route on my own, should the need come. I sighed and pressed on.

Finally we made it to an imposing lacquered door. There were no markings of any kind, and it was hard to tell where one structure ended and another began, if those structures were indeed distinct.

"This is it," said Simeon. "Pay the man."

I handed the teenager some folded shillings and he shamelessly checked the amount, then grinned widely, saying "One love, my brother" and rambled back toward the beach.

My heart was jumping, my sternum felt like it had been bandaged too tightly, and Simeon had positioned himself behind me, no longer my fixer and ombudsman but my second-in-command, fading back so I could take the lead.

I curled my toes in the sand and reached for the buzzer, but Angie grabbed my wrist mid-press.

"Wait!" she cried, a streak of panic in her voice. "I'm not ready. Oh, um, I don't know if I can do this ..." She held my wrist and looked at me with unblinking lemur eyes.

Again, and of course, I had been so wrapped up in my own head, confronted as I was by the delays and ancient memories induced by Simeon's side mission—not to mention the impending existential rupture behind that door—that I hadn't really thought to consider Angie and whatever emotions she might have been experiencing. "I feel kind of awful" she had written on the pamphlet, and those words were stuck in the corners of my mind: I shuddered at being the cause of this feeling, though certainly I was.

"What is it?" I said, projecting a masculine calm I didn't feel. Simeon had slunk back to the other side of the alley, was examining a brass medallion inset on a door there, embarrassed by the outburst.

Angie began talking rapidly, something she did when nervous: "What if Audra is here? I don't know if I can be civil to this woman. I've known this was a possibility the whole trip, I've been psyching myself up, but now here we are and I don't know what I'll do if I actually see her. What if I can't be polite?" Now she was the one breathing heavily, a role reversal in terms of our general relationship, and it calmed me a bit to soothe her.

"It's OK," I said, "It's all right. Why are you getting yourself worked up? She's probably not even here, remember? Supposedly she's AWOL."

This did seem to settle her and she looked right at me, downturned mouth agape, the lines in her forehead deep. "This woman had your child and never told you? What kind of person does that? Not a good person."

I felt a surge as I realized that Angie was looking out for me, that in her moral expansiveness anxiety was surfacing because she might not be able to contain her ire on my behalf. Audra, a woman Angie had dubbed "bougie" and "self-impressed" when I had told her stories about the YSL handbags and red-soled Louboutins; Audra, with her clarity and index funds, was in many ways the antithesis of Angie, and I had once wondered if there was the slightest twinge of envy in these dismissals of the dark-haired specter of my past.

But then, in that moment in the sand, poised at the door of possible oblivion, Angie's minor breakdown; the crack in her normally energetic though collected exterior, made me trust her in a kind of fullness I hadn't felt before, something beyond mere affection that I couldn't quite name.

She was sucking water from a warm bottle and breathing through her nose.

"Remember," I said, "we're supposed to be focusing on this girl, you said to focus on this girl, because whatever her mother did or didn't do isn't her fault." (That last was something my sister had said to me, and I had been waiting to repeat to Angie at an opportune moment.)

She finished the water, inhaling wetly. "No," she said. "Of course you're right." (*He He* breath.) "I've got a hold of myself now. Yes, OK, do it!" Meaning press the buzzer.

"You sure?"

"One hundred," she said. "Engage."

I took a conscious breath myself, straightened my back and felt the sweat worming down my spine. One more quick glance to Angie and I pressed the buzzer and she held on to my arm and neither of us exhaled for the moment of silence before the slow sound of interior latches disengaging could be heard, and the heavy door creaked open.

Immediately Angie's death grip on my arm loosened as we both saw the person staring back at us, not Audra or the girl or even the hirsute Imam that had been conjured by Cubby. Instead we were faced with a frail white woman, perhaps seventy-five or better, wrinkled in that special leathery way I had associated with those lifetime sun worshippers in Palm Springs or Boca Raton. She stood tottering on thin white legs, her white arms perceptibly tremulous, knocking the carved wooden bracelets and necklaces hanging around her white wrists and neck.

"Yes?" she said.

I stammered, saying I didn't know if we had the right place but we were looking for Petra—and at that moment I realized I didn't know her last name, and so said Wester.

The woman held onto the side of the door with both hands, appraising us. Finally she spoke more than one word and I realized she had a mild Scandinavian accent: "Audra and Petra are not in at the moment."

"*Oh!*" said Angie, too loudly, an exclamation of relief that we'd found it—or that she wouldn't be facing Audra imminently, or both.

I said—and how strange the words—that I was the girl's *father*, that they were expecting me because it seemed she was having a bit of trouble in school. "So here we are."

At my disclosure the woman untensed considerably, peeking around Angie and me to size up Simeon, which she did in a fraction of a second, but Simeon noticed it, and then she invited us all in.

I was surprised to see that inside was truly a world apart from the shaded alley: there was a massive entry room sumptuously appointed with hand-hewn chairs with cane backings, which I later discovered were made right off the wharf, and an abundance of wall art, photographs of dhows, woven artifacts, beaded linens.

"What a beautiful place," said Angie.

The woman asked that we leave our flip-flops and bags, and then indicated a shallow stone cistern in which petals floated, directing us to rinse the sand from our feet. Beyond this entry was an expansive courtyard with a kidney-shaped pool and palm trees, and I suddenly recognized that the open spaces in Shela were all within walls, which explained why the village had first seemed only a veiny spread of alleys. Around the pool were planted patches of grass and flowering shrubs, and stone patios were arranged with chaise lounges and conversation tables; a hammock was strung between two trees.

As this woman was no Imam, this was no bare madrasa where children memorized all the emission points of the tajwid.

Angie whispered, *what is going on?* and I was pretty confused myself.

The woman said to follow her and we went around the pool and up some steps to a second level and an open-air sitting area overlooking the courtyard. In the center was a long wooden table and turquoise-cushioned banquettes along all the half-walls. She invited us to sit, and a delicate man with a tight, taciturn face appeared, crisp in tennis whites and pomade.

"This is Johnny," she said. "And I am Margit. Welcome to my guesthouse."

Angie, Simeon and I introduced ourselves, and I explained that we had come from Nairobi that morning.

At this Margit looked puzzled, or discomfited. "I'm sorry to hear you've traveled all this distance, but Audra and Petra, they're away. They're unlikely to return any time soon."

Johnny had gone to seek refreshments and returned with impossible speed, bearing a tray with a pitcher of guava juice, a teapot and various glasses and cups. He set them before us and whispered unobtrusively to find out what we wanted.

"Do you have any idea when they might be back?" I asked.

"Could be weeks. A month or more. One never knows."

I let that sink in, feeling surprised, aggrieved, reflexively calculating how much the flight had cost Cubby and how much the trip had cost me so far. Above all, I had the rising feeling, probably unjustified, of betrayal—plus I was confused about why Margit insisted on the pronoun "they" when the girl had emphasized that her mother was AWOL. I asked Margit if perhaps they were somewhere else on the island and she said no, they lived at her place when on Lamu, but they had both left two or three days prior, international travel, Dubai or New Delhi and they'd probably be gone for weeks.

I turned to Angie, but she was as bewildered as I was, wrenching up her lip into a W. Simeon was engrossed in his minty tea, still serene, his thoughts obviously elsewhere. Margit smiled trimly, again as though embarrassed for me.

I gave Margit the abbreviated version of the story, about the emails I had received, about never having known anything about the girl even one week prior, about feeling an obligation to come to Kenya because she had claimed distress, had implied that she was in a dangerous situation, almost that she was being held against her will in some dirty-floored pressure cooker of Islamic fundamentalism. At the mention of Islam, Simeon chuckled knowingly.

Now it was Margit's turn to be puzzled. "But her father's in the foreign service."

Angie and I looked at each other. "Well," I said. "I'm not."

"How strange," said Margit, squinting at me. "You know what? Now that I look, I can see the resemblance."

Audra and Petra had been with her going on two years, she said, and when they first came, the guesthouse was much busier, but Audra had laid out a whole month in cash, in Euros, and since that time they had been permanent residents, more or less, taking over two of her best suites. Even if they were gone for entire months, Audra still paid, so they kept some belongings up there and Margit had the rooms cleaned and the linens changed as she would for any guest.

"But now," she said, waving a sun-spotted hand over the empty courtyard, "of course there is virtually no one else, because of the troubles, and so Audra has turned out to be a lifeline." But Margit didn't know what Petra could have meant about being in school. Audra had hired a tutor for her, she said, groping for an explanation, an English gentleman who lived on the mainland, his family attached to some sort of mission there. Audra paid him to come four times a week and he instructed her for hours, brought her books and magazines from Mombasa.

Just to be clear, I asked her again about a school, about this girl being held against her will or in a bad situation, and she looked pained and told me that Audra never would have stood for anything like that, and besides people on the island were free to do as they pleased.

This was all baffling, and that idea of an elaborate joke flitted across my mind again, even though such an explanation no longer made sense. At the very least I had confirmed that the girl actually existed. Now I knew she was real and that, at least from Margit's perspective, she resembled my physically. And yet I was even less sure about why she had written me. Where were the hairy-chested men angling after a child bride? Where were the pyramids of Soviet-era assault rifles? Where was the impending doom? And Audra certainly didn't seem AWOL. Why had the girl lied?

There didn't seem to be any need for my presence since by all appearances this girl was living in semi-permanent boutique luxury on a resort island, waited on and privately tutored between shopping trips to the gold souks in Dubai.

Angie squeezed my hand with an expression somewhere between I Hope You're OK and Sorry We've Wasted All This Time, and I was more mystified than ever about what we were doing. I had spent the last week resolving to swoop in and save the day, to the extent that I was able to do so, when all along some small voice inside me kept insisting that if I knew anything at all about Audra, it was that she was capable, methodical in her decision-making, and would therefore have never put herself in a position where she or anyone else she cared about would need intervention from the likes of me.

Margit, though, was intrigued by the whole scenario, and wanted to know if we were staying the night.

It occurred to me that I hadn't planned any accommodations, so accustomed I had grown to following Simeon's lead. Looking around, Angie and Simeon seemed eager to settle in, and so I said sure and Margit said splendid, told us we could freshen up and then we'd have some supper. It was probably around 7:00, although the equatorial sun was still blazing, and when Margit started describing the house specialties, I realized I was starving and Angie said *oh yes* and we were suddenly warmed by her hospitality.

We all followed her again, this time up another set of stairs, to a floor with rooms on each end. Margit said the meal would be ready whenever we were, and Simeon thanked her and disappeared into his room. Angie and I went to explore ours: it was a real luxury-type room, dominated by a four-poster bed made of teak or some other tropical wood and hung with gauzy mosquito netting, at that moment rolled up into draping arcs and tied with satin ribbons. There was a ceiling fan, which I switched on, and a balcony that looked not onto the courtyard, but onto the water where the tan-sailed dhows were coming in from a day of fishing. Our backpacks had already been brought up and placed on a luggage rack.

"This place is absurd," said Angie.

"No Audra," I said. "No girl."

Immediately she regretted the comment about how nice the room was, or seemed to, and swept over to debrief, handing me a bottle of water.

111

"Drink," she said, and I gulped the water.

"See?" she said. "You're white as a sheet. Hydrate." She sat on the edge of the bed and patted the spot next to her. I sat down. "Let's review," she said. "Petra is an actual person. Which I knew. Check. She does seem to be your daughter, since she looks like you. Check. But she's not in trouble, so there's more to the story there."

"Or she's just a liar," I said.

"Or she's just a liar."

"Definitely she lied about being here on Lamu. And about my being in the foreign service. Or Audra did."

She put her arm around me while I hunched with the water in my lap. "I still think you did the right thing," she said.

Her body radiated heat even as I felt turned inward. "My god, you stink. I stink. We both stink."

She shoved me away. "Yeah, well, fuck you too."

"We will deal with this post-showers," I said. I jumped off the bed with purpose while she splayed out, arms thrust above her head looking stunned or perhaps merely exhausted. I turned on my heel as she shrugged a little shrug to herself and rolled over to grab her camera, checking what she had recently shot.

In the bathroom, one end was filled with an open shower. It was one of those small things that almost made you cry, and I pulled the door closed for some brief privacy. The contrast to Simeon's suicide shower was profound, and I snorted out a laugh while turning the heavy brass tap. Out came a hard stream of water wonderfully hot, a miracle for me in that context, and I was overwhelmed and wobbly-kneed as I kicked off my shorts, tugged off my shirt, and staggered into the tiled space, collapsing on a bench as the jet hit my chest, the gritty spray dancing off and stinging my welling eyes.

—

When Angie and I reappeared at the big table, it was set for dinner with placemats and napkin rings and even multiple forks. There were oscillating fans and diaphanous curtains untied at stone columns and the scent of fried garlic wafting in on the breezes.

"Swank!" said Angie, quoting Dolores Haze.

Margit and Simeon were sipping white wine, absorbed in what seemed like an intense conversation. She urged us to help ourselves to glasses, and I caught the end of Margit saying that she had actually remembered when Simeon's brother had died because it had scandalized the island, there having been, she believed, shoddy police work involved. Simeon looked pained, insisting that he merely wanted a headstone, that it didn't matter what the circumstances had been so long ago.

I noticed Margit had changed into more formal attire, a billowy dress with embroidered flowers, and had put her hair up, secured with chopsticks. Angie's hair was up, too, and she looked tanned and relaxed and enthusiastic about the adventure. We toasted, and food was brought to us that turned out to be really excellent, a number of courses, from fruit salad with mangoes and banana garnished with hibiscus petals, to a light cream vegetable soup. The main course was whole crab caught off the coast, steamed in a gingery garlic sauce with coconut rice.

"Am I starving, or is this delicious?" said Angie.

As we ate, we filled one another in on our backgrounds, Margit explaining that she had come to Lamu from Trondheim in the late 1970s with her husband who had since passed, that their dream had been to open modest guesthouse, and they did, but that with the troubles her financial future was looking less certain.

Angie was listening avidly, pressing Margit for details, and as she was speaking, it dawned on me that she had most likely told these same stories to Audra when they first met, that Audra had eaten at this same table, many, many times, had probably held the very spoon that I was at that moment using to bring the soup to my mouth, had certainly handled the fork with which I prized sweet strings of crabmeat. I had a strange sensation of synergy thinking this, wondering if the girl's spine had been pressed against the rigid back of the very chair in which I was sitting, Margit clearly having always seated herself at the head, presiding over the table as matron of the establishment, and it was not the first time that I would feel simultaneously remote from and close to Audra and her daughter, as though cupping my eyes on the wrong side of some smudged partition, watching them mouth words I could not understand.

Over dessert of cream and custard, a leisurely meal's worth of conversation and background under our belts, Margit began talking about them.

"Precocious" was the word she used first about Petra, then "headstrong." "Clever." When they had first come to Shela, Margit told us, Petra was moody, sullen, lashing out at Audra in front of other guests, holing herself up in her room, refusing to come down for meals. Audra was annoyed or chagrined, Margit wasn't ever sure. "She knows how to fall in line," Audra had said to Margit. "And she will."

"In truth," Margit said, "the entire situation was somewhat perplexing, these Americans with their pricey luggage turning up to live in little Shela. Very few Americans come here, even before."

On their first night, Margit had taken a meal with Audra, Petra sulking in protest, and Margit had learned they were not on holiday at all. Audra had said she was on temporary assignment, that she was connected somehow to the deep-water port then being planned for Lamu, to be the largest in East Africa, contracts having already been awarded to construction firms headquartered in Hangzhou. At this Margit had bristled, because like every other hotelier on the island, she was opposed to this port because she thought it would ruin Lamu's distinctive character, turn it into Güllük or Abadan, devastate sea life. Not only that, but the government was repossessing something like a half-million acres of land from farmers in the area. There were a handful of true squatters, she admitted, but they were being lumped in with the tribal peoples who have lived there for hundreds of years, the whole thing a shakedown in her opinion. But Audra had assured her nothing was set in stone, that there were detailed impact studies yet to be performed, that consultants such as herself were there precisely to increase revenues for everyone, to relocate people to more fertile tracts of land and to protect sea life from even the tiniest PPM of industrial contaminant. "Lift all the boats," Audra had said.

Margit was bluntly skeptical, but she liked Audra, was impressed by her polish and the way she spoke so fluently about the history of the region, the way she seemed to have an index at her fingertips of all the issues that only locals would care about. She was gone from the guesthouse most weekdays and some nights, Margit unsure where, but, she supposed, to consult with the engineers or marine biologists or financiers or Chinese executives, who were so frightened by the Muslim environment that they walked around Lamu Town with fatigued guards armed with machine guns, much to the amusement of the island's residents. Audra herself had no fear, seemed instantly to have contacts all over the archipelago, and Petra inherited this confidence from her, in the days following their move finally venturing from her room in daylight hours to sunbathe and even chat with other guests. After that she made friends quickly and would accompany families, usually European, on their excursions to the beaches or the ruins on the windward side of the island. She spoke three or four languages, Margit discovered, and seemed to know all the latest pop songs from these people's home countries, something that struck Margit as exceedingly unusual for an American.

During that first high season, said Margit, Petra had seemed contented, appeared even to thrive on hanging around an international set, having chaste romances and then keeping in touch with boys with slender fingers because that was for her a mark of sensitivity. Her life became slightly more structured after Audra had hired the tutor, but the more Audra pushed her to succeed, saying that she would already be at a disadvantage for college applications because of her unconventional background, the more Petra would become frustrated, childishly nasty, saying yeah, and whose fault is that? During the first low season, and especially after the troubles, when the island seemed to have shut down and Audra was paradoxically gone more than ever, Margit began to worry about Petra's isolation, not a problem, she said, for an old woman at ease with the sun and some novels, but not so healthy for a young girl, who so clearly blossomed when interacting with people, who was greedy about new experiences.

"Although Shela is beautiful," said Margit, "it can be hard for a young girl." Petra had made a couple of girlfriends from good families, but they were never allowed too far beyond the eye of their own mothers or aunties, so she was left either helping them with cooking or other chores, or else sitting in their homes and playing video games; since these girlfriends were certainly not permitted to be alone with boys, Petra was by proxy isolated from them herself. Eventually Petra started hanging around the beach boys who ran leisure cruises and subsisted on supplying illicit things to European tourists. When Audra had caught them all smoking hash, the consequences were dire. This had led to a period of frosty relations between mother and daughter, something Margit knew well since for the past few months she and Petra were practically the only ones in the house, Audra away for increasingly long stretches of the day and night, Johnny and the cooks finding supplemental work on the mainland.

Margit had begun to view Petra as an adoptive granddaughter, and despite her white lies and combativeness had grown fond of her, and they baked and watched movies together—her own grandchildren, she said, refused to watch anything old, but Petra couldn't get enough of those corny beach blanket films—and Petra made her jewelry from seashells and coral and they had begun to raise a pair of cockatiels. Petra had even pleaded with Johnny to stop poisoning the feral cats who lived around the guesthouse, and Margit, who had previously viewed them as problems to be solved, had relented and together they made a sanctuary for them in an unobtrusive corner. Petra brought them scraps every night.

By way of conclusion, Margit said she thought the girl was an impressive young woman. "You should be proud."

"I have nothing to do with her," I said quickly.

Simeon made a joke and everyone laughed.

"Is it lonely," asked Angie, "being here by yourself?"

Margit looked toward the kitchen door and said that the great thing about running a guesthouse, in normal times, was that you were always meeting new people, but that now it was an adjustment, especially without Petra there.

For whatever reason, I was focused on the off-hand way Margit had used the term "white lies" in connection to this girl—was it merely a white lie to claim she was suffering under the knuckles of murky Islam when she clearly wasn't?

Simeon was now asking about the new port Margit had mentioned, wanted to know about the turtle populations, and I stopped listening as I wrestled with the possibility that my absence from this girl's life had caused a kind of tangible damage, caused her to think it acceptable to lie to draw me, a functional stranger, around the globe.

I drank some more wine, but didn't contribute much as they continued on about illegal trawlers, nests in dunes.

Angie was fascinated by Margit in the way she was attracted to any older woman who seemed to her "independent"—as in, artistic, worldly, eccentric—and wanted to know all about the logistics of leaving everything behind in your country to start a dream in a new one. This was of less interest to Simeon than what was happening with the turtles, and he said he was turning in. I took the opportunity to say that I was wiped, too, and was heading up to bed. Angie moved to come with me, but I insisted that she stay since she and Margit were clearly hitting it off.

"So you just up and moved?" said Angie with admiration, tapping the table for emphasis.

———

In the room, I brushed my teeth using bottled water per Margit's recommendations and stripped to a pair of boxers. I really was drained from the travel and heat and the emotional strain of building this girl up in my head, imagining the possibility of seeing her and having her see me—and then from having that possibility taken away as a door opened.

I figured out that in order for the mosquito netting to be effective, I had to unfurl it then tuck the bottom edges underneath the mattress, creating a creamy womb that shimmered against the ceiling fan. It lulled me to sleep right away.

I gasped awake in the dead of night, sweating, my heart racing, unsure of where I was. Disoriented, I batted the netting, then remembered. Angie was sleeping next to me in shorts and a tank top. She was a very heavy sleeper, and I considered for a moment nudging her so we could talk out what had or hadn't happened. But she looked so contented, on her side with a curled fist tucked under her chin, breathing gently around her mouth guard, which made her lips protrude ever so slightly, so I left her alone. Instead I slid from the mosquito netting as quietly as I could and caught a breeze out on the balcony.

It was pleasant there, the starry sky so huge and clear that I could actually track satellites arcing through space.

What a disquieting experience, discovering more about this girl, who was becoming a little less flattish and faded in my mind, her personality taking shape so that she was transforming, slowly but surely, from a mere notion on a screen to a round character who might one day become, if I ever actually succeeded in meeting her, a real person.

In that moment I had an idea.

I pulled on a shirt, grabbed the metal flashlight that had been provided in the nightstand, and silently padded out of our area of the guesthouse and around to another set of stairs, which I knew led to Audra's floor because Margit had said so. The courtyard was silent except for the gusts in the fronds and a trickle of water echoing from somewhere. I stole up the staircase, stealthy and not feeling too guilty since I hadn't seen Audra in fourteen years and she had decimated my heart anyway, and this girl was not yet for me a person of substance whose privacy could be violated.

As expected, the upper floor was open, even larger than ours because it was on the top level, the penthouse, a wrap-around terrace with cushioned chaise lounges and doors on either end. The outer area didn't appear to contain any personal effects worth investigating, so I went to the nearest door, which like mine had no lock, and pushed in. What I was looking for I didn't know, just some usable clue, so I beamed the flashlight around the room. Moonlight was coming in through the open shutters, so I could see well enough.

Judging from the disarray and clutter, I guessed it was the girl's room. The bed had been neatly made, surely not by her, and there was evidence of efforts to stack piles of clothes on chairs, but it was clear this was a doomed attempt to reign in a space whose normal state was chaos. I beamed around the walls, over a poster of some shirtless soccer star I didn't recognize, but then was startled to see tacked up on another wall two old-fashioned album covers, Joni Mitchell's *For the Roses* and Leonard Cohen's *New Skin for the Old Ceremony*. I spoke aloud unintentionally: "What?"

A searing sensation came over me, as it was hard to process what I was seeing. Why would she have these particular albums, two of my favorites, when in my experience even college students evidenced only the dimmest awareness that vinyl records had once existed? That old Pynchonian feeling crept back in. I inspected the albums more closely: the edges were blunted with use, although they appeared empty. Around them she had lots of things hanging on nails: beaded necklaces and bracelets, feathers, a blue ribbon embossed in gold German writing I couldn't understand. I wondered how Margit felt about her putting holes in these walls.

I kept moving. On a small dressing table, there was a box spilling over with costume jewelry, a brush tangled with hair, nearly empty perfume bottles. In the mirror's frame she had stuck a small ticket of photographs, the kind you get in carnival photo booths, and I finally caught a monochrome glimpse of her, all big teeth and snub nose scrunched in a series of contortions. I bent down to get a closer look and was shaken to see echoes of my brother Benj.

I looked a long moment, never touching the photo ticket itself, then let my attention wander to a tiny folded tee shirt, under which I discovered a creased copy of *A Fan's Notes*. This was another shock as I had read and re-read that novel in high school, during the height of my Cohen phase, and it had recently been object of a half-hearted cyber recovery campaign on my part, as in I had tweeted out how under-appreciated it was. The searing sensation intensified—was there finally some sort of telepathic bond between this long-lost daughter and me? Or was this a mere masculine fantasy, that such a connection existed when I myself had done absolutely no parenting at all? Was I over-interpreting? How could you not notice, for instance, that this girl had set up her own "save-the-cat" operation, even though I remember distinctly Audra once telling me that cats were "weird"? Whatever it meant, her taste seemed abnormal for someone her age: where was Harry Potter or the latest effeminate pop star?

As in my room, there was an open storage shelf, crammed with more clothing, mostly bathing suits in lime and animal prints, as well as board games, shoes (although who could wear them in the sand?), damp paperbacks, a stuffed giraffe, a filthy blue deer. I did a cursory walk-through of the bathroom, whose counter was a junkyard of quarter-filled bottles and jars, but when I eyed what seemed to be some European version of maxi pads, I retreated, unwilling even to confirm that first glimpse.

Still flushed and convinced I would find no definitive explanation of her emails amid the unnerving emblems of Baby Boomerdom, I went back downstairs and into the gauzy cocoon. Angie hadn't budged. I laid listening to the visible whir of the fan for a long time, Angie occasion-ally turning over with a whimper, and I thought about the Chelsea Hotel, about that scene where Exley interviews for a job, hoping that this girl at least had a sense of humor.

—

When I broke through the mosquito netting the next day, Angie was already up and gone. I was experiencing a strange sense of newness, numb newness, not simply because I was in a foreign place, which was part of it, but because my life was expanding in ways I didn't understand.

I showered again, because I'd sweated all night, then wandered down to find Angie. She was on a laptop at the dining table, where an array of fruit and pastries had been put out.

"You're alive!" she said.

"Technically," I rasped.

"There's coffee." She was wearing a bright red and yellow headband and a huge necklace with wooden beads the size of lemons. Her camera was next to the laptop, its strap snaking out among bottles of sunscreen and tins of lozenges.

I must have been staring at the necklace because she explained without my asking that she had traded with Margit, that it was hand-made locally.

I said it was festive and asked about internet.

"Yeah, of course. I was just researching about the island. It's only a page in the book but there's actually tons to see."

I scooted up next to her and poured myself a cup of coffee. "What time did you get up?"

"I don't know. Early. I went shopping with Margit. You wanna check your email I'm guessing."

She turned the laptop toward me, and I navigated to my webmail program, fully expecting something from the girl, some explanation of why I had come 8000 miles to "rescue" her or "present" myself or whatever it was I was doing there—only to find an empty room and some album covers.

I had a hard time getting the page loaded. In fact, Angie noticed my hands were shaking as I tried to type, and she said I should get some water in me before the coffee, and she poured me a tall glass. Water was her answer to everything.

"Don't worry," she said. "It's filtered. I already checked."

I sucked down the water while waiting for the webmail program to load. Angie described shopping with Margit. Finally my inbox appeared in jagged fits. There were emails from both Cubby and my sister, and I clicked into them briefly. Their substance was essentially the same: Had we made it without major bodily injury? Had we met the girl? How did Audra look? (from Cubby). I scrolled through the morass of personal loan offers and phony Calls for Papers that never seemed to diminish, but found nothing from the girl. I thought this was a mistake at first, on my part, that I'd missed something, and then went meticulously back through everything, and even checked my Junk folder to ensure nothing was hiding there. I flipped the laptop back around to Angie.

"Am I blind?" I said. "Is there really nothing? What the hell?"

"Take it easy," she said, peering into the screen with care. "I don't see anything, except from your sister and Cubby."

I felt it was bullshit, said it was bullshit. Outrage was the proper response. I snapped the laptop shut and skidded it across the table and Angie told me again to take it easy. On what planet was I supposed to take it easy, I was saying, when some random girl writes me "out of the blue," asks me to come to Kenya, and foolishly I do so, and then she's not even there. And she's a liar. There was a basket of napkins on the table, and I realized I had taken one out unconsciously, was twisting it in my fingers as I raged.

Angie refilled my water, a server's reflex, and did her best to project empathy, even as I knew the ruined napkin was evidence that I was being histrionic and unreasonable—yet the more I worked myself up, the more it seemed as though I wasn't actually controlling my behavior but rather watching myself at some remove.

I stood up and elaborated all the wrongs perpetrated against me, I couldn't help it, felt a real righteous justification, and I railed more about the general unfairness and shittiness of the situation, and Angie nodded and frowned sympathetically, a bartender's reflex, and waited for me to calm down.

"I'm sure she had her reasons," she said after I stopped raving.

"What's that supposed to mean? What *reasons*? To screw me over? This was a waste of time! Money!"

Angie stirred some sugar into her own coffee serenely, a monk in the face of an onslaught of zealots from a distant valley. "Take a load off. We don't know her story is what I'm saying." She clinked her spoon on the rim of her cup and looked at me. Her Zen expression put me off my rage for a moment and I counted to ten, then sat back down.

"We know her mother hasn't abandoned her," I said steadily. "We know she's not in some fundamentalist Islam type scenario."

"But we know she's your daughter"—I glared at her—"and we don't know what's in her head. I was a thirteen-year-old girl once upon a time, and I can tell you, it's no picnic. I can't imagine what it must be like living on this island with your mom and an old lady, not knowing the language, and then having to rush back to Dubai or wherever at the drop of a hat. I mean, imagine how hard that would be."

"I guess," I said, sulking. Probably she was right, but I hated admitting it, a fact that got me down even more because I associated that kind of intractability with masculinity, toxic masculinity, and yet there I was, sulking and intractable. I knew it was a stupid dynamic, but that knowledge didn't make it any less difficult to break.

Ultimately, Angie was forced to be gentle with me—something I also hated, but accepted—and we had a much cooler conversation about what to do next. She convinced me that there was no point in fleeing Lamu in disgust (my first impulse), and we decided that we would stay another couple of days, and if there was no word from the girl, spend a few days in Nairobi before heading home. That way, as Angie put it, we could "salvage the trip." In general, she didn't have the funds to travel as widely as she had dreamed, and so was determined to see as much of Kenya as possible.

"So let's motivate to do some exploring," she said.

"What exploring? Now?" I was still embittered and wasn't ready for anyone to have any fun. "I say we chill by the pool and see if they have any of that palm wine."

Angie had been bussing the table while I picked at some pastries, but at that she stopped, as if shocked. "Are you insane? We've spent all this money and time to get here, the least we can do is enjoy ourselves."

"I thought it was unsafe. What about the kidnappings?"

"I had a long talk with Margit about it this morning. She insists that now Lamu is the safest place in Kenya." Apparently, Margit had explained to Angie that since the incidents, the Kenyan armed forces had gone into Somalia, the navy did regular patrols, a radar battery had been installed along the coast, and a curfew had been instituted so not even fishermen were permitted on the water after dusk. "Plus there's something like 200 Kenyan Special Forces stationed along the road to Mombasa, so we're good."

"I'd rather stick to the pool."

She stood up straight, indignant, but playing up this indignation for dramatic effect. "Well," she said, "I'm going with or without you. I'd rather it be with you but suit yourself." She started gathering up her camera with the full knowledge that she had me over a barrel, that I wouldn't let her traipse around by herself. Besides, I was a little curious to see the island, even if I didn't admit that directly to her.

"Let's go explore," I said.

Angie filled a small daypack with waters and sunscreen. Her guidebook had only the one outdated page on Lamu, mainly listing various festivals that weren't happening currently, but her online search was fruitful, and she had gotten a wealth of insider tips from Margit. She created an itinerary that involved wandering—"wandering with purpose," she said. I said it sounded fine. I hadn't seen Margit or Simeon all morning, but as we were preparing to leave, Johnny materialized from somewhere and said he would take us down to the water.

We did a reverse tour of the twists and turns that had led us there the day before, and once we were back at the greened-over beach, Johnny pointed to a path along the sand past the breakwater. All we had to do, he said, was follow this packed dirt path and it would take us to Lamu Town. "When you get back to Shela," he said, "just say to anyone 'Orchid Club' and they will know the way."

Angie was pumped, waved as Johnny trudged back up the alley, and we began to make our way to Lamu Town.

"I think he and Margit are an item," she said casually, when Johnny was out of earshot.

"What?" I said, incredulous. "He's like forty. And she's seventy."

"She's seventy-three," she said.

"You're crazy. What makes you think that?"

"I don't know. Little glances. The way she introduced him. It's a vibe."

"Doubtful."

"You never notice anything."

"Hmph," I said ambiguously.

We found the old corniche path to Lamu Town and Angie made us walk slowly and deliberately, with the idea that this would allow us to "take everything in." Lots of people were on the path, mostly men in kikoi and tee shirts, some in kofias or tarbooshes, fewer women in hijab. Angie kept saying "tarboosh, tarboosh, tarboosh" to cheer me up, and it was working because her goofiness was so straightforward and unapologetic.

As we walked she would smile and wave, the men would look embarrassed, and the women would shoot Angie knowing sideways glances. Between the villages, set amidst what looked to be jungle thickets, were enormous fenced homes in various states of ostentation or disrepair: some were ultra-modern with stainless steel doors and camera arrays, others had that crumbling charm I associated with colonial times, paint flaking and salt ravaged, vegetation creeping over where it shouldn't.

When we made it to the town proper, a riot of life and color opened before us, and I said to Angie that she could do a whole book of travel photos here. There was the museum where we had stood in the shade while Simeon told us about his brother. There was Lamu Fort, with its ramparts and ocean views. There was the sugar cane vendor and the old men gambling in the square. There was a market crowded with wooden stalls offering every kind of tropical fruit I had ever known about, and many others I didn't, plus nuts, potatoes, dried herbs. There was an indoor part of the market, much hotter and closer, a stinking fishmonger and butchery displaying whole prehistoric dorado and ruby-pink filets of tuna, alive with people hacking away at goat and sheep carcasses, breaking them down to sell each part individually. Men jostled, made deals, shouted over one another, the women squatting to inspect particular cuts before committing to purchase. There was a general lack of refrigeration, and clusters of flies swarmed on hunks of resting meat. Angie bent over in imitation of the local women, examining a sheep's head encrusted with busy insects.

"Look," she said of the flies, "they're wringing their hands, wringing their feet."

I felt a wave of nausea coming over me, had to get out of there due to the smell, and Angie teased me, saying "Don't kill the fly!" before we retreated to the outdoor market.

We stopped to regroup and chug some water. Angie was digging everything, taking photos and pointing out a wall made of coral, a cop in a burgundy beret, a cat stealing a minnow carcass from a scrap heap. She was impressed by the shadows cast by filtered sun coming in through the ragged awnings over the shops. Maybe because of my remark about her doing a travel book, she pointed out the awnings, drawing particular attention to the blue plastic sheeting strung from smoothed branches.

"You notice those sacks?" she said.

"Not really."

"They had something similar to them in Cambodia," she said. "They're everywhere here."

She pointed out that the donkeys we had seen being led along the path from Shela were slung with these sacks, made not of a material like burlap or jute, but of acrylic or polypropylene woven on high-speed industrial looms to mimic jute. She knew this from Cambodia, had once had an idea to do a whole series on the Sacks of the Global South. Many people considered them superior to natural fibers, she said, because they would not degrade, a problem for the great Pacific garbage patch but a boon to those communities who would have otherwise seen their grain rotted in storage facilities before it could be distributed. These sacks were all the same size, twenty-five kilograms, the weight a grown man could comfortably bear on his back, and yet in

Lamu they were widely repurposed, slung not only over donkeys but filled as sandbags, used as shade, or ripped and tied as warnings to the ends of jutting rebar on unfinished projects.

Angie was right: the more I looked, the more I saw them. She angled under the polypropylene ceiling of a spice business and took some shots, saying that this was the sort of thing that would interest her, to do a book on the many varieties of polypropylene sacks in Kenya.

"Look where it's worn," she said, "how the light comes in like stained glass."

We spent the afternoon wandering with purpose, ambling around town as Angie hunted for polypropylene sacks in various forms. We stopped to buy Cokes. We chatted with security guards, kept an eye out for Ali Ecstasy. Angie discovered a curio shop, hurried past by everyone else in town but us, which had an assortment of spears and wooden boxes made there on the island. The proprietor showed me a string of red beads, trade beads, he said, for my wife, and I bought them for Angie. Outside, we saw what must have been a Chinese executive flanked by fatigued guards with machine guns, and snickered because Margit had mentioned this character, or one like him.

When it seemed to be cooling off, more people emerged from their homes, but we decided to make our way to the wharf with the intention of heading back to Shela. There we encountered a surprising sight: two large white men, unmistakably American, waiting on the pier for a water taxi to be pulled around. They noticed Angie and me, were checking Angie out unsubtly, and she strode right over to say hello. They were each well over six foot, knocking on six-foot-four in fact, with whole relief maps of muscles, unintentionally twee tribal or barbed wire tats, and near crew cuts, one blond, one dirty blond. They were dressed in camo cargo shorts, olive drab form-fitting tees, and identical wrap-around Oakleys.

"What's up?" said the dirty blond one to Angie.

"What are you guys doing here?" Angie asked.

"Sightseeing," said the blond. "Tourism." They didn't ask about us, but still weren't shy about eyeing Angie up and down.

I noted the oversized duffels at their feet. "You guys military?" I asked.

Their faces both flushed as pink as those tuna filets in the market, and they mumbled naw, naw, *tourists*.

"So where you headed?" asked Angie.

One of them repeated the question back, then said airport. "We're just tourists heading to the airport," said the other one.

They were none too bright, but it didn't really concern us, so I tugged Angie by the elbow, told them to git-r-done, and we picked our way down the path back to Shela.

"Bizarre," said Angie.

Again we passed the jetty in progress, surrounded by the sweat-beaded laborers, still working, stripped to the waist, heaving carts of rubble and propelling them forward blankly. Kids were splashing off an unused dock, and they hooted and whistled until Angie waved at them, returning it with embarrassed glee. When we got back to the beach we recognized, the teenagers in board shorts and soccer jerseys were again loafing in the shade, and the Rasta one who had led us through the alleys strutted up happily, saying what's up my man and eyeing Angie even more openly than the blond giants.

"Call me Mohammed Starlight," he said, and wanted to do a complicated handshake.

Angie hunched forward and adjusted the straps of the daypack so her breasts were less pronounced and I asked Mohammed Starlight if he could possibly take us back up to Orchid Club.

"Not a problem, my man," he said.

As we walked through the shifting and shard-studded sand, he looked around conspiratorially and wanted to know if we partied, if we wanted to buy a little something-something, and I realized, again belatedly, that these were the beach boys from whom Audra had restricted her daughter. With a sidelong glance I studied Mohammed Starlight, his sun-bleached bands of hemp bracelets, vaguely familiar to me from the nineties, cowries, the mane of tousled hair with streaked highlights, the sickly-sweet smell of coconut oil emanating from his chest, the gold hoops in his ears, and I understood Audra's stance on the matter.

When we reached the lacquered door, I held out some folded bills, but hesitated before putting them in his open palm, clearing my throat, trying to sound casual, and asking him if he knew the white girl who lived there.

He gave me some line about "Mohammed Starlight"—third person—knowing everyone on the island, and I said in that case maybe he could do me a favor and sort of steer clear of the girl in the future. But it may have come out wrong because he was immediately, melodramatically offended.

"What is this, man? Racist shit?"

"No," said Angie, though it was unclear if she was saying "no" to me or Mohammed Starlight.

I had somehow ceded the moral high ground in three seconds and so was suddenly playing catch up, assuring him that it didn't have anything to do with race but everything to do with the little something-something he was peddling.

At that he looked relieved. "Eh, is *that* all," he said. "OK. It's called socialization. You know, people really need to chill."

"How old are you?" I asked.

When he said twenty-two, I reminded him that the girl was thirteen. He assured me he had only made himself available because she seemed lonely, and referred to the one time she had wanted to go to the Police Canteen, noting that he'd refused because even he knew it was no place for a young girl, unless she was charging for it. "You feel me?" he said.

I didn't really know what he was driving at, but I did know that for whatever reason, as the conversation developed, the idea of Mohammed Starlight introducing this girl around to Lamu's surfer underclass was becoming less and less appealing. "Just keep in mind that she's a child and you're an adult," I said.

He found this hysterical. "All right, sure, if you say so. An adult."

I pressed the wad of money in his hand, he counted it shamelessly, and Angie and I went inside.

"Look at you," she said as we shook off our flip-flops to rinse our feet in the cistern.

"Look at me what?" I said.

"Fatherly instincts."

"Fuck off."

We found Margit and Simeon chatting around the big table. Johnny appeared from nowhere, as he always did, interested in our impressions of Lamu Town. We described the highlights, and showed Margit the beads we had purchased, acknowledging that they were probably made in China, but she examined them and concluded that they were quite real, that she could tell because the insides were a certain shade of white. They were trade beads, she said, used for purchasing human beings when Lamu and Zanzibar were the centers of the Indian Ocean slave trade. Historical pieces that we should keep.

"Damn," said Angie. "Well I won't be wearing those for fashion."

Simeon was looking relaxed, loose-limbed, again sipping some mint tea. He said he had been over to Manda Island to have a look at what was being done to help the sea turtle population. There was a conservation trust, founded by a white woman but administered by locals, whose mission was to guard the turtle nests in the dunes, so they had a team of guys who patrolled different parts of the island looking for egg poachers or trawlers who might snare mature turtles. This was really wonderful, Simeon was saying, because sometimes people didn't think long-term about ecological concerns, he had seen this firsthand, and in his opinion such initiatives were marks of an advanced society.

Angie mentioned the encounter with the blond and dirty blond hulks.

Margit sighed and brought a hand down on the table, saying they were U.S. military, that there was a camp on the far side of Manda. "Not officially," she said. "But it's there."

Johnny started to say that there were certain places you couldn't fish because the navy had made it forbidden, but it was really the Americans, and Margit said they were likely special forces, there as part of some sprawling effort to deal with the warlords in Somalia, and this was why nobody was really worried about pirates anymore.

"So what is the plan now?" asked Simeon suddenly. "Since your daughter is not here?"

Angie and I recounted our discussion from the morning, but tentatively, realizing that we should have asked Simeon for his input then. The "options," as we now framed them, were to have Simeon leave and simply hang on at Orchid Club for the next few days, hoping Audra and her daughter would turn up, or head back to Nairobi with him, and then probably go home from there. I had all summer, but Angie had to be back at work in five days. We had purchased return flights for then, figuring they could be changed if necessary.

Also, I had no idea what Margit was charging us to stay there, and the mounting expenses were inducing a different kind of anxiety. Finally we all decided that we would stay another night, because the next day Ollie's headstone would be ready, and then barring major email revelations would return to Nairobi, then home for Angie and me.

The whole trip seemed to me then defeating and pointless, but what else was there to do?

—

Angie and I spent the rest of the time in Lamu walking the dunes and exploring the ruins on the windward side of the island, as the girl had done. We ate well. Angie bonded with Margit, promising to write her and even to come back to visit. I slept in a hammock and drank palm wine. Simeon got notes from the turtle conservationists and called his wife.

There was only one flight a day to Nairobi, and Simeon made arrangements. When it was time to leave, Margit seemed sincerely sad to see us go. At first, she refused any payment at all, but Angie balked, and insisted that we pay—that I pay—which was irksome but I didn't say so, and finally Margit agreed to let me give her $500. As I handed over my credit card, I kept telling myself that it had to have been a fraction of the true cost for the three of us, in normal times, but it still stung.

Once our packs had been invisibly brought down to the front entry, Margit gave me that singular embrace of a frail elderly woman, the kind that requires you to bend over and hug very gingerly, as if handling too roughly would cause her to break, and I was aware of her liver spots against my skin. Angie sniffled and ensured that they had each other's contact info.

Margit was positive everything would work out with my "family."

"No doubt you will see Petra soon," she said. "Children have a remarkable capacity for forgiveness."

Johnny materialized to send us off, I tried to detect again if there was anything between Margit and him, but couldn't, Angie lingered too long in her goodbyes, and at long last we were back down at the beach, where sure enough Mohammed Starlight and his pals were loafing. He put in a call to another friend, who showed up within minutes in a splintery motorboat. I gave Mohammed a bill or two and reminded him, light-heartedly, about our agreement, and he yawned and said he knew that he'd better "keep his nose clean" or else I'd turn up and "bust his kneecaps."

Back on the wharf in Lamu Town, I was already soaked through with sweat and probably heat rashed, Angie kept saying she hated goodbyes, and we followed Simeon down an alley to the stone mason's shop. He had red hair and a glass eye, this stone mason, and had polished a small granite block, maybe twice the size of a mailbox, and etched in Simeon's brother's full name, the dates of his birth and death, and a cross. Simeon thought the job was perfect and stared at me expectantly, as though I were going to shell out for it. Angie was behind him, and shrugged without him seeing, so I stood there trying to look clueless.

After an uncomfortable interval, Simeon reached into his own pocket and counted out some bills for the stone mason.

"It's really well done," I said, but I could tell he was annoyed.

When the mason was paid, he called in a teenager with a handcart, and we all loaded the headstone, secured it with some strips cut from polypropylene sacks, and proceeded to the Methodist mission at the top of the hill. Being the greatest fixer in all of East Africa must have meant that Simeon was equipped with an unfailing sense of direction because he seemed expert on the confusing route up the hill, even though he had only walked it twice in thirty years. He led us there with no missteps, striding confidently without the help of Ali Ecstasy, the teenager bumping the handcart over cobblestone or dragging it with effort through sand, Angie after that, still commenting on the way the doors were carved or the coral visible in certain walls, while I brought up the rear, constantly adjusting my sweaty straps, thinking I overpacked.

At the top of the hill, the minister seemed to be waiting for us, wearing a dark suit and clerical collar. We heaved our way with some difficulty to the spider-webby slope where Simeon had buried his brother, and three of us, Simeon, the teenager and I, got the laden cart through the vegetation before finally making it to a spot where someone had already excavated a rectangle where the headstone would go. Angie took some furtive shots while we fitted it into place, and Simeon found a spade that had been leaning nearby to backfill and tamp down the soil. The minister delivered a brief prayer and benediction, and Simeon stood to mumble something about his brother being at rest, then what seemed like a prayer in his language. He asked Angie to take some shots of him posing next to the headstone.

"Can you email that to me?" he said.

"Not a problem," said Angie.

The teenager was assertively bored, so Simeon gave him a handful of coins, and he trudged off with the handcart. The minister invited us for tea, but Simeon regretfully declined, saying we had a plane to catch, and then tried to give him some money, too, which the minister refused. I leaned against a tree awkwardly, batting off ants that had marched onto my arm and wondering if Benj's grave was being properly maintained. The cemetery where they buried him offered various packages and tiers involving perpetual care, weekly weeding and grass clipping, fresh-cut flowers, flags for veterans, and though I never knew the details, or what they could afford, I remembered my parents arguing about these tiers at the time, opposed in their ideas regarding what constituted money well spent.

Simeon cast another long look at his own brother's headstone, then said we had better go, and again he led us back down the hill, never making a false turn.

5.

ANGIE AND I had three days in Nairobi before we were to fly back to the States. After surviving 540 Air's E-ticket return flight into Wilson, Simeon recommended the Hilton, expensive but comfortable, suitable for us. When he pulled his muddy Nissan Patrol up to the hotel, an enormous box of a building, several stories high but with a cylindrical tower in the center, shooting up twenty or thirty more stories, guards ambled over to sniff around. There was a serious security perimeter, and they questioned us suspiciously, these guards, asking if we had reservations and Simeon lied and said we had, and they searched the backseat and luggage area, ran a stick with a mirror on the end around the vehicle looking for bombs attached to the undercarriage. They even trotted a Belgian shepherd around before letting us through the gates and into a parking lot.

Simeon was shaking his head, but I was somewhat heartened, quietly noting that the security at both domestic airports had been compara-tively light, realizing also that he had probably chosen this fortress because he questioned our abilities to survive the capital on our own. He was telling us that the concierge could help with airport transfers, that we could take all our meals in the hotel, and I began to feel a little insulted by his lack of confidence in our independence.

I think Angie was insulted too. "I lived for a year in Cambodia," she reminded him. "We'll manage."

"I'm sure," said Simeon.

Once we had everything unloaded, Simeon said he was sorry that he couldn't stay with us, but that as we could well imagine, he had respon-sibilities back in Kajiado.

"There's no way we could have made it to Orchid Club on our own," I said.

Angie said she hoped the headstone had brought him peace.

Simeon waved off any further mention of his brother, then steered me toward the matter of his fees, which he didn't bring up directly. "Of course," I said.

He produced a neat invoice with an oniony yellow carbon copy underneath. The fees turned out to be much higher than I expected, and I suspected that he had folded the cost of the headstone into them anyway. I had to duck into the lobby to pull out tens of thousands of shillings from an ATM at exorbitant rates.

Simeon pocketed the wad of bills self-consciously, then clapped my shoulder and gave my hand a long slow shake, telling me it was a great pleasure to meet me and that he hoped we would have the chance to visit Kenya again to see the real sights. Angie wanted to give him a hug, said to say hi to Mrs. Karanja and Theophilus and that she wanted to come back and visit, that he should come see us in the States. I said that, too, knowing neither of those things would ever happen.

"Don't forget to send those photos," he said to Angie, then climbed in the Patrol and drove off, again without ceremony.

Angie and I were on our own. We had our backpacks X-rayed, handed over our passports to be photocopied, then found our room, which was musty and oddly laid out. Angie had already planned our activities in the city. First on her list was Nairobi National Park, "The World's Only Wildlife Capital," a game park in the center of town. It was about $3 for residents and $35 for tourists, and she called down to have the concierge arrange transportation for the next morning. That afternoon we walked over to Uhuru Park, landscaped with palm trees and dotted with rusty stands where you could buy Fanta or ice cream. There was a modest reservoir with paddle boats for rent, but the lawns around it were generally under-watered and the park sparsely attended. The neighborhood around the hotel was livelier, a noisy hub of office buildings with business types shouldering others out the way on the main sidewalks; but if you turned down the side streets, you would find microworlds where labcoated men and women cooked street stews in huge steel stockpots over open flames, where scrappy guys pulled car-tired rickshaws overloaded with polypropylene sacks, where people sat on upturned buckets shooting the shit out of view of the banking conglomerates who had their East African headquarters around the corner. The concierge had intimated that it would be unwise for us to conduct ourselves alone at night, and so stinging from the fact that Simeon had been right, we took our first meal in one of the themed restaurants in the hotel, having been offered buffet coupons at discounted rates.

The next day the concierge informed us that Nairobi National Park had to close due to some unspecified emergency; Angie was disappointed but resolved to make the best of things regardless. The concierge then tried to sell us on a "slum tour" of Kibera, and Angie lectured him on poverty porn. We did Carnivore instead, an obligatory tourist restaurant. We went to Westgate Mall and the Karen Blixen Museum because Angie was a huge *Out of Africa* fan.

"How could you not be in love with Robert Redford?" she exclaimed, and when I pointed out I was nothing at all like Robert Redford, she said it was merely pretend, a romance.

"I thought it was a memoir?" I said.

"I'm talking about the movie," she said, and we left it at that.

The old Blixen estate was wood-paneled and very colonial. Angie was having a great time.

—

On the night before we were supposed to fly back to London and then home, I made the mistake of stopping in the business center to check my email. It was a mistake because during those few days in Nairobi, I had willed myself into forgetting what we were doing in Kenya in the first place, had tried instead to enjoy myself, as a tourist, with my girlfriend, who kept saying that we were having a "once in a lifetime" experience. Of course I couldn't totally purge this girl from my mind, of course I felt there would be ramifications of all this—I just told myself it would come later, that I could worry about it later, as I would my compounding credit card bills.

Then I checked my email. There was, in fact, something from the girl:

> OH MY GOD, I am SO SORRY!!! Right after the last time I wrote you we had to leave for India all of a sudden and I just saw your email that you were actually coming. That was shocking. Mom had a work emergency and we left last minute. There's internet here but it's a major pain so I can't really check it easily. Mom doesn't know I wrote you but if I knew for sure you were coming I would of made her stay in Lamu until you got there. SORRY!! Supposedly we'll be here two or three weeks minimum so if you want to come out here since you're already in the area (ha ha!) that would be completely awesome. I'm sure my mom would be blown away! Word to the wise though: it's not *as* nice as Lamu so don't expect ginger crabs because I know that's what Margit served you. If you can get your hands on GPS this address should get you here: Woodburn House, Bela District, Bihar, India.

After all I had been through, now she thought I would simply pick up the goose chase and head to India. The balls! I printed out the email at the cost of 225 ksh, about two dollars, and rushed back to the room in a semi-blind rage.

"Look at this shit!" I cried, barging in on Angie, who was just beginning to pack. I threw the paper at her and found a beer in the minifridge.

Angie read the note slowly, not engaging me right away, and I drank half the beer to calm down.

"Can you believe the stones on her?" I said.

"Well…" said Angie carefully. "I mean, this does explain-"

"Explain? How? You can't ask someone to fly halfway around the world and then just not be there. *And then* ask that person to wing off to India. This is crazy!"

"It's a heavy lift, I grant you. But from what she's saying here, it wasn't her fault. It doesn't sound like her mother is giving her much say in things, so maybe she thought she was going to be in Lamu, but then her mother took her to India. It says there was a work emergency and they had to leave suddenly."

"I know what it says," I said, too bitterly, finishing the beer. "If we can believe anything coming from her."

"Mmm," said Angie, now suddenly lost in her own head. "India, though. Bharatavarsha. Jambudvīpa. The legitimate holy land. The Buddhist holy land. Dharmabhumi." She brandished her three-fish tattoo.

"Huh? What are you talking about? Are you insane? Clinically? There's no *way* I'm going there, holy or not."

"I can't go, which is a real bummer. But you could easily change your ticket."

"Are you feeling OK?" I said. "Seriously. Are you malarial? Any other delusions? Here, have a beer." I cracked one for her and a new one for me.

"I still say she clearly wrote you for a reason in the first place, like maybe what she was saying about Lamu wasn't entirely true, but she reached out to you because she had some need."

"And I did my supposed 'duty.' She wasn't there. So."

"So? Your responsibility is done? Dead."

"This beer is basically piss water. Tusker was better."

"Interesting that you wouldn't want Mohammed Starlight giving her hash on the beach," she said, smiling.

"What? That's just common sense. That's a long way from going to India."

On top of everything else, the piss water wasn't even really cold, but I drank it anyway.

We went around like that for the next hour, during which time she presented a series of arguments that seemed calculated to wear me down.

For instance, she said if I were a woman, if I were a long-lost *mother*, the story would be very different and there would be no conversation about "responsibility."

She had baroque defenses of the girl, whom she theorized was being put into an impossible position by her mother. Her evidence? Angie had often been put into impossible positions by her own mother.

She said she had always thought of me as a person capable of "moral generosity," even if I didn't demonstrate such capability on a regular basis. I didn't press her on exactly what she meant, as it felt a little accusatory.

"What if did go," I said. "Out of spite?"

"A questionable motivation," she said. "In terms of moral generosity."

Finally I did admit to her, to myself, that I was curious about this girl, about her situation with Audra, about how I might factor in her life.

Maybe, I thought, there was some invisible thread of obligation tethering me to the girl, because an unknown part of me did want to go on to India, despite how illogical it was. Was it moral, or dumb?

I said this, though not in so many words, and Angie brightened considerably.

"You see there?" she said, walking over to me slowly, swinging her hips. "That's what I thought you might say."

She came within an inch of my face, kissed me, then pushed me onto the bed seductively, knocking her half-filled backpack to the floor.

Down at the business center, we worked out the logistics of getting from Nairobi to Woodburn House, Bela District, Bihar, India. Within mere minutes we discovered that the Bela district was in the north-easterly part of India, and that the closest major airport was Patna. It was hard to determine via Google Maps what was there—the machines in the business center were maddeningly slow and we were only able to see a suggestion of a village in some hills that had the name "Bela." We weren't totally sure if we had the right location, nor what in the world Audra would be doing there. It appeared, at least from the vantage of the internet, to be nothing more than a rural quilt of greens and browns, a few tertiary roads but no large cities or even towns. Puzzling. We took notes, and after further searching, I found I could get a visa in Nairobi at the High Commission of India, which, it turned out, was within walking distance of the Hilton. There were flights to Patna via Doha.

As had happened when Cubby made my arrangements for Kenya, the sequence of future events seemed simple, but I was stymied by the very last part of the trip, the inches on the screen from Patna to the Bela Hills. "I won't have a Simeon," I said to Angie. "How will I get from the airport to Woodburn House?"

"You have something better than Simeon," she said. "You have experience."

She Googled and found that those inches onscreen translated to fewer than two hundred miles. "Unclear if there's a rail connection," she said. "So you rent a car. Look." She discovered an agency in Patna advertising "a fleet of magnificent cars that can suit all purposes and pockets." Still I distrusted my abilities, despite said "experience." Angie wrote down the rental agency's phone number because you couldn't book anything through the website. She was trying to keep things light and positive.

"I'm so envious," she was saying. "India. What a time you'll have."

After I'd booked an appointment at the High Commission of India, called to reserve a car and change my flight (at an inflated fee), we had dinner in the fanciest restaurant in the hotel. Technically it was a fare-well dinner because Angie was heading home in the morning, and I was staying in Nairobi another day to sort out my visa and mentally prepare myself for India. She was misty during the meal, and kept saying that she was proud of me, kept repeating she was proud of me, to the point that I was sort of offended, as though she hadn't really believed I'd had the moral fiber to fulfill my "responsibilities" or "obligations" or what-ever other label she and Cubby and my sister put on the situation.

During dinner, Angie got buzzed and started asking sideways questions about Audra, fishing around to see if maybe I was still interested in her, after all these years, and how I felt about seeing *her*, aside from the girl. This was out of character for Angie, as she wasn't a romantically jealous person, but I thought it was a legitimate thing to wonder about, and the way she worked around the topic indirectly only endeared her to me more. Typically she was much more secure than I was, and this small doubt was a twisted indicator of how she felt about me, and I assured her then that I only had eyes for her, that Audra, distant Audra, was so long ago as to be just one or two glimmers in my memory.

"That's good," she said. "Because I made you a Valentine."

She pulled from her pocket what looked like a four-folded newspaper page and pushed it over to me with a smirk.

I smoothed it open to find a page she had indeed torn from a newspaper, from the "Crazy World" section of *The Sunday Standard.* It was from an article titled "Woman Who Cut Off Her Husband's Manhood Says Men Still Want to Date Her," a profile of Lorena Gallo, formerly Bobbitt, twenty years later. Over the text of the story Angie had drawn with a Sharpie an old-timey heart and arrow. Inside she had written: "Will + Angie 4-Eva."

"Very touching," I said. "Very understated."

"I'm so glad you like it," she said, mock-sweetly. "I picked that paper up off a table in the lobby, and boom: there's this story. Who knew they knew about Lorena Bobbitt all the way in Africa?"

"I'll treasure it always," I said.

—

We had to get up very early so she could make her flight, and she insisted that I not accompany her to the airport because it would be a waste to pay for cabs there and back. She hated goodbyes, as she again reminded me, and we did a teary scene in front of the doormen and bellhops and assorted other service people who seemed to have nothing better to do than gape at us as we waited on the taxi. I tended to shut down during goodbyes, and embraced Angie rigidly as she wiped away tears and second-guessed the wisdom of my going to India alone.

"Maybe it's dangerous," she sniffled.

Now it was my turn to reassure her, and I said what could be dangerous about a country that wouldn't even harm a cow?

She laughed a snotty laugh, and the taxi was there. She agreed to email me as soon as she got home, and I agreed to email her as soon as I got to wherever it was I was going.

I packed her in the taxi, she blew her nose, I shut the door, and the taxi honked its way out of the parking lot and into the street. Angie was gone before I knew it.

The shock of being alone didn't fully register with me as I spent the day in bureaucratic hell at the High Commission of India, whose officials, I discovered, didn't share my sense of urgency regarding visa processing. After languishing in a line that seemed for others mere suggestion, I was told that it was the wrong time of day to initiate a visa application, despite my appointment, and I had therefore to return later that afternoon during a certain window of time, then and only then, at which point I learned that if I paid a special fee, I could pick up my visa later in the evening, during a certain window of time, then and only then. I did all this, and when I returned for the third time, the cherry on top was that I owed another $50 "expediting fee," payable in USD at the counter, which may or may not have been a bribe.

Once I had visa in hand, I went back to the hotel's Business Center and answered the emails from Cubby and my sister. I told them much the same thing, in fact cut-and-pasted most of my reply, explaining what had gone on in Lamu, that Angie was now home or almost home, and that I was going on to India, and was unsure about the internet access there. I also sent another email to the girl with all my travel details, assuming she would be unable to check it. Angie had agreed to take over cat care once she got back, and I emailed my neighbor to that effect, since he was stopping in a couple of times a day to feed and water them.

That night, exhausted, I ordered room service, drank a six pack of Tusker, and crashed early because my flight to Doha was at the very crack of dawn.

—

At the front desk just after sunrise, I could see it was not yet fully light outside, and ambiguous as to whether the haze in the parking lot was morning fog or pollution. The clerk informed me that beyond the meals and room, I had been billed almost $300 for my use of the Business Center, so I sucked my teeth and put $1,145 on my credit card for three days in Nairobi, not counting the touristic outings we'd done, and flopped into a stifling cab for the airport.

I was wheels up surprisingly quickly, with time enough for a mere cup of over-priced coffee, had a seven-hour layover wandering the duty free area of Hamad International in Doha, where they had gleaming Jaguars and Benzes parked among the gold-leafed kiosks stocked with perfume, chocolate, and bottles of Yamazaki fifty-year single malt whiskey, priced at $13,000. I thought Cubby would like it in Qatar. In a food court I had what was probably the best hummus of my life, which isn't saying much, and watched news coverage of Thabo Makgoba gliding elegantly into the hospital where ninety-four-year-old Nelson Mandela lay critically ill. After a rocky flight out over the Persian Gulf, Iran, and Pakistan, we landed in brown-skied Patna, almost clipping the tops of some trees as we did so.

It was June 27th and I was on my own.

6.

ON THE SPECTRUM of airports, Jai Prakash Narayan International was somewhat less impressive than Jomo Kenyatta. We parked far out from the terminal, which looked like a temple, and had to walk across the cracked and patched tarmac in soupy heat, nearly as bad as Lamu, avoiding the team who had already set to work unloading the plane, oblivious to the civilians in their midst. We were herded inside to a shabby, fan-cooled immigration room where an official swiped my passport, stared at the computer screen and then me, and stamped my visa without asking any questions. After that, and despite the industriousness of the cargo handlers, I waited endlessly for my pack, and then left baggage claim in search of the car rental counters. I was glad to find instead a man holding a placard with my name on it.

The man had a slight stoop and was impeccably suited, and he introduced himself as Mr. Kumar. He wanted to be the first to welcome me to Patna and let me know that he would be the one taking me to the car rental offices, which were not located on airport grounds proper.

Mr. Kumar offered to carry my pack, but I refused, and followed him outside, into what to me seemed utter bedlam: crushes of people dealing with massive amounts of luggage, including steamer trunks, women in various kinds of wraps soothing tear-streaked children, young Turks duded up in blue suits shouting into their phones, old men dispensing advice to their prodigal offspring, everybody in sandals; the road in front gridlocked, cabbies spitting brown jets from their windows and wiping mouths with the backs of their hands, every driver of every vehicle honking, honking, jockeying for an inch or two of progress, whether to load or unload, all watched over by a youth in fatigues hunched behind an emplacement of sandbags, a large caliber machine gun mounted on a bipod and trained on nothing in particular.

Mr. Kumar pushed through all this without looking back, to an SUV with a scorpion hood ornament poised at the curb, silent and still amid the noise and rush. He opened the rear door for me, then climbed in the front passenger seat. Not having Angie there to check my wilder anxieties, I imagined that Mr. Kumar was mafia, that his crew had somehow snatched my information from cyberspace and had sent him to pluck this clueless yokel from the airport and secret him to an undisclosed location. If so, the joke was on them, because this yokel had a negative net worth, and didn't foresee the college coughing up significant ransom money for anyone below full professor. But then I noticed an Ambi-Pur oil wick clipped into the air conditioning vent, an insignificant detail, but for some reason its presence totally calmed me—because I simply couldn't believe violent mafia types would have air fresheners in their SUVs.

The driver didn't acknowledge me, and Mr. Kumar didn't introduce us, but was instead very curious about why I was hiring a self-drive vehicle, an enterprise I could tell he considered foolhardy, at least for me.

As the driver battled and beep-beeped to navigate us away from the airport, almost killing a bicyclist, I was beginning to see his point.

Their company could arrange drivers and guides as well as cars, Mr. Kumar was saying.

"Are you perhaps going to Bodh Gaya," he said, bent around in an attempt at eye contact. "Because we offer full-day car and driver packages at attractive rates. If indeed you were going to Bodh Gaya."

As he was saying this, we merged into an unreasonable density of buses, trucks, cars, rickshaws, motorcycles, bicycles, pedestrians, animals, sometimes people squatting over small cooking stoves on the shoulder, children running with makeshift kites, not watching where they were going, crooked men straining with overloaded carts, cows plopped down when and where they pleased, all this happening with little visible regulation, and I was tempted to take Mr. Kumar up on this offer, except I wasn't going to Bodh Gaya, wasn't necessarily sure where I was going, nor for how long, so it did not seem feasible to hire a driver.

"As long as you have GPS," I said. "I should be fine." He assured me that they did indeed have the latest in GPS technologies.

I believed then that with the advent of GPS, it was impossible to get lost.

Of course this wasn't necessarily true.

After nearly colliding half a dozen times, we made it the mile or two to Mr. Kumar's office, in a strip mall. The mall looked newly-constructed, with a restaurant on one end, a mobile phone store next to that, an empty retail space, and our destination at the far end, all fronted with floor-to-ceiling glass. There was an unpaved parking lot roped off like a freshly-seeded lawn, and some knee-high piles of rubble where a sidewalk should have been. Otherwise the building could have been part of any mall in the valley.

"Watch your step," said Mr. Kumar as he led me over the rubble.

Once inside I was instantly grateful for the blast of air conditioning, but the office itself was just a couple of impersonal desks and chairs and some poorly-photographed travel posters. One depicted what looked like a hangar-sized, white-washed beehive, and Mr. Kumar caught me looking and explained that it was the Golghar, the regional granary built by the British in the 18th century, now a tourist attraction.

I said it was my first time in a city that boasted a granary as its main tourist draw.

"We're unique," he said.

He produced a manila folder with some forms in triplicate. As he started explaining that these were all standard forms, I saw that they were principally in Hindi with just a smattering of English, such as the heading on one, which read AGREEMENT TO LEASING A MOTOR VEHICLE. I expressed my concern to Mr. Kumar that I could not understand ninety-five percent of what he wanted me to sign, but he argued that it was a technicality, that these were standard forms.

I signed where he indicated, a little too blithely—but at that point, I was all-in.

There was a manual card imprinter, deposits in rupees I didn't really follow, and a GPS in a zippered nylon pouch.

We went back outside, to the half-cobbled lot. The car was red and compact, the size and general look of an old Geo Metro, only buffed and late model, called a Maruti Alto. He looked like a proud papa, like Cubby with his Benz, as though this was his own personal possession that he was lending me, so I tried my best to seem really impressed. There was no sort of tutorial or inspection: he just handed me the key, wished me good luck on my journey, and went back into the office. Again I was alone.

To be honest, I was slightly concerned because it was a right-drive vehicle, and the shifter was accordingly to the left of the driver. I was able to drive a manual transmission no problem, but I'd never done so with my left hand. I looked around to see if there might be a suitable practice area, but unfortunately there was only the lot, just large enough to bring cars in and out, and then the road beyond, a blaring, exhaust-spewing kill zone of screeching buses, nimble rickshaws, suicidal mopeds, plus a bunch of mini cars that looked like mine, though filthier and more dented.

Inside the car, I spent some time fiddling with the GPS, skeptical about whether it would actually register the address I had, but to my relief, it claimed to know. In the time it took to punch in the address, a crowd of five or six guys had gathered from points unknown to see what I was up to. This development, combined with the blazing ambient temperature, meant that I was already sweltering, and I switched on the engine to reveal that the climate control system, boasting knobs fancier than on my Tercel, blew only warm air, that this economy model had no AC as such, and so cursing I rolled down the windows and resolved to get going, if only for air flow issues and to escape the onlookers.

The fundamentals seemed to be the same as in other cars I had driven, except for the flappy-eared statue of Ganesha stuck to the dash. The presence of that elephant head, with its swagger of a trunk and belly-dancer eyes, well-fed remover of obstacles, encouraged me to plunge into driving, and I successfully backed out without stalling, the men in the crowd retreating in wonder, as if stunned that the machine had grumbled to life.

As I turned, I learned further that there was no power steering, and so I muscled myself around hand over hand to ease out of the lot. But I stalled heading on to the road, much to the amusement of my audience, who *huzzahed,* and I swore and waved off their attempts to advise me, instead focusing all my mental energy on getting away in one piece.

I prevailed, edging methodically onto the narrow shoulder, occupied by the lesser stream of bicycles, mopeds, pedestrians, and a dog or two—and then finally out on the road proper, the left-hand shifting going better than I expected, the flat voice of the GPS already telling me to make a turn in five hundred meters.

But I had a problem. The fuel gauge was not even on E—it was beyond E, the needle in that abyss past the E hash mark and touching the nothingness of the plastic instrument panel. I tried not to panic, but I seemed already to be enraging other drivers as I slowed to scan the area for gas stations. Rickshaws buzzed around me and even the hulking dump trucks were chugging up on my rear in clouds of carbon monoxide, threatening to nudge me into a ditch if I didn't step on it. The GPS had a British accent and kept insisting I turn immediately. I didn't, because I spotted what looked to be a gas station up ahead, it was sure enough, and I glided in, simultaneously relieved and hotly shamed that I had forgotten to exchange any money at the airport.

An attendant appeared, and I asked him where I could find an ATM, but he didn't understand, seemed not to speak much English, and so I pantomimed with my wallet and the useless Kenyan shillings, and this language he knew and pointed to a bank across the street. I patted the hood of the Alto, indicating that he should keep an eye on it for me, and darted across, Frogger-style, almost getting creamed because not a single driver adjusted their speed in any way whatsoever.

The bank had a telephone booth-sized space built in to the front where an ATM beckoned. I had to swipe my card to open the door and was greeted with a glorious wall of air conditioning. I pulled out 10,000 rupees, not positive as to what that translated to in dollars, dashed back across the street, and directed the attendant to fill the car. There was a mini-mart attached to the gas station—emphasis on "mini"—as it only had some racks groaning under bottled water and motor oil, and I had the presence of mind to buy a few liters of water for the trip, one of my more prescient moves.

I paid the attendant, who made change from a rainbow cabbage wad in his pocket. He wanted a tip, so I gave him a couple of bills, how much I still wasn't sure, but he seemed happy and thanked me in sudden English. I pulled back out, and the GPS was demanding a U-turn, which I knew to be impossible, but I came to a roundabout a couple of blocks down, and so was able to turn around and get back in the right direction. Although the GPS did not offer an estimated time of arrival as my Garmin did, my destination was only 298 kilometers, roughly 185 miles, so I figured I would be there in three hours, five or six o'clock local time, no problem.

That turned out to be an optimistic estimation.

It took me the three hours just to make my way out of town because there were seemingly endless backups caused by ill-staggered construction projects in varying degrees of completion. After some time I could see the muddy Ganges off to my left, past a low-slung part of town, and then I was directed to turn onto 83, the Patna-Gaya Road, which promptly narrowed to a single lane due to some improvement work. As traffic slowed to stop-and-go, there were teams of policemen, construction workers, and apparently otherwise uninvolved children with switches who were shouting at vehicles to wait their turn, and those vehicles would venture forth anyway at the smallest opportunity.

After I made it to the outskirts of Patna and out on open highway, the drive was relatively straightforward as I passed rolling farmland, cultivated patches of fields in various shades of green, occasionally coming through a village or township, these places always built clinging to the

contours of the road and forever populated by people carrying baskets
or lengths of pipe, or simply leaning on mopeds and chatting, inches
from speeding buses, unconcerned, some again cooking on makeshift
stoves or hatching deals in the shops lining the road. This all against
backdrops of thatched stalls selling cigarettes and batteries, once in
a while improbably punctuated by a gleaming three-story KFC or
massive administrative building, and as I made my way south, near
where, according to Angie, the Buddha had attained enlightenment, I
was feeling pretty good about myself, thinking that it was no big deal,
this traveling the world. I even stopped at a KFC-imitator for dinner.

Once I got south of that chromed hive of fried familiarity, however,
things got more complicated.

I drove for another hour or so, and the GPS led me off highway, first
to a lesser macadam road, then after many twists and turns, to a shod-
dily maintained unpaved road that gave way in spots to what was little
more than a dry riverbed hardly wider than a footpath. It skirted fields
and wound around rice paddies before finally bringing me to a tiny
village. There the road opened so I was driving through a dusty square
stacked on one side with terra cotta pots for sale probably forever, a
few plastered-block buildings standing out among the predominantly
mud-brick structures, people slouching under awnings made from
blue tarps or pot metal, staring at me. Finally I passed through to the
other side and came to a crumbling concrete building, and the GPS
announced that I had arrived at my destination. The caved-in roof and
busted-down walls gave me the nagging sense that I was in the wrong
place.

Still, I had come that far, and so investigated. I walked up to find a
family tending a sputtering fire near a droopy tarp shelter, watching
me as I approached. I waved and said hello and asked if they perchance
knew the whereabouts of Woodburn House. They just stared at me,
and a shirtless man carrying a hoe came from somewhere and started
speaking to me in a toothless wheeze, not exactly shouting, but
displeased I was on his turf. I thought it best to backtrack to the Alto,
and tore out of there as his hoe transformed into a halberd.

Shaking slightly, I crept back through the village, looking for any indication that Audra had been there, but could see no reason for any outsider to have ever ventured there, unless those terra cotta pots were collector's items. Clearly the GPS had malfunctioned. It was starting to get dark, and I worried about my ability to navigate the crater-filled road at night. I drove for a long time, unsure if I was on the same roads I had come in on, the GPS now dispensing redundant advice as I made some desperate guesses, and darkness seemed to fall all at once.

As the sun set, I was on a dustcloud path of not merely ruts but whole miniature canyons, and I knew there was no way I could ford them in the darkness without compromising an axle or the toylike tires, and so was effectively grounded, the blackness much more profound than I had ever expected, my feeble headlights illuminating a little pool in front of the car, but not penetrating enough to be trusted.

I reeled through some relaxation exercises I knew to prevent myself from completely losing it and made my peace with the idea of camping for the night. I pulled off as much as possible, but there was some crop planted right to the edge of the road, so there wasn't much I could do. The headlights had attracted an alarming array of insects with seemingly prehensile pincers, as well as thousands of screaming mosquitoes, and so I hunkered down inside the car, at first with the windows rolled up, which created a type of low-intensity oven. After a few minutes I had to rig a vent system with a tee shirt blocking the gap so I could at least have faint air circulation. Though demoralized, I had a stomach full of fried chicken and a cache of water, so I was reasonably sure I would survive the night.

Sealed in there, I started imagining I was trespassing on somebody's land, that farmers would emerge from the brush Simeon-style, armed with rifles and staves wanting to kill me and steal the Alto. And who would stop them? Who would know? The rental company would make an insurance claim for the car; Angie would just never hear from me again; at a certain point my sister would wonder if I had died and investigate; the buyer at the college bookstore would start dispatching irate emails reminding me that I hadn't yet put in my orders for the fall; in September, Mark would start texting with increasing urgency; and once I hadn't shown up for my classes, the school would file a missing person's report and I would be declared M.I.A., and they might be able to reverse engineer that I'd last been seen outside Patna, Bihar interacting with the cashier at Indo-Chik. But probably not even that.

As the night deepened, I put the seat back as far as it would go—not very far—and had plenty of time to think. It was probably the most wide open and remote place I had ever been, and I'd gotten there in five hours from an international airport, having traveled from Pennsylvania to Queens to London to Nairobi to Lamu to Nairobi to Doha to Patna and now here, where exactly even my GPS couldn't say, having lost myself in the final tiny fraction of the trip, the reality of contemporary global travel, which made it so easy for those with that enchanted combination of citizenship status and money to move from urban center to urban center, usually in seamless air conditioning, tracing the circulation of capital. Beyond that, you were on your own. Not too much capital around there.

So what was Audra doing there? ("There" assuming I was generally where I was supposed to be; but who really knew?) On the road, I had kept an eye out for evidence of industry, had noted mills and factories in the distance, but once off the main highway, I'd puttered through smatterings of villages, many of which had only one or two brick structures, a medical clinic or school, while the rest looked hand-constructed from rough cut lumber and corrugated zinc; or, in the farther afield spots, mud bricks with reedy roofs, moss blooming in the chinks. There were plenty of domesticated water buffalo hitched to yokes, bent women tending to charcoal fires, yet the further I pushed off the highway, there was little modernization to speak of, maybe a narrow-bodied tractor every once in a while and not much else. Dusty vistas and tortured, rain-starved trees. What in the world could Audra possibly be doing?

It hadn't escaped my notice, of course, that I didn't know Audra at all, hadn't spoken to her in fourteen years and had even then only seen what I had wanted to see. And her daughter, she was the barest figment, a composite of adolescent girls I'd read about in novels or seen on TV and in the movies—since I didn't know any in real life—fleshed out and made idiosyncratic by a few words on a screen and a rented room full of knick-knacks, pubescent emblems of taste. I was starting to wonder again if I had any business "there" at all. Despite Angie's arguments, however Audra had structured her life was her concern, it was she who had chosen to rear a child on her own, she who was the mother, raising a girl for thirteen years, bonding with her, checking off developmental milestones, worrying about vaccines, protecting her from harm.

For whatever reason, I pictured all this happening in San Francisco, that Audra click-swished down Fillmore with the most expensive stroller on the market, drinking vanilla lattes with some MBA'd mommy group, but in truth I had no idea even where the girl had been born, or where they had lived. I couldn't say what kind of baby she had been, whether she had been an agreeable toddler, whether they got along, or fought, or what—or if—she thought of me. I couldn't say much.

Van Gogh once remarked of Frans Hals' paintings that he used twenty-seven kinds of black. This occurred to me as I watched the varieties of darkness in the night, drifting because I was exhausted and over-heated.

The girl had written me.

Blackness almost shimmered.

Against all indications of my life to that point, I had come. Thanks to Angie for that one. Straining to distinguish black from reflections of black in the glass, I saw textures like ink or smudges of coal dust comprising what seemed then multi-dimensional oblivion. And still it was hot even with the sun vanished. I wondered what Angie was doing at that very moment. What time was it in Pennsylvania?

Curtain.

The sun awoke me the next day, and I squinted to discover a couple of dhoti-wrapped men with huge gnarled staffs shuffling around the Alto. I scrambled out of the car, lest they start banging on the hood and cost me my security deposit, and tried to account for myself. These men were ancient and ropey and deep-creased, tiny and thin but muscular, not unthreatening to me then, given my situation.

They assessed me for a moment, then unleashed a torrent of disgust because I was blocking the narrow road, which seemed in daylight to be more a livestock route than a thoroughfare for cars. Where is the highway, I kept asking them, but they only gesticulated gruffly, like the monk in Mount Baldy: get out of here. I gestured: that way? Or that way? The elder one seemed on the verge of exploding, and he shook his staff to the east, and I thanked him, bowing like a moron, my only defense, and drove off. I saw in the rearview mirror that they were kicking around in the spot I had camped for the night, incensed, looking for evidence of some deeper transgression.

I drank water to settle my cramped stomach and bumped around on dirt backroads all morning, sometimes encountering gaggles of geese or herds of goats, or else variations on my two dawn visitors, none of whom were helpful. Everyone stared openly, suspicious of the interloper.

Eventually I did find a paved road, and then it wasn't long before I came to an outpost slightly larger than the back-country villages, which is to say there were two-story edifices, motorized vehicles, and people. I found what looked to me the ritziest establishment in town, a brightly-painted building with a sign, partly in English, that read "Veg Restaurant." I went inside with the intention of asking for directions but ran into a language barrier right away. Why, I thought with ragged indignation, have an English sign if you or your employees were not able to speak English effectively? I was in the process of writing the address in big block letters on the back of a campaign flyer, when, mercifully, a diner came to my aid.

A fleshy-eared man with thick glasses and a Nehru shirt, he looked to me like an angel, and asked if he could assist me.

Everything came pouring out of me at that moment, and I must have seemed half insane, having slept in the car, having driven around blindly for hours. If the man was taken aback, he didn't show it. He studied the address I had written down, then said that part of my problem was that I was in Jharkhand, not Bihar.

"Another state entirely," he said, looking up at me over his glasses.

"Another state!" I repeated, too loudly, thinking of an altered mental state, and the other patrons were now even more shameless in their regard for what I was doing there. They whispered and pointed while I cursed the GPS.

"Listen," said the man in the Nehru shirt, "I can see that you are agitated but technology has its limits. Let me call someone but you calm yourself."

"That would be great," I said quietly.

He put in a call on his phone, speaking in another language, making notes on my campaign flier. When he finally snapped the phone shut, he informed me that he had found the place for me, that it was perhaps an hour by car, but that I would never find it on my own. "Your GPS will be worthless in this case."

"What else is new?"

"Perhaps I can arrange for someone to take you there, but it's a very strange place to be going at any rate."

"Everything about this trip has been strange," I said.

"I can see that," he said, indicating in a general way that I seemed unkempt, unwashed, potentially offensive. He made another call then invited me back to his table.

He introduced himself as Mr. Nigudkar and ordered me an overcooked meal of vegetables in heavy sauces, but I didn't care. He told me he was a "merchant"—he used that word, old-fashioned—said that he sold safety matches and was looking to set up a match factory in the area.

"American?" he asked, and when I confirmed his suspicion said that one of his sons had studied chemical engineering at Purdue University in West Lafayette, Indiana. The other lived in Düsseldorf, and was dating a German woman, a situation of which he did not wholly approve.

"Are German women considered morally loose?" he asked.

"I really couldn't say," I mumbled, sopping the veggies with some roti.

"This is not how we do things in India," he explained. "We do not 'date.' I never 'dated' my wife. But we have been married thirty-six years."

"Maybe he's just experimenting," I said.

He went on some more about his non-dating life and the match factory, and eventually a rangy boy of maybe fifteen showed up, spoke briefly with Mr. Nigudkar, and was introduced as Dilip. Mr. Nigudkar said Dilip would guide me to the place.

"He knows where it is?"

"You'll find it."

I tried to give Mr. Nigudkar some money, but he shushed me, and in fact insisted on paying for my meal.

"Please," I said.

"No no no. You are a guest in this country. But maybe a little baksheesh for Dilip. His family is very poor and his father was killed. A friend of the family."

"And you're sure?" I said, unconvinced.

"I am sure."

—

It turned out Dilip spoke very limited English—limited, as far as I experienced, to the word "here." He sat up straight in the Alto, thin legs jutting forward, hands chastely clasped, eyeing all the pedestrians outside with a newly-imperious eyebrow lift.

Once we were pulled out, Dilip would say "here!" to indicate a turn, and in this way we drove for another hour or so, on the highway, then off again, through secondary and backroads that were similar to the ones I had traversed the day before. He peered ahead anxiously, alertly, craning his neck and furrowing his brow as he considered landmarks. A couple of times he patted my hand to indicate that we should slow or stop, and would crank down the window to shout at whoever happened to be on the side of the road, called to them as though they were family, rattling off staccato sentences that would invariably puzzle the walker, who would then approach cautiously, peer over at me skeptically, and then turn back to Dilip to work out our next series of moves.

At long last, after we had wound our way up into some low and forested hills, we came to a prominence overlooking a village of only a few concrete buildings and a cluster of mud-walled structures.

"Here," said Dilip, pointing to the far side of the prominence.

There loomed a large white house in a European style, old, maybe a hundred or two hundred years. Looking stately and Edwardian in that landscape, the house reared up three stories, had dormered windows along the roof, and a half-moon balcony on the second floor, under which a portico shaded the main entrance. It was obviously in disrepair, as paint was blistered from the siding, shutters hung off-kilter or else were missing, and a couple of windows were boarded over. It didn't exactly look abandoned, though, for despite the shabbiness, the place seemed lived-in and projected an aura of bygone gentility, however disconnected it seemed from the surrounding countryside.

I pulled into a driveway of sorts, beyond two plaster lions and iron-work guarding the entrance. I noticed fresh tire tracks in the clay, but there were no other cars at the house, and the air was stone quiet after I turned off the engine.

Dilip hopped out immediately and sat on the hood of the car. I steeled myself a bit, got out, and pulled a wad of bills from my pocket. Still not entirely sure about the exchange rate, I pressed a bunch into Dilip's hands.

"Do you want to come inside?" I said to him. "Maybe there's a phone and we can call someone to get you."

Shuffling through all the bills with glee, Dilip flashed me a gappy smile and crooked thumbs up, then gestured toward the house.

"Yes," I said. "Do you want to come inside?"

He gave me another thumbs up, then turned and flip-flopped back down the driveway without another word. I watched him shamble past the plaster lions, then disappear down the hill toward the village, apparently with a private plan for getting wherever he needed.

"Okaayyy," I said aloud, realizing that I was delaying turning to the house.

This was it—or it wasn't, given recent events, and I didn't know whether to expect Audra and this girl or another dead end. What was another few thousand dollars to a well-heeled academic such as myself?

Finally, after staring at the front door as though it would open on its own, I took in as much oxygen as I could, then strode up the path leading to the house, running my hands across the empty stone cisterns that had once been elaborate planters or fountains. There was wrought iron fencing everywhere, like defense systems, rusting but still foreboding. Somehow the place reminded me of the decaying refinement of Grey Gardens, the East Hampton estate fallen into squalor and made famous by the Maysles brothers' documentary about Big Edie Bouvier Beale and Little Edie Bouvier Beale, aunt and cousin of Jackie Kennedy, who spent their adulthoods shut in that mansion in homemade diklos and haywire browline glasses, replaying long-ago parties with ambassadors and industrialists as their cats sprayed priceless paintings left forsaken on the parquetry. Which made me wonder if this mother and daughter could possibly have gone similarly batty under the circumstances Audra had created. I put the odds at 50/50.

As I made my way through the yard, my heart was thumping and my breathing labored. I steeled myself again, then went up to the portico where I could see at the far end of the porch a man showering some potted plants with a watering can.

He must have heard the car and the one-sided conversation with Dilip, but he acted as though he hadn't registered my presence at all.

"Hello?" I called.

He turned toward me utterly unfazed, as though he'd been expecting me.

"Good afternoon," he said. "Please go on inside."

I felt the need to explain myself, and my heart was really racing and I called out that I was looking for Audra and Petra and he nodded languidly, still watering the plants.

"Yes, indeed," he said. "Please make yourself comfortable."

I studied the hefty door a moment, stalling, then turned the handle, glancing over at him to see if it was all right. But he had already wandered around a corner with his watering can, unconcerned, and so I pushed open the door.

Inside was a soaring entry hall, dark and dramatic with richly-stained woodwork. Cool, but not crisply so, un-air-conditioned but an immediate relief from the heat outside. It smelled, incongruously, like chocolate chip cookies were baking somewhere. I shut the door behind me and felt as though I was standing in pools of shadows.

At the end of this creaky entrance hall was a wide staircase with an intricately-carved banister and newel, and I was deciding where to go, if I should maybe ask the guy out front or follow the scent of the cookies. On the walls were huge portraits of lordly looking white men in red sashes and medals, self-assured, portly Masons probably with ruddy faces and elaborate bristling mustaches. Between two of these paintings was a closed door, and I thought I could make out the faintest sounds of a woman's voice beyond.

The door was a pocket door, and I slid it open to find a library lined with empty shelves of nearly black, oiled wood.

It took me a second to register that at the far end of the room, behind an expansive, executive-sized desk, stood Audra, talking on a cell phone. She was facing away from me, but I knew it was her from the hair and the voice and the unmistakable bearing; she was displeased with the person on the phone and making that known. I stood in silence, paralyzed by a kind of shock.

After half a minute she turned to check a binder on the desk, and then saw me. Although she must have been shaken by the apparition from her past, she hardly missed a beat so far as the person on the line would have been concerned because she just said she'd call back, pushed the phone screen, but then dropped it with a clatter.

"You ..." she said, as if deflating.

The years hadn't been that bad to her: a little bit stouter, maybe, but certainly Audra. She wore drawstring linen pants and a tank top, no shoes, and as she came around the desk I noticed that she still kept her toenails pedicured and painted, which struck me as both odd and impressive, her keeping up the toes way out in the sticks. Her hair was in a ponytail, and as she neared, I could see streaks of gray pulled in, and a few more crinkles around the edges of her eyes. Overall, though, she seemed remarkably the same Audra, wearing what looked like the same diamond studs in her ears, and she carried herself with the same poise, even after seeing me materialize in remotest India and dropping her phone.

Suddenly in her presence, I was hopelessly self-conscious, and I threw back my shoulders to stand up straighter. I hadn't showered in a couple of days, my hair was greasy, thinner since I'd known her, plus my face was peeling from a sunburn. Nor had I applied my usual confidence-boosting regimen of creams and serums. I'd been wearing unchanged underwear for longer than I was comfortable.

"The guy told me to come in," I said, lamely.

She had regained her composure almost immediately, and I could tell she was evaluating, calculating. "I have to hand it to you," she said.

She came through a set of wingback chairs separating us and held her arms open, a move I would have thought uncharacteristic of her, especially after all that time, but I followed her lead, hoping that I didn't stink too offensively. Stiffly we embraced, a sensation at once foreign and familiar, as some subconscious part of me recognized her scent, took me back instantly to driving in her car and my reaching over to change the radio, she saying "no Mexican," this I recalled, but the shape of her body had long been estranged from my muscle memory. She stood back to take me in, concealing behind an expression of eerie equanimity what had to have been soul-shifting disbelief. But she didn't show it. As always, her self-control was remarkable.

"You look like shit," she said. "But good in a global sense."

I asked, in my dumb nervousness, if the house we were standing in had been a hill station.

She said something about hill station being an imperialist term, I didn't really listen because I was far from one hundred percent in control of myself and thought I might have a coronary because my heart seemed to be pumping harder than normal or at least arrhythmically.

She could see I was flustered, wanted to know if I needed to sit down, but I said no, that I was just hot and tired from traveling and she shrugged, not exactly buying it, and said that in any case she was sitting down so I might want to, too. And so we settled into the chairs, and I was grateful to be off my feet.

"That daughter of mine is crafty, no?" she said, smoothing out her pants over her knee. "When did she reach out?"

I breathed through my nostrils a second and was calm enough to tell the story.

She seemed mortified that I'd been to Lamu, said mainly to herself that it represented a certain amount of resolve, my embarking on this trip, but then she paused as though remembering something, then told me in a businesslike way that she had never intended to upset my life, but that a child was one of those "disruptors" you really couldn't account for.

"X factor," I said. "And you never told her about me?"

She ignored that last part and deflected by offering me a drink, then got up and went to the door and shouted down the hall for tea. She went around to the desk and picked the phone off the hardwood, examined it for damage.

"Just let me know if you need to use the facilities," she said. "Trust me, they're the best you're gonna get for at least a hundred, hundred-fifty kilometers."

I knew that I needed a shower but said "I'm fine" in a clipped sort of way.

"Suit yourself," she said.

The guy who had been watering the plants glided in with a tray of tea and cookies. He left them on the table and Audra came back, sat down, and poured me some milky chai.

"I did what I thought was best at the time," she said, answering my earlier question. "Remember we were living on opposite coasts, and I knew you were sort of put off by the idea of kids, what with your brother. And I didn't want to derail your PhD."

"Right," I said, not having remembered discussing Benj with her. "But wouldn't that have been for me to decide? I was planning to move to DC."

"Maybe so," she said, "but I wasn't exactly working from a known playbook. This was all improvisation." She had a feeling that she couldn't quite understand, a feeling that told her if she didn't have that baby then she might not ever have a baby. Biologically, of course, she could have, but it was a feeling, not a rational calculation.

I didn't react to that information. My exhaustion and coursing adrenalin were starting to balance each other out and I recalled some moments when Audra didn't seem all that comfortable in the province of feeling, and so what she was saying made a perverse kind of sense. Hard to know how she was interpreting my silence, but I thought I detected a flicker of apprehension dance across her face, if just for nanosecond, and I sort of enjoyed her not knowing what I was thinking.

"You ever get married?" I asked.

"There was a guy in Frankfurt," she said. "Fortunately we didn't go through with it because he turned out to be like a caricature of a German male."

"What does that mean?"

"Petra thinks she's funny," she said. "She ordered me this tee shirt online that has a pair of turntables on it, and it says 'Spinster.' Get it?"

I drank my tea, which, counterintuitively, was cooling me down.

"So fill me in," I said.

After she learned she was pregnant, she told me, she knew she was going to keep the baby, but that she would have to break it off with me, felt that really instinctively, and so she did, and the call was one of the hardest she'd ever had to make. Taking maternity leave would compromise her reputation as a team player at the consultancy, not ideal, she said, and she did so against the counsel of her father, who warned her it would read as weak and used the term "wedlock," which had deeply pissed her off. Once she became undeniably pregnant, her bosses did take her off high-level accounts, her father was annoyingly prophetic, and she noted this and began to strategize, and when it came time to have the baby she went to Maryland to be near her mother, not because she figured her mother knew what she was doing but because she, Audra, so profoundly did not know what she was doing. In that particular instance.

Petra was a name she liked because it seemed worldly, like you wouldn't necessarily know the nationality of a Petra, and as a bonus it was a small way to appease her father, Peter, who thought the whole situation was ludicrous and would have preferred a grandson anyway.

Jump to the hospital scene: after hours of torment, there was that moment like what you saw on TV when they really did hand you a swaddled baby, and in Audra's case it had been what she called "ecstatic terror," and she thought to herself she would tackle Project Baby 1.0 in much the same way she would tackle any complex, multi-layered problem. She had money and mandated leave, but very little sense of what the practical day-to-day of having an infant entailed. But she knew she could master the associated tasks because that's what she did, breaking apparently insurmountable challenges down into their constituent parts.

"A child is not a challenge," her own mother had said gnomically, and it irked Audra that her mother did seem to know a few things, her general lunacy notwithstanding. In spite of herself, Audra admitted a whisper of reluctant admiration for her mother because she felt destroyed physically and emotionally—mere days after Petra's birth, she, Audra, began to sob unpredictably, now second-guessing herself and her abilities to raise any child, let alone her own child. This was all to be expected, her mother explained, seemingly content to get up every few hours in the night. Audra appreciated that logically, but hormonally it was a different story, doubt would rear like a knife in her chest, and she sort of understood why people shook screaming babies, although she herself would have never done so.

What order of sin would it be, she started to wonder, to leave the baby in the care of her own mother and find a job in Singapore or Hong Kong? Her mother had little else going on, being a grandmother had suddenly infused her life with clarity of purpose, and the tiny being wouldn't know the difference anyway. Audra would be free again. Win-win, on paper.

But then after those first weeks, such fantasies of flight were eclipsed by the recrudescence of certain feelings from her girlhood, when her mother had inflexible ideas about how daughters ought to behave and be seen, meaning for Audra uncomfortable ballet recitals and a debutante ball, both of which included taffeta, and now she had an irrational phobia of taffeta. There was a morning, she said, watching her mother rocking Petra in the glider she'd special ordered, when she realized she was on the one hand exhausted, grateful for her mother's enthusiasm and newfound energy, on the other increasingly suspicious and probably personally resentful of the way Petra was already being tracked into a 1950s ideal of femininity, the starting point a knit pink cap someone fitted on her the very morning she was born. The final straw was the day Audra discovered that her mother had ordered a huge pre-pasted wall mural featuring a pink-on-pink castle design, as in for princesses, accented with glitter, and in that instant her sense of maternal insufficiency was overtaken by a resolve to raise her daughter on her own terms, in a realm far distant from that particular princess castle.

When her leave was up, she learned that her position on the San Francisco team had been given to someone else, a move that was no doubt illegal, but she was offered as solace an extended assignment in Germany, technically a promotion, and she thought that might be a way to both remove herself from her mother's sphere of nuttiness and to ensure Petra's upbringing would be more interesting and less insulated than the one she herself had had.

"You probably think that was crazy," she said. "Moving to Frankfurt with an eight-month-old when I didn't know anybody there, when I didn't know anything about eight-month-olds. You're thinking: maybe I was just using this baby as an experimental *fuck you* to my mother?"

I didn't say anything. She was on a roll, and I was fascinated to hear that she had ever been afflicted by anxiety or any modicum of self-doubt, since I had only ever known her to project iron capability. But that was a long time ago.

"It *was* crazy," she said. "It was. But I decided to throw caution to the wind. I'd spent my life achieving, at HBS and all that, and I knew if I took the safe route I would actually be doing a disservice to Petra. The career motivation aspect was there, sure, but I felt for some reason that since it was just the two of us, I might as well go fully unconventional."

They spent nearly five years in Germany, a place that ended up being a kind of transition from the States to her more far-flung assignments, and she had proven to herself in the tidy and well-lit suburbs of Frankfurt that she could raise a child on her own, outside the U.S., subsisting on tepid doner kebab and inexpensive beer. Petra had a full-time nanny, that was unavoidable, but Audra spent all her free time with her. Petra learned German and even a smattering of Ukrainian, as this nanny came from outside Luhansk, and was able to attend a real-life kindergarten.

In the meantime, Audra said, she had been given more and more responsibility in Western Europe, found herself flying off during the week, and so when Petra was five and Audra was offered a chance to move to Istanbul with the promise of no travel, she jumped on it, and put Petra in the International School where all the diplomats' kids went.

But the world being what it was, they were in Turkey only six months, and their life worked like that over the next years, as they moved more frequently, to places like Athens, Ayacucho, Anuradhapura, Kathmandu, Lamu, and this most remote part of India. The alchemy was balancing routines and stability with exposure to new people and places, which Petra seemed to thrive on since it had been her natural state since birth. Audra had been confident, she assured me, that her daughter was in good hands because there always seemed to be networks of people, however small, on whom she could rely if called to Lahore or Juba or some other place she would not bring a child, insured to the gills but wondering if the international courts would tangle her will in probate should something happen to her—like *Bleak House*, she said.

It hadn't been the easiest life, she admitted, for reasons that were all too readily imaginable, and there were exasperated moments when she threatened herself with returning to DC and marrying a hedge-fund type and moving to McLean and death; but the older Petra got, the more Audra marveled at her ability to adapt to insane conditions, to find consolation in solitude or to make friends effortlessly, having after a month been integrated into whatever social scene there was, bringing home animals and securing them permanent homes when it was time to relocate. Difficult as it was for Petra to be constantly changing schools after building relationships with teachers and her classmates, Audra could tell that she was coming to rely less on others and more on herself, remarkably comfortable in locales or social situations from which Audra-the-debutante would have run screaming for fear of the unfamiliar.

Although I knew part of the way she framed all this was defensive, an argument for living that kind of life, as she told it to me, all the years that passed between us acted as a screen, a version of that phenomenon where people unburden themselves to total strangers in ways they never could to family.

"So what is your job, exactly?" I asked.

She said she was acting as an advisor of sorts to developing economies, which is why she was there, and it didn't get more developing than "underserved" Bihar. Her team had set up a co-op to help women sell whatever they could make with their own hands—they connected them, by way of a complex supply chain, to the global economy. She had a whole micro-finance operation, too.

"It's a female empowerment thing," she said. "But let's be honest, it's also PR for the company, like the kind of PR you couldn't buy if you wanted to. And Petra loves it."

What was "the company," exactly, I asked, and she said vaguely "one of these international holding companies."

Suddenly it occurred to me that healthcare must have been an urgent concern out there. "What happens if someone is bitten by a cobra?"

This she thought was funny, and I saw her laugh for the first time in fourteen years. "What? Like Nag and Nagaina? I follow you. I mean, there are hospitals."

She explained that she carried a kind of super platinum health insurance, meaning that if she or Petra ever had a serious accident or acute life-threatening illness, they would be flown by helicopter to the nearest third-level hospital. From Lamu the contractors at Simba could get her to Djibouti if the situation were really dire; from here a chopper could get to Aastha Lok or Ranchi within the hour, depending on the winds. Certain private hospitals in Kathmandu and Anuradhapura were decent enough. She spoke like someone who had really been flown around in choppers in those parts of the world, and so therefore had to worry about wind velocities and favorable landing conditions. Petra had her tonsils out in Nairobi, and they evidently had competent orthodontists there as well.

I sat absorbing all this a moment, and something seemed to strike her, and she suggested that I go clean up, because Petra was due back soon and I didn't want to present as the Great White Hunter emerging unwashed from the bush.

"And you don't smell great," she said, "to be honest."

She wasn't wrong. I went and got my pack from the car, and the watering can guy, who she finally introduced as Rakesh, took me upstairs to an old colonial-style washroom and showed me how to operate what he called a geezer so I could have warm, if not hot, running water.

I remembered that pseudoscience myths held that because cells in the human body have finite life spans, as they regenerate, we become new people every seven years—this isn't literally true, of course, but it occurred to me as I tried to process what had just unfolded.

An insistent voice in my head kept pointing out what Audra *should* have done or *would* have done, and I had heard that voice even in the very moments I sat across from her, listening to her speak and do things in real time. What a strange experience of simultaneity, disjointed simultaneity, because it was as though I had expected her to emerge whole-cloth from 1999, a hologram sprung from my fraying memory. The version of Audra I had constructed in my mind over all that time was suddenly overlain with present-day Audra, real-life Audra, who had become a new person twice over in fourteen years.

I wasn't completely able to handle all the information flooding my system, but had the fleeting feeling that it wasn't surprising Audra had never been married, that it hadn't "panned out," as she had put it, with the German, because certain parts about her that I had repressed—her need for perfection, for example, her attendant propensity for criticism—had come edging back as she described what she considered the highlights of Petra's childhood, and I recalled how this drive for perfection could manifest as a compulsion for control, as her vocal exasperation regarding those whom she dismissed as not "on point," as she had always said.

There were times, I remembered then, when perfection itself seemed more important to Audra than actual human relationships, and I wondered what effect his may have had on her daughter, I mean our daughter.

I retreated again into a shower.

7.

WHAT TO EXPECT after I ventured back downstairs? Benumbed, my encounter with Audra still bleeding into my consciousness as I shaved, deferred somewhere from the forefront of my mind, I knew my shallow experiences with my nephew could hardly have prepared me for interacting with Petra. Seldom was I around children, and I'd never really been around a thirteen-year-old, except when I myself was thirteen, miserable years I'd just as soon forget.

I concentrated on shaving, trembling, and as I scraped and screaked, was confronted by how haunted and haggard I'd become. For lack of sleep or heat rash or cinematic sweep of a dozen years compressed into an hour's conversation, I was hollowed out and spent, nicking myself in a swirl of strawberry-and-cream. I patted down my face, then turned to the arsenal I needed now more than ever, cleansing carefully to defy age, working around my tissue-stanched cuts with cotton balls soaked in toner, doubling up on Liquid Collagen in the vain hope some elasticity would bounce back to my dry and sun-spotted skin. I doubled up on the Ultimate Age Defying Cream, too, air drying between coats, fanning myself like a swooning belle, then tried to do something with my hair, which managed to be both limp and greasy in the humidity. I stalled in this way for as long as I could, touching up in the antique accordion-arm mirror that began refogging almost as soon as I had wiped it clear.

I shook out my clothes as best I could but was forced to pull on wrinkled khakis and an even more wrinkled collared shirt. After making myself as presentable as I was going to be, I thought of Angie and her willingness to drop everything and wing over to Africa with only the thinnest of plans; I thought of my sister and her clear-eyed admonitions; I thought of that photo strip I had seen in Lamu, big teeth and nose freckles a ghostly echo of my poor brother Benj. I thought of Audra abandoning me and then her mother, absconding to Europe and then parts unknown, always with a child in tow, diphtheria, giardia, heat stroke, cobras, wind velocities, orthodontia, insurance premiums, and whatever else had defined their lives.

What *was* I doing there?

When I felt I had dithered long enough, I picked my way down the stairs, trying to quiet all the noise in my head. I assumed Audra would be waiting for me, impatient, drumming fingers, but when I returned to the library, it was empty, the scent of her soap or shampoo still lingering.

I started to snoop causally around the desk: over an old 1930s blotter were stacks of binders and detailed land surveys; a 19th century brass barometer stood on the edge next to a sleek world clock from Sharper Image; strewn among the binders was a headlamp on an stretchy band, mosquito repellant and pepper spray, a ceramic mug with Harvard's Veritas shield that I remembered from before, uncanny again. There was a dish with paper clips and unfamiliar coins, a lethal letter opener, a framed photograph of Audra and her daughter standing beside a yoked water buffalo and knee-deep in paddy water, wearing identical sunglasses and looking amused.

That's as far as I got because activity erupted in the entry hall: the front door heaved open and a sharp sing-songy voice called out, wanting to know whose car it was out front.

Stomping, banging, and the fortified door swung closed with a thud.

I turned to see a coltish girl burst breathlessly into the library, still yelling about the car and flinging a backpack at a wall, all one continuous action before she noticed my presence next to the desk.

Initial impressions: lean, spindly-limbed, deeply tanned, with Audra's thick black hair, although in miniature. Seeing me, her mouth popped open cartoon-like, true unexaggerated disbelief, but she shook that off in a second, not tamping her shock into equipoise like her mother, but instead running across the room to leap into my arms, and she was unexpectedly light, squeezing then almost throwing me back, pushing me with her arms and jumping on one foot to take me in, saying "What?! Is this for real?"

I put out my hand awkwardly and said it was nice to meet her. She shook it limply, suddenly dubious, then slunk back looking up at me. I smiled and shrugged, and she tugged on her bracelets.

"Here I am," I rasped.

At this she hopped back as if yanked by a cord and then began talking manically, almost to herself.

"I can't believe this. I know you said you would come but deep down I didn't believe because the internet isn't reality, a lot of people say a lot of things and if you don't expect anything you can never be disappointed. That's Alexander Pope. Oh, this is a dream. Have you seen my mother? She's going to lose it. Naturally, she's going to murder me."

I stood there as she talked frantically, in mild shock probably, and I felt nearly paralyzed myself, taking her in: she moved with lizard-like darts, looked like a mix of Audra and my mother, in fact she had the exact nose as my mother, and Audra's gray-green eyes, and of course that hair, dark but then sun-kissed enough that I reflexively wondered if Audra was now dyeing her own hair. She was at the age where she was all lanky limbs, elbows and knees, big teeth, her spray of Benj's freckles even browner from the sun.

She had a way of carrying herself with conviction, and despite the bounding around the room and incessant talking, I could tell immediately she had inherited her mother's confidence. And she was hyper-articulate like her mother, even in her jumbled monologue pronouncing her hard consonants distinctly.

As she went on, expressing astonishment that I had come so far around the world, I pulled myself together, thinking that there was no reason to be nervous in the company of this person, who was a child after all, and I mustered all my years of deep reading in humanity's collective wisdom to say something profound, or at least identifiably fatherly; I think it was *how are you*, or some variation thereof.

She wrenched her face up and looked at me as though peering over glasses she didn't have. "How *am* I? An existential question! Flabbergasted, but doing fine. I still can't believe this. How are *you*?"

"Are you glad I'm here?"

She jerked her head, looking as though about to cry, but didn't. "Obviously. I'm just so flabbergasted that you actually came out here. This is massive. Huge. How did you get out here? That must be your car?"

"You do know that your mother never told me?" I blurted out, and as soon as I did, I realized I was maybe throwing Audra under the bus. But it was the truth.

She said she had discovered as much, her mother's line had been her father was in the foreign service, but in recent years she had "confessed" to actually having gone to a fertility clinic. But then Petra had unearthed a trove of documents in a manila envelope and started an investigation that had led to her emailing me. She told me all this in a rush of minute detail.

Was that what I had amounted to in Audra's life, an anonymous donor?

"I just want you to know," I said, "that I never abandoned you. Because your mother wanted to raise you on her own. It was her decision to make."

"I know all about my mother," she said. "No surprises there." She kept pulling at her bracelets. "This is too weird."

"One question," I said. "Why the story about the Islamic school? I thought I was walking into a *Black Hawk Down* situation."

She stared at me. "I don't know what that is," she said. "But I figured you would never do it if I just emailed and asked you to come to Kenya. Obviously, I Google-stalked you once I had your name and all that. I started keeping up with your Twitter, but I never followed you officially—it just seemed like, you just seemed like you had your life, and you were tweeting all this stuff about books and being a professor, and it seemed like your life was so great and that I would just be messing everything up." She hesitated for a moment, looking at the floor. "You just didn't seem like the type of person who would care about your daughter."

Then she did start to cry, but only started, and immediately stifled it.

Suddenly I felt very small, because what she was saying meant that I wasn't merely an abstraction for her, the far-away figure who had never been in the picture, blurry enough to be idealized to contrast the reality of her mother, whose daily parenting spelled discipline, boundaries—no, I was someone who had taken greater shape in her mind from afar, and what she was able to study, my meager academic website, my self-congratulatory tweets, suggested to her that I lacked the emotional depth to take seriously an honest request from a person I had co-created, however unknowingly.

This girl, this thirteen-year-old, had surmised (correctly) that only by tapping into the vaguely Islamophobic attitude that had settled around the edges of my generation's collective unconscious would I respond to a cry from the dark, because deep down I believed, even without admitting it to myself, that somehow I could rescue her from an undemocratic fate.

It was soul-shattering, the knowledge that in virtue of just being myself I had let her down.

I looked at her as thoughtfully as I could, trying to muster something to say, but was at a loss.

Thankfully at that moment Audra strode in, having changed into a dark linen pantsuit, saying dinner was served and shooting Petra a severe, pointed look that said *you and I will talk about this later* (meaning me). I excused myself and made my way on watery legs up the stairs and to the only refuge I knew in the house, the bathroom, where, as the lock clicked resonantly, I tried to prevent the tremor in my lungs from shaking into an all-out panic attack.

I sat on the toilet, my skin stinging, trying to do my breathing exercises.

I hadn't noticed a special or immediate connection to the girl and was wondering whether this whole trip wasn't the most ill-considered thing I'd ever done. She seemed agreeable enough, though a little theatrical, and I couldn't help but notice her smell, ripe and metallic from a day in the sun, and I tried not to be put off, to label the odor a stench, but it was a visceral response, and horrified I thought I'd come around the world at great expense and nothing paternal had kicked in, confirming my fears. This is where my mind went: her smell. Where was the metaphysical flowering of feeling? Why was I so emotionally shrunken?

I sat there for some time, ten minutes, with each passing second oozing more oily sweat because I knew I was making myself look bad, was being rude, and my chest constricted further as I hunched over on Audra's retrofitted toilet.

After those minutes, thanks to bitter experience with such moments, I was able to calm myself down by focusing on my breathing, cool air coming in, warm air going out.

I drank some water from the bottle I'd left there, regulated my heart rate, and went out to face the music.

Wobbly, I went down the stairs, my stomach turned.

Wiping my forehead again, I found the dining room, wood-paneled and equally vast as the library, where an enormous table had already been set for three, candelabras and napkin rings and salt spoons. Everything OK, they wanted to know, and I said yep, just the normal travel-related digestive issues.

"Montezuma's Revenge!" said Petra. "The old Aztec Two-Step."

"Please stop," said Audra.

"Blitzkrap," said Petra. "Delhi Belly."

"I'm not going to ask you again," said Audra.

I took a seat and tried to act like an adult.

We were served by Rakesh and another, younger boy, who wordlessly filled our glasses and brought us roast chicken and vegetables, and though it seemed strange to me, Audra was a natural servant-haver, offering discreet directives over her shoulder, explaining to me that there was a limit to how much curry a person could eat, assuring me that she preferred American staples like steak and potatoes but that their cook refused to prepare cow of any kind, which Audra nonetheless sourced from a Halal butcher on Church Road in Ranchi.

"So I grill steak on Sundays," she said, as though it were a necessary irritation.

Petra sat with one leg tucked under her and had dug in unceremoniously.

"I might become a vegetarian," she said, eating chicken.

In my weakened condition I was unnerved to be enacting a kind of ghostly colonial ritual, to be served by the native help who drifted in and out of the room as conversation flowed around them. In this context the meal unfolded, and I prepared to have Petra give me the third degree, ask me all about my origins or how Audra and I had met or what my average day as an English professor was like.

Instead, it was a strange, mock version of a normal family meal: Audra said to her daughter why don't you tell him what you've been reading, and Petra said *The Myth of Sisyphus* and what did I think of that, and I suggested she read *Siddhartha*, fitting given where she was currently living—plus it seemed to me about right for her age group.

"Did you know wet curry isn't actually indigenous to India," Petra said. "If by indigenous you mean that regular people ate it 500 years ago. Because I happen to know it was developed to suit the Brits when they were running things since the 1700s."

"That hadn't come to my attention," I said.

She wanted to know how many countries I had been to, and I started counting them up in my head, but it was fewer than eight, and she said that she'd been to thirty-two countries and lived in eight.

"Not too shabby, huh?" she said, and I agreed it wasn't too shabby.

During this part of the meal, Audra mainly observed, but I saw that they had a kind of sublingual communication system and were carrying on another conversation with layers of meaning and implication that I could only guess at. Reeling through my mind, grasping for how Rockwellian family dinners went, I realized that I had never really experienced them, due to the divorce. What I remembered was lukewarm Burger King at my dad's, or my mother pouring Kessler into commuter mugs of ginger ale and having my sister and me walk to the gas station for sandwiches.

Surfacing nothing from my childhood, I did recall those grown-up dinners when Audra had met my parents. Once, she had stayed in San Francisco for the weekend, and I wanted to show her off to my dad; I hadn't planned to introduce her to my mother, since there seemed to me little point, but Audra was curious, so we did them two nights in a row on a three-day trip to Southern California.

Audra had rented a muscular German sports car, steel gray and aggressive, and we screamed through the Pacheco Pass, then down the 99, blurring the vast agricultural fields of the Central Valley. There were refurbished school buses shuttling migrant workers from dormitories to geometric plantations, other ghosts of the past, and even as Audra was laser-focused on driving, smoothly overtaking everything on the road, she seemed to be analyzing the scenes flashing by our windows, and remarked that twenty-five percent of the state's water supply went to growing almonds and alfalfa hay, most of which was shipped to China, and that sooner or later even the deepest of aquifers would run dry. "People never see the big picture," she had said.

We met my dad and Valerie at his favorite Italian restaurant where he knew the waiters, and given that these were the Clinton years, as soon as we sat down he made a crack about whether grad school was helping me to uncover the meaning of "is," and he elbowed Valerie and winked at Audra with a sparkly eye, as though they were all three in on some conspiratorial joke at my expense, and that's how the rest of the night went.

The following evening we went to my mother's townhouse, but Ted wasn't around, and she pretended to be excited to see me, something she sometimes did in the presence of others, and at a certain point when Audra had excused herself to go to the bathroom, my mother popped open the miniblinds with her fingers, appraising the BMW and wanting to know where Audra got a car like that. When I said Audra had a Harvard MBA, that was all she needed to know, and I could tell she was suddenly nervous about her ketchupy meatloaf, and throughout the meal she kept apologizing for her run-down divorcée furniture and mismatched table service, and Ted finally stumbled in after we had finished eating, smelling boozy, leering at Audra and pumping her for thoughts about some penny stock he had heard about because they had a Vegas trip coming up. That's how that one went. Audra never met my sister.

Half a year later, sliding into a shallow depression, I made the mistake of telling my dad over the phone that Audra had broken it off, and he said: "No real shocker there, you weren't exactly in her league, pal."

As I looked at Audra now, I was beginning to see her anew, a lightness on her face as she joked with her daughter, Petra's toothy features breaking into a laugh as she made a pun or told some story about a friend, always looking slyly at me, to see if I was getting it, and although their unspoken conversation was largely unintelligible to me, the connection between them was plain, something beyond a mere maternal bond and forged no doubt in the crazy situation Audra had created, carting her daughter to strange points on the globe, from city to hamlet, having her learn German and Ukrainian and probably Swahili and Hindi or Tamil or whatever the local language was around there. I felt my outsiderness acutely, as though I were a tourist peering into their real life together, which in a way I was.

But Petra, she kept trying to draw me into the conversation, mugging for me, cracking jokes, and I couldn't help but be impressed by how sharp she was, how she could move from topic to topic with a kind of fluidity that most of my students would find difficult to sustain. She sat with one leg tucked under her, a natural booster seat that made her appear taller, more elongated in the chair, even as she hunched slightly and Audra reminded her to sit up straight.

After the main dishes were cleared by the silent butlers or valets, Petra slapped her palms down on the table, was seized by a bolt of inspiration, jumped up and flew over to a heavy oak sideboard brimming with begrimed carvings: triumphal oak wreathes, lion heads, three-dimensional cornucopias spilling fruit from its doors. This she flung open releasing poofs of dust, antiquated whorls of atmosphere, probably, and bent in to rummage around noisily.

"Let's read from the book," she cried from the depths of the sideboard.

"Let's not," said Audra wearily.

Ignoring her, Petra found what she was looking for, slammed the door shut in another Krakatoa of dust, and walked a book around to the table, holding it like a relic.

"This came with the house," she said to me, scooting her chair closer to the table and tucking a leg under. "*Mrs. Beeton's Book of Household Management.* Ever heard of it? It's from the 1800s but it's full of all kinds of information."

I delivered my best interested expression.

She thumbed through it, then picked out a passage. "Here," she said, reading: "'Something more than an abundant diet is required to keep the mind and body up to a standard sufficiently healthy to admit of a constant and nutritious secretion being performed'—this is about breastfeeding, to remain healthy during breastfeeding," she summarized, "'the mother ought to drink *malt liquor!*' What? *Noooo.* Too much. Mom, did you get plenty of malt liquor in your diet when you were breastfeeding me? 'For the best tonic and the most efficacious indirect stimulant that a mother can take at such times, there is no potation equal to *porter* and *stout*, or, what is better still, an equal part of porter and stout.' What is porter and stout?"

I said beer and Audra gave me a look that mildly chastised me for encouraging her.

"Mom! Did you get plenty of malt liquor and porter and stout when you were breastfeeding me?"

Audra made a remark about all the liquor in China.

Petra went on to tell me that her mother said the book represents everything wrong with the way we view women in the West. "There's something in there about how the most important aspect of femininity is knowing how to manage household duties. It's great."

Audra reminded her that they were supposed to be reading the book ironically.

"Yeah, it's 'ironic,'" said Petra. "Listen to this: 'The nine or twelve months a woman usually suckles must be, to some extent, to most mothers, a period of privation and penance.'"

Audra made another joke about Petra's teeth being privation and penance, but still Petra carried on without really listening.

"So, *Daaad*," she said, putting girlish emphasis on the final word, drawing it out. "Speaking of Victorian attitudes, what's your opinion on boarding school?"

"Please," said Audra.

I said, catching Audra's severe look: "I don't even have an opinion."

"Yeah," said Petra. "So you'll start to notice these brochures lying around from Rosey and College Alpin Beau Soleil and Institut auf dem Rosenberg and places like that. These are supposedly the most expensive boarding schools in the world, like 95 or 120 grand *a year*. Supposedly Kim Jong un went to the one in Köniz, and that's the worst one she's considering."

"We've been over this," said Audra, rehearsing an old argument for my benefit. She said Petra could go wherever she wanted, but that they had to get more systematic about her education.

Petra said something about being "edjumacated" and Audra said she needed to "matriculate" at a top-tier university, an Ivy or their equivalent.

"Well," said Petra to her mother, "you're not the one who'll be shipped off to Switzerland to learn to ski with the Hereditary Grand

Duke of Luxembourg." She turned to me. "They actually list 'notable alumni' in their material."

"Will," said Audra to me. "You're a professor. Isn't it important for students to have a solid high school education if they want to get in to a good university?"

"Uh," I said. "Admissions really isn't my department."

"The answer is yes," said Audra to Petra. "You want to go to these hot schools you've been talking about, you can't just have a transcript written on the back of a napkin."

"I'll be a non-traditional applicant," said Petra. "It'll make me stand out."

I interjected, inanely, to ask her what she wanted to be when she grew up.

"Probably either a diplomat or a C.E.O."

I nodded, again inanely, and she asked me how long I'd be staying. I was about to say I didn't really know, but Audra said that we'd worry about that later.

Rakesh brought in dessert of sliced fruits and rice pudding, and Petra had the idea of playing a game of Scrabble—before anyone else could say anything, she unfolded her leg, jumped off again, and disappeared down the hall.

"She'll want to challenge the English professor," Audra said, somewhat unenthusiastically.

"I wonder how my life would've turned out if I'd gone to boarding school," I said.

"Ha. You and me both."

Petra came back in with a Scrabble board already out of the box, the little bag of tiles resting on top. It was a round teal version with the playing square in the middle.

"Didja know there's a Scrabble Association of India?" she asked me, shaking the tile bag on the far, unset side of the table. "Last year they had the tournament in Bangalore and the top prize was like ten or fifteen thousand dollars. *Dollars*, not rupees."

"Wow," I said.

"Come on you guys," she said. "Come down here!"

She was busy arranging the board, was eager to have us do an activity together, reminding me of Hayley Mills in *The Parent Trap*. Audra twisted her mouth and narrowed her eyes, as though considering, but still shifted down to the far end of the table without a word, and so I followed suit. Petra had set up three stations and was shaking the bag again so we could draw tiles.

Right away I was gripped with anxiety because I wasn't sure what the etiquette was regarding whether or not to let Petra win. I had memories of the scant few times that I had played board games with my dad, who was utterly ruthless in Monopoly and Risk, getting to the point of dominating the game but refusing to allow anybody to surrender, so we would have to play out the slow, inevitable death for the final hour, my sister or I finally exploding in frustrated tears. I couldn't remember if we'd ever played a game with the five of us, but later with my sister and me, Dad had made clear his belief that a noble throwing of the game on his part would only lead to his kids feeling coddled, wouldn't toughen them up to the realities of war or capitalism, and I always vowed that if I ever got stuck playing a board game with children I would go easy on them. But still I wasn't sure what to do in that situation.

Audra leaned over her tile board, tucking a strand of hair behind her ear and concentrating on her letters, so again I followed her lead, rearranging my own tiles but uncertain how hard to play.

As it turned out, I had worried for nothing because the game didn't last very long.

After her second play, Audra rifled through the bag for more tiles and Petra flicked her head like a hawk.

"Hey!" she cried. "What're you doing?! You're cheating!"

"Let's not be ridiculous," said Audra.

"She feels in the bag for blanks!" Petra said to me pleadingly. "It's cheating."

"Would you stop?" said Audra.

"Don't try to cheat," Petra muttered, hiding her tile rack with her forearm, and Audra warned her that we could stop playing that very minute.

Petra made a miffed grunt but played her turn, and the game unfolded without incident for a few more turns. I decided not to take a dive because Audra seemed not to be taking a dive, and Petra was holding her own, although behind score-wise. She played somberly, as though it mattered, and hovered over the board to scrutinize all the words I set down. But when Audra played a word containing both X and Y on a triple word score, Petra exploded just as I had at her age, or a little younger.

"You can't do that!" she cried. "I was gonna go there!"

"Sorry," said Audra. "Them's the rules."

A furious complaint ensued, also strangely familiar from my childhood, in which Petra accused Audra of being unfair because she *needed* that triple word score if she ever hoped to catch up, and Audra said there were no futures in Scrabble, and as Petra convulsed in a rage, she reached for her glass of juice but instead jostled the board so the tiles shifted in a jumble from their spots.

"Oops," she said flatly.

"What a spoil-sport," said Audra.

This enraged Petra further and she said that it was pointless to play anyway when people decided to cheat.

"I think you're tired," said Audra.

"Actually, I'm wide awake."

"Why don't you head up to bed?"

"Because I'm wide awake."

"Go!" said Audra.

Petra pushed away from the table, too abruptly, and said fine, that she didn't want to play with cheaters anyway, and warned me to keep an eye on her mother. "She doesn't play fair."

Audra glowered and Petra made a sour face and sulked out of the room.

I had been quiet through this, not wanting to overstep, unsure if the outburst was typical or an acting out because I was there. After Petra had stomped loudly up the stairs, Audra turned to me with another groan, waving a hand over the wrecked Scrabble board.

"She can be a real fucking brat sometimes," she said. "You still drink vodka?"

We moved back into the library, where she had a liquor cabinet under lock and key. Rakesh came in with a bucket of ice and Audra said it was a luxury around there, the ice, not easy to get, but she got it, and mixed us some simple vodka and tonics. Back in the wing chairs, staring at the stone fireplace as though it roared with life, she apologized for Petra's behavior, saying that probably a lot of things were running through her head.

I said, echoing Margit, that she was "at that age," not really knowing what that meant specifically.

"She's been at that age a while."

I made a joke about the angel of in vitro fertilization blessing her with a visitation.

Annoyance flashed across her face, again detectable just for a nano-second in the deepened creases at the ends of her mouth, but then she relaxed a bit.

"I know it sounds cold out of context," she said. "But it was a game time decision." When Petra got old enough to ask, she went on, they were still living in Frankfurt, and there were lots of American military personnel at her school and Audra just said that her dad was doing special missions for the army. The older she got, the more Petra pressed her on it, and finally Audra said that she had made up the part about the army. Years went by and she felt there was a kind of truth in the lie. She thought that at a certain point, it would have just muddied the waters to get into it all with Petra.

"But then she uncovered your trove of secret documents," I said.

She swirled her glass. "You must have had a heart attack when you got that email from her. I know you were always adamant about not having kids."

I was going to say something about how my ticket was punched on that front, was in fact in the middle of saying this, when she took a deep breath, a big swallow from her glass, then looked me dead in the eye, and she did this so seriously that I actually trailed off just to absorb the stare. Her eyes were gray-green and penetrating.

"Don't take this the wrong way," she said evenly. "But I'm not positive it would be productive for you to be in Petra's life right now."

This was a little wounding. And what did she mean, *productive*? I reminded her that they lived about 7800 miles away, which I knew because the internet said so, that 7800 miles was a direct measurement but there was hardly a direct way to get there, so in practice it must have been much longer, the point being that it didn't really seem reasonable to say I could disrupt her life, did it?

"Is it optimal?" she said. "All this bouncing around? We won't know until she's thirty-eight. And as far as you go, I don't want her to be disappointed. I'm trying to focus her—she has to stay focused on applying to these schools. I don't want her derailed."

I reminded her that Petra was the one who had asked me to come, reminded her that I was just trying to "do the right thing" (I was flailing at that point), maintained that I would have moved to DC back in the day, that I would have married her and raised a child and generally done what a man was supposed to do.

She seemed surprised at that last declaration and blew a bubble or two back into her drink. "I'm not going to bullshit you," she said, "but I wasn't convinced you were in a place to handle a child back then. Or now."

Maybe not exactly news, but still it stung. When we knew each other, I was of course aware that we were on different planes professionally, she having conquered school and the corporate realm, I barely surviving on part-time work and assistant teaching, infantilized by the academic hierarchy—but respected, or so I thought, by her. Maybe not so much.

Now, hearing her doubts, sitting in that rigid wing chair and holding my sweating glass of vodka, all I could think to say was: "How come you didn't give me the option at least, let me decide?"

"Because," she said, "it was my decision." Q.E.D.

"Why were you with me in the first place?" I blurted.

"Will," she said. "Why get into this? I don't want to hurt your feelings."

I sucked down the rest of my drink and said that I had just one feeling, that it was impossible for her to hurt that lone feeling.

She sipped thoughtfully. Because it was fun for her to be with someone who marveled at those parts of her life she took for granted, she said. At the time she was horribly burnt out, was on the verge of a mental breakdown in fact, even the very night we met was working in her room until absurd hours, compiling reports upon reports, without the energy even to change from her work clothes and then came that thumping from somewhere, the last straw, and she stormed the lobby with the intention of getting somebody fired. But then she saw me standing there in that tuxedo, fresh-faced and oblivious, disheveled but looking at her with naked lust in a way that made her feel wanted, something she hadn't exactly felt amid the brutality of that particular assignment in San Francisco. She decided to let herself go with it, to fuck me and see what happened. She expected a one-night fling, but it turned out that I was quick-witted enough to amuse her, snarky in a way she appreciated, and she discovered that taking me around to all the restaurants and bars in town was a release valve for her, the only way she could unwind from work, and she was grateful for a space to be freewheeling, to show me a good time and spend her money on things that were frivolous and irresponsible. It made her feel like a girl instead of a bloodless shark who always had to be aggressive, to keep moving to stay alive. It was nice, but it wasn't reality.

She was making it sound like I was nothing more than a distraction for her.

"No," she said, "you weren't, no." She said clearly I was a special person—which is something she had said to me fourteen years prior—but she also knew that it wouldn't work between us long-term, that when we were together it was like vacation mode, not real life. She had realized this, but then discovered she was pregnant, and thought the best course was to rip the Band-Aid off, callous as it sounds, and she never wanted to hurt me.

At first, I hardly heard what she was saying. I wanted to counter with all the good times we had had, and so asked if she remembered hiking Muir Woods, when we had stumbled upon that rambling bar, the Tourist Club, and we had to become members for the day so we could hang out drinking beers under the redwoods. That afternoon I had been transfixed by watching her look into the woods as though in meditation. She wore a gray shirt and white puffer jacket tied around her waist, with her sunglasses pushed up on her head, and tiny gold hoop earrings, not her usual diamond studs. Did she remember? Or when we stayed overnight at that lodge in Sausalito, and sat on the second-story porch watching all the tech guys pull up in their insane cars, and it was so windy and cold but we didn't care because a valet had brought us a blanket and we were bundled together on a bench. Or when her HBS friends had those Giants tickets and we all went and the weather was perfect and she wore a black and silver baseball cap her girlfriend coveted because it was an exclusive from an Italian designer known to everyone in the group but me?

As I said all this, she was shaking her head gently, eyes dewy but somehow distant, and it was clear that she did not remember those moments at all, said as I recounted them that they sounded familiar now that I was describing them, but I knew she was just trying to make me feel better, to soften the reality that our time together was simply not as profound for her as it had been for me, an unserious frolic she recalled fondly, but without much emotional investment.

"Is there internet access out here?" I said suddenly, thinking of Angie.

She looked past me a moment, nodding, then slowly rose and went back to her desk. From a file cabinet she pulled a fat laptop with hard rubber bumpers and a briefcase handle, the kind you saw on construction sites or in photographs of modern warfare.

"This will run through the satellite dish," she said, handing it to me.

The laptop was weighty, heavy duty, and I made a face indicating that.

"Sand used to be an issue with the old machines," she said. "But these are pretty good. Have it at. I'm fading here." She stretched, stifled a yawn, and lingered in the doorway before heading to bed. "Just make sure to power it down when you're done," she said, and dissolved into the unlit hall.

I hadn't budged from the wing chair, and sat with the computer in my lap, listening to Audra climb the stairs, her footfalls echoing in the main hall, until a door was closed somewhere and the library was plunged into the silence of a just-closed museum. The oily bookshelves seemed to absorb both light and sound, and I opened the laptop with the intention of letting the solitude inspire me to write a detailed letter to Angie.

Things loaded with surprising speed, and I was treated to the usual barrage of emails, mainly bureaucratic announcements and those financial services offers I hadn't yet opted out of. There were emails from Angie, Cubby, and my sister—and an anomalous one, from the Provost, titled "time for a quick chat?" The Provost had emailed me probably twice in my years at the college, so it was somewhat alarming, and upon opening it I learned that he wanted to "touch base" with me about my Psychopathology in Literature course; apparently his office had fielded a "couple of inquiries" from "concerned stakeholders."

I recalled the phone conversation with the mother I had all but forgotten amid my recent adventures, wondered in my exhaustion whether she was an important donor, and then recognized how depressing it was that I could be so far away from that speck of a college, on the other side of the globe in a derelict hill station beyond the reach even of GPS, and in a matter of seconds could be yoked again to the pettiness of my stupid everyday life.

I decided not to respond to the Provost. It was summer, after all, and I opened Angie's email instead. Instantly I almost felt her there with me:

> Will!
>
> I'm dying to hear all about India! Did you make it all right? Did you meet Petra? Tell me everything!!

Getting back home was mostly uneventful, except for one thing that happened in the airport in Nairobi. I was going through security and I got randomly flagged. Annoying since the guards didn't seem to really care one way or another, but not the end of the world. So they poke around and take a few things out—including your favorite, my birth control. The guard proceeds to just leave the pills on top of my stuff as he's looking for the nail scissors or whatever they saw on the X-ray machine and this guy, a white dude, an American, who happens to be milling around the security area being nosy sees the pills and then turns to LECTURE me about birth control being a "holocaust" against the "pre-born" and that he didn't see a wedding band in the first place, and I'm like *what in the actual fuck is happening right now?* I just stare at him as he's reprimanding me—this obese white dude older than my dad, who's sermonizing to *me* about my own private birth control and I wanted to take my nail scissors and stab him in the eye. But I didn't. I politely told him that it really wasn't any of his business and he said it was "God's business." *Then* I notice his polo, which had a logo for some overseas Christian evangelical organization and I realize this guy is like acting out Victorian colonial fantasies about bringing the One True Religion to the natives of Africa. Pitiful. The way he spoke to me, like he just looked through me with his dead-fish eyes as though I were not a thinking feeling human being—I mean, it was scary, and I shuddered to think of what he was saying to people in Kenya, and what he would be working on back home—banning birth control like they banned alcohol, probably. This guy would be all about it.

But except for that, Mrs. Lincoln, it was smooth sailing back home. I picked up your car no problem and it started just fine, as I predicted. The cats were totally insane when I got to your place. I talked to your neighbor—but I forget his name. Ramon? Ray. Reggie. Murgatroyd. Anyway, he said he stopped in twice a day but they were still loved starved. He didn't change the litter, which was pretty foul but I took care of it and you owe me big time for that. Your snake plant was knocked over but it survived and they managed to unravel an entire roll of toilet paper and it was pretty much across your whole apartment. I don't know if it just happened or Ramon just didn't clean it up or what, but I got a good laugh out of it. Par for the course. Got your mail too and there didn't seem to be anything out of the ordinary. I'm here now and Kick and Lad are zipping around like maniacs. Gozer is cowering from under the coffee table, standard. Essie is curled up right by me on the couch purring.

Anyway, I had a great trip, even though the circumstances were strange, to say the least. I can't wait to really sit down and study what I got there, shot-wise. Maybe I can do that coffee table book? Will, I hope you were able to find Petra all right and that it's a positive experience for you. I really am proud of you and I can't wait to hear all about it. Write me back whenever you get a chance to let me know that you're alive.

Missing you already!!

xoxoxoxo

Angie

In starting to tap out a reply, I realized that I was tired enough for my brain not to be working, realized that although I had planned to send Angie a rich and big-hearted message I was nodding off, for all that had happened to me over the last several hours, and I just managed to say that I was in India, was alive, barely, and had found Petra and Audra, that it was an unreal experience that I couldn't fully articulate in words, but that I would write her again just as soon as I had the chance.

I wrote that email with my last reserve of energy, then grunted and creaked and dragged myself up to my room.

—

The next morning, my door rattled with zealous banging.

"Are you decent?!" cried Petra from the other side.

I was still bleary, clawed at the mosquito netting, disoriented.

"Coming in," she said, still knocking as she pushed open the door. She was already dressed and scrubbed, bearing a mug of coffee. "Mom claims you take it with cream and sugar."

I actually took it black, but it hardly mattered.

She handed me the steaming coffee then recited what was clearly a memorized mea culpa: "I would like to apologize for my behavior last night it was totally uncalled for and I'm embarrassed that you had to see that especially on your first night in town."

She got through it, eyes cast on the floor, and I imagined Audra standing over her in the kitchen, wagging a wooden spoon as she committed the speech to memory.

"I haven't given it a second thought," I said, then added a quick thank you for the apology because I knew dimly that children were supposed to be validated.

She looked up and said really, and when I reassured her, she broke into a toothy smile. "Well then get ready," she said. "Because we have a big day ahead of us."

Throwing off the pain of apology, she began humming around the room, saying that my backpack was uncool, that Rakesh had taken my laundry to the laundry lady, that she was so excited to show me around and introduce me to some of her friends.

I noticed she had applied bright red lipstick, not very neatly, and colored her cheeks with what I guess was too much rouge, so she looked borderline clownlike, and I wondered why she made herself up for me. I wasn't fully awake.

The coffee was watery and mild, but when she asked, I said it was tasty. I told her I'd be with her in a minute and she bounced out so I could pull on some clothes and splash water on my face. I rubbed in some Age Defying cream and sunscreen, and ran a comb through my hair.

Downstairs, a spread of yogurts and boiled eggs was laid out in the dining room, and as I ate, she said she wanted to clarify that her mom would never knowingly cheat at Scrabble and I said I gathered as much.

"Where is she, anyway?" I said.

"She's off," said Petra, "on one of her 'errands.' We'll see her later."

"Why aren't you in school?"

She laughed as though this was a dumb question with an obvious answer.

After breakfast, she led me out the big house, where Rakesh was clipping the thorny blood orange saplings planted in pots around a patio in back, even as the rest of the yard looked unwatered yet overgrown, clumps of yellowing elephant grass and a couple of ferny tamarind trees whose pods were scattered in the dirt, having been breached and harvested by squirrels or their equivalents. It was already hot, and the air had currents of cooking smoke and cinnamon.

"Ah, Bihar," Petra said broadly, imitating Harrison Ford in *Indiana Jones and the Last Crusade.*

She couldn't wait to show me everything, and I followed her down a packed dirt trail leading in the opposite direction of the way I had driven in, winding through a valley and around another low hill. Walking around that hill, we encountered a swampy gully filled with garbage, mostly semi-disintegrated water bottles and plastic bags, and when I paused to peer in, Petra explained that it functioned as a dump for the people living in the immediate area.

"Human waste," she said, "that goes somewhere else. This is household waste."

Slimed-over water trickled through the lowest part of the gulley—a frog leapt in. "Splash," said Petra.

It was only nine or ten in the morning but was far more humid than I was used to, though not quite coast-of-Kenya humid. I had easily sweated through the back of my shirt while Petra seemed adapted to the environment, hardly flushed as she walked, pointing out virtually undetectable lines through the grass, leading off into forests where, she said, people harvested tendu leaves or bamboo, depending on the time of year.

"A guy we knew killed himself out there," she said. "Due to despair."

In just ten minutes of walking, I had already drained my bottle of water, feeling generally out of shape, and looking, I'm sure, a little wrecked. Petra would glance over to assess me, watching me catch my breath.

"Mom says only mad dogs and Englishmen go out in the noon day sun," she said.

"Words of wisdom," I said in fits.

We came upon a clearing of well-trampled dirt around a two-story cinder block building. It was newly painted lime green and had a steel door and stone lattice in the windows instead of glass. An Indian flag flew from a pole, and a sign read "Bela District Female Enterprise Co-Operative" in English and Hindi. Some round-bellied children were waving sticks and running around in the dust, dressed only in fraying shorts. Petra seemed to know them all, joking briefly in I guess Hindi and they squealed when she produced an old-fashioned rubber ball from her bag. "Ball," she said in English, holding it aloft.

When they had repeated ball, ball, ball to her satisfaction, she tossed it in the air and they scrambled to catch it, then swept at it with their sticks like half-sized cricketers. Petra introduced them as Vishwanath, Snehal, and Ravi, and proceeded to explain in intricate detail their relationships to one another, and apparently, to a couple of women Petra knew. I said hello to Vishwanath, Snehal, and Ravi, who shrank behind Petra shyly, clutching at the cuff of her shorts with nail-painted fingertips. Petra snatched the ball from one of them, feinted playfully, and tossed it into the grass. They ran after it shouting. Then she gestured grandly at the humble building as though it were a palace. Nothing to do but follow her inside.

It was an open room with a low door at one end and a wooden ladder poking up through a hatch in the ceiling. There were several tables with dried grasses, metal trays and what looked like jars of paint or dye, ribbons, spools of fine-gauge wire. A lone woman, wearing a lavender and red sari over a blouse, sporting a dime-sized gold nose stud and enormous glasses, was bent over a project at the farthest table. She seemed both exasperated and self-conscious that we were there, but after Petra spoke with her briefly, she lit up and came out from behind the table, stooping slightly, took my hand in both of hers and smiled, talking non-stop.

"This is Amrita," said Petra. "She's welcoming you and saying it's an honor to meet you. I told her you're my dad, which is why she's laughing like that. They all know me here and they thought you were dead. So this is a big deal."

Amrita was radiating, just sort of resting my hand in hers and lightly massaging it, inspecting me with narrowed eyes as though I were a rare object. I hunched awkwardly and tried to appear likeable.

Petra said something else, and Amrita raised a hand and shuffled back to her table, resuming her labor, still chatting with herself and shaking her head, but good-naturedly, as though she'd had a stroke of luck she couldn't quite believe.

As she did so, Petra explained that Amrita was weaving placemats from what they called kusha or darbha grass. This grass was very famous in India, Petra said, and it grew around the nearby lowlands if they were swampy. Amrita and several other women from the village harvested it, and then had their special drying and curing methods that made it suitable for weaving. They use the grass for everything, she said, prayer mats, rings, even medicine—her mother had a zig-zagging basket back at the house that was woven right in town from kusha grass. From an economic point of view (to paraphrase what Petra was probably parroting from Audra or someone else), the problem was that there was little local demand for these traditional baskets, but when Audra established the Bela District Female Enterprise Co-Operative, women from the village—Petra called them "artisans"—could suddenly hope to connect their goods to larger markets.

Audra knew a distributor in Ranchi who had a connection to an exporter in Mumbai, who in turn got hand-made goods on ships to wholesalers in Europe and North America. This distributor had analyses showing the market not for baskets, but for hand-woven placemats, had proven-winner designs and color palettes from his guy in Mumbai, and so the co-op worked with Amrita to get her an unsecured loan of 10,000 rupees, capital to purchase the right kinds of non-toxic dyes and the trays and other equipment. With Audra advising her, Petra herself had helped Amrita negotiate a deal with a local delivery company to get her placemats on the monthly truck to Ranchi, and in this way, Amrita was now supporting herself and her children.

Petra knew all the numbers cold, and ran through them for me, saying that Amrita could make on average two mats per day; if she were paid Rs145 per mat, she grossed about Rs7,200 per month, minus Rs1500 for shipping costs and another 500 for dyes and other supplies, netting about Rs5200 per month, around $83.

"This is *a lot* of money for this sort of work," said Petra. "Mom's company provided her with that microloan to get her started, that was like $160, and she's able to pay some back each month, and now she's an entrepreneur. The banks around here, they won't give loans to people like her, so she was stuck picking leaves and they always get screwed on that. But now she's got her own business, she's plugged into the globe. She's trying to bring in her sister, which could double production."

"Is she married?" I said.

"The old story," said Petra, sounding old herself. "Her husband went away for the chili harvest and never came back. That was three years ago so she's assuming she's pretty much on her own."

"What's in it for your mom's company? To set up this little co-op way out in the middle of nowhere."

She spread her arms: duh! "They make money! These are loans. They're just tiny loans, but they charge interest. People like Amrita almost never default. Multiply it times a million."

It was like talking to a forty-year-old banker, and as she spoke I was noting a characteristic of Audra's that had worn off on her—a kind of brash, affected confidence that may or may not have been warranted, as though knowledge in one area somehow made you an authority on whatever subject you happened to bump into.

She had walked over to Amrita's table, wanting to show me something, and the older woman took Petra's hands in hers to guide her fingers in the cadence of weaving, a lesson that had obviously been ongoing because they resumed in the middle of a particular technique, Petra working in earnest, but frustrated at her own clumsy attempts to replicate what Amrita had been doing so effortlessly. At a couple of points Amrita let out an admonitory sigh, repositioning Petra's fingers, and Petra would shake her head, impatient, wanting to get it right immediately. Amrita was tsk-tsking no, and Petra was getting increasingly red-faced as she concentrated, then I guess became fatally flustered because she broke from the table and said "Forget it! I can't do it if you're watching."

"I get the idea," I said.

She muttered something to Amrita, then took me to the tiny back office: a Queen Anne roll top desk with lacey fretwork along the top, mismatching filing cabinets, and a calendar depicting some henna-bearded guru. She explained that Audra let her keep track of certain accounts, including Amrita's, and then checked her work before forwarding it on to the company.

"She calls it real-world training to supplement the poetry about birds and churches in ruins."

"Probably smart," I said.

After saying our goodbyes to Amrita, we left the building, checked in on the kids who were avidly defending the ball from one another, and then set off on another barely-visible trail. Through the clutches of trees were small cultivated fields with men knifing metal tillers through soil or guiding an ox yoked to a cart, the wheel following the hoof.

We came around more low hills and on to a trampled clay road around which a few buildings were clustered. Compared to the villages I had been through so far in India, this one was noticeably quiet: a courtyard of sorts set with brick pavers where a few old men sat and chatted under canvas awnings. There were wooden stalls or carts offering underweight vegetables, phone cards, or ubiquitous paan, but their sales didn't seem brisk. Goats were bleating in a wooden pen, being listlessly watched over by an ancient woman slumped on a bench under a dusty tree, fanning herself with a newspaper.

"Everybody's out in the fields," Petra explained, taking me over to a white building with a drippy red cross painted on the side.

"It's admirable," I said suddenly, "that your mom's company is investing in the people here." I waved around. "Clearly there isn't much opportunity otherwise. I know she said it was mostly PR, but still."

Petra paused at the door to what must have been a clinic, looking as though she were deciding whether to tell me something.

Finally, shading her eyes because the sun was behind me, she said: "You don't *really* think my mother would be out here in BF India just for some microloans so a few women can sell placemats to IKEA? I mean, do you?"

Put that way, it did stretch belief, but given my twisting emotional state, I have to say that I hadn't thought too much about it. Wasn't it exactly the sort of project profiled in those achingly-scored documentaries designed to elicit donations from Westerners to the less-lit corners of the globe? There were always portraits of a woman very much like Amrita looking fragile and forlorn, huge eyes saying *help me! I'm helpless!* because it was more satisfying to imagine your money going to a specific person rather than an abstract cause.

I was sweating ignominiously. "So why in the world *are* you here?" I said.

Before she could answer, someone threw open the clinic door—a young man, college-aged but enormous, bulging with muscles, well over six foot, wearing basketball shorts, a tight black tank top, and beat Chuck Taylor knock-offs. He bustled around the doorway, chiding Petra for being early, speaking in heavily accented English.

"Just visiting," she said. "I wanted to introduce you to my father. Dad: Pradeep, Pradeep: Dad."

Instantly he lit up just as Amrita had, turning to me and saying it was a pleasure to make my acquaintance, nearly crushing the bones in my hand with his huge paws.

"Certainly I never thought I would meet you," he said.

He held the door open for us, and I followed Petra through an empty waiting room, then down a corridor past closed doors stenciled with numbers, to a concrete-floored room in back. She was explaining that a doctor came through there once a month, but that otherwise it was shut up. Pradeep was paid by the state, she said, to make sure nobody steals the machines and medicines that were locked away there. I asked if it was a state clinic or a private clinic, and she said a little bit of both.

In the back, I saw the room was furnished only with a sleeping pallet on the floor and a couple of chairs and crates used as tables. But there was, surprisingly, lots of weight-lifting equipment: a padded bench for chest presses, with a rack hand-fashioned from pipes, a chin-up bar in a corner, and even a rubber gym mat along one wall. There were a few actual dumbbells, too, as well as plastic buckets filled with cement that had been attached to steel rods, makeshift curl bars. The entire back wall was corrugated metal, but on the others Pradeep had posters of body builders and a slate board on which was chalked a crude chart with "arms," "chest," "legs," "back," and the like consisting of an X-axis, and M T W TH FR SAT SUN a Y-axis. A splotchy full-length mirror was propped up in view of the rubber mat.

"Pretty cool, huh?" said Petra, giving Pradeep a demurely downward look, and he tried not to let his pride show.

"I am able to do cross-fit and weight training here," said Pradeep. He asked me if I knew about cross-fit and I said I did.

"It is more about proper form," he said, "than fancy equipment."

Petra said that Pradeep trained some local people, and that he was making a name for himself.

This embarrassed him, and he mumbled something about the gym being modest and that he just wanted to get people interested in fitness. In Patna, he was saying, they had the Patna Weight Lifting Association, so why not there?

"And he wants to compete," said Petra. "Professionally."

"It is my dream," said Pradeep, "to compete in the GCG."

"The Glasgow Commonwealth Games," Petra translated.

I tried to detect if they were exchanging any meaningful glances. I asked them how they met, and Petra mocked me, saying that I was already being protective.

In fact, her lipstick seemed then excruciatingly bright, a beacon, a lighthouse.

After a few seconds, during which Pradeep looked worried or guilty, Petra explained that he was Amrita's nephew, and she and her mother knew the whole family. "Everybody knows everybody around here."

Pradeep laughed nervously, but at Petra's prodding, he proceeded to show me around his jury-rigged gym, not wanting, I thought, to seem vain about what he had accomplished, but nonetheless proud of his tiny domain. Each time we got to a new piece of equipment, he would demonstrate how to operate it, leaning back on the bench to knock out a few chest presses, or gripping the rod attached to the two cement-filled buckets and doing some slow bicep curls. After each demonstration, he would invite me to try it, assuring me he would assess my form, but I always refused, saying I wasn't in a good mental space for a workout, which was true. I was winded from just walking around in the heat.

He had a chin-up bar bolted diagonally across one corner, and as he jumped to rip out ten or twenty pull ups, I stole a look at Petra watching him, the muscles of his back and shoulders flexing through his shirt as he executed one fluid pull up after another, seemingly incapable of being winded himself, and she had a kind of bemused expression on her face that I couldn't quite parse. Unquestionably he was too old for her, and yet was just as obviously a vast improvement over Mohammed Starlight.

He kept going on the bar for a minute or more—an eternity in chin-up time—and I pretended I was marveling at his athletic prowess when I was actually studying Petra: her bemusement blossomed into admiration, which at last broke into a pop-eyed, foundation-caked grimace, and she shook her head, clapping, saying OK, OK, that's enough He-Man showing off. Pradeep dropped himself back to earth and turned with a broad grin, breathing normally, his shirt still bone dry.

Looking at his shoes, he said that any time I wanted a workout while I was there, I could come to him, and he would get my heart pumping. "I have a whole system," he said.

"He did a boot camp with Mom," said Petra, "and it just about killed her."

She was looking at him with what seemed deep affection, throwing an empty water bottle at his head, and he parried with a forearm chop.

"Gotcha!" she said.

At that moment a lower part of the rear, corrugated metal wall began to shake, and then a fragment, apparently moveable, was peeled back, and a boy appeared. I thought I recognized him from the co-op yard. He was sweaty and stinky and excited, immediately delivering a long and complicated message, and Pradeep nodded sympathetically, exchanged a few words with Petra, and then turned to me.

"We are invited to my Auntie's for a meal," he said.

Petra shrugged, saying that Amrita must have dropped what she was doing to welcome me.

I said a meal would be delightful, and Pradeep said something to the boy, who gaped at me for a long minute, in exactly the way Cubby's kids would gape at me, then abruptly scurried back into the sun.

"Country text messaging," Pradeep joked, replacing the moveable piece of wall.

—

On the way to Amrita's place, Pradeep pumped me with all kinds of questions about life in the States. They began innocuously enough as he wanted to know whether I knew who Arnold Schwarzenegger was (I did) or Flex Lewis and Branch Warren (I didn't); or what sorts of issues, politically speaking, the right and left tended to debate. After I counted off the usual petty list, strange to a non-American, he pressed me on guns, asking was it true all of us owned guns and did I think it necessary for ordinary citizens to carry weapons in order to combat terrorism or the government?

What did he mean by "the government"?

"These Occupy protestors who were in New York City. Would they rise and act if they had enough weapons?"

"I don't think so," I said. "But then again, you never know."

He said that political power comes from out the barrel of a gun, noted that the U.S. had traditionally been allies with Israel (I said that was accurate), and then wanted to know what my government's position was on the fact that Israel was providing weapons and training to the Indian government, drones and thermal imaging equipment, which was then sometimes turned on their own citizens.

I said I didn't really have an opinion, but clarified that he was talking about "terrorists," that he was saying that the government might use those Israeli weapons on "terrorist" camps.

"No no," he said. "Not terrorists. What about Palestine? This is true occupation, is it not?"

"Pradeep," said Petra. "Forget it."

"Yes," he said, and we had arrived.

———

Amrita's place was a tidy homestead with whitewashed mud walls and a thatched roof. A makeshift pergola had been fashioned by stretching a green tarp out from the eaves to two wooden poles attached at either corner. A blanket or rug had already been partially set with bowls and other dishes covered with lids or pieces of cardboard. Twitchy chickens were pecking around and she had a leafy vegetable garden fenced with a matrix of axe-hacked branches. I was looking forward to getting out of the sun.

Petra went right inside like she owned the place while Pradeep and I waited in the shade of the tarp, and I wondered how and why he was so informed about the goings-on in the States. Although he was somewhat fuzzy on the specifics—such as the improbability of Americans in 2013 ever being able to overthrow their government—I suspected that it must have been through chats with Petra that he had come to expand his world view beyond the chin-up corner. He smiled at me self-consciously then looked at his feet.

Petra emerged from the house with Amrita and several others, all of whom she seemed to know, all of whom greeted me enthusiastically, if not exactly in fluent English. One of them produced an aluminum watering can and poured me a tall tumbler of water, Pradeep assuring me it had been thoroughly boiled, was therefore safe to drink, for me. After a whirlwind of translated introductions—Amrita's two daughters, a cousin or uncle, and a couple of others who had appeared from around the property—we all arranged ourselves on the blanket in the warm shade of the tarp, and Amrita toddled out with a mammoth cast-iron pot. One of the daughters scooped red rice into bowls, and Amrita ladled in saucy chicken. There were plates with vegetables, lentils, other kinds of rice.

"Amrita doesn't care about ceremony," said Petra. "I mean she has everybody eat together, men and women, so she says please enjoy."

The food was delicious, and I held my bowl up and smiled at Amrita, indicating that I enjoyed its taste. Buzzing discussions erupted among the others, so I focused on my food and trying to bring down my core temperature. Sometimes when you're walking in the sun, you don't realize how thirsty you are until you stop moving, and I accepted cupful after cupful of water from Amrita's smiling daughter. Petra floated in and out of the conversation, and on the occasions when people seemed to be including me, I looked to her for translation, but she said that she could only follow a small part of what they were saying, as they were speaking mainly in Gondi.

"They're talking about Pradeep's father," she said. "Amrita's brother. He thinks the weight lifting is selfish."

They talked while I had another helping, Petra interjecting when she could. The flies were thick and fearless, but I tried to make friends with them, thinking of Angie.

After everyone had eaten, the daughters had cleared the dishes, the flies following them off on unknown currents, while everyone else bowed out, so it was just Petra, Pradeep, Amrita, and another man about my age who had been introduced as Vimal, a "relative." Vimal had initially struck me as out of place under the tarp as he was neatly-pressed, with a starched collared shirt and close-toed shoes, when everyone else but Pradeep was farmer casual and in rubber sandals. His skin was stretched tight across his skull, so you could see his temporal bones through his closely cropped hair. He was slurping tea and speaking lowly with Amrita, eyeing me, or so I thought, and then turned to address me directly.

"My apologies for being discourteous," he said in faintly British English. "I have not seen my cousin in months, and we were just catching up."

I was startled to hear English come out of his mouth because when we had first been introduced, he merely shook my hand brusquely and nodded as everyone else had, so I assumed he didn't speak my language. My surprise must have been evident because he apologized again and said that it often took him some minutes to adjust in his mind to speaking another language.

"And what is it you do, sir?" he asked.

I explained that I was an English professor, and he seemed impressed, then confused about what I was doing so far out in the countryside.

"You are not, I take it, a missionary," he joked.

"He's out here for me," interrupted Petra. "He's my father."

His expression implied that he had already known this; he smiled crookedly and called Petra *didi*. "You are the famous young woman we've heard so much about."

Pradeep coughed on a chunk of fruit.

"And you are Mr. Vimal Pottai from the forest," said Petra, and I couldn't tell if she was being rude or self-possessed.

He repeated back what she had said in an amused or sardonic tone.

"Uncle has business interests down in Dandakaranya," said Pradeep quickly, recovering. "But I never said he was *from* that place."

"What kind of business are you in?" I asked Vimal.

"I coordinate things," he said tightly. "And you, didi," he said to Petra. "Where is your mother, the equally famous Madame Wester?"

"She's out coordinating," said Petra.

"You are her husband, sir?" he said to me.

Now it was my turn to cough, and for whatever reason I reddened. "Just visiting," I said. "Not at all."

"Ah," he said. "I see. Then it is fortuitous indeed that we were able to take a meal together, as I too am only visiting."

I asked him what *he* was doing in the area.

He considered this question for a long moment, looking from Amrita to Pradeep, then finishing the rest of his tea before answering.

"Are you familiar with ore and mineral extraction?" he asked, not pausing to hear my answer. He explained that the area was "blessed" with iron ore, bauxite, sponge iron, and that it would be highly lucrative for certain anointed corporations, in partnership with the state government, naturally, to set up large-scale mining operations in the vicinity. It wasn't a gold mine, he said, it was far better than a gold mine, for with the proper equipment and manpower, countless tons of raw material could be produced by the hour, could either be refined there or shipped as is to the Port of Paradip, a mere 600 kilometers away on new roads, to be loaded onto freighters bound for China. And yet, he went on, you see no mines or steel refineries in this region. In Jharkhand they have Bokaro Steel City, an entire industrial metropolis built from nothing in the 1960s by Nehru, financed by the Soviets. In Chhattisgarh and Orissa, he said, there are other issues, but here we have subsistence farming and the young nephew founding his weight lifting association.

Pradeep coughed again and excused himself, and it was not clear, to me at least, if he felt slighted or merely wanted to stretch his legs, but so intense was Vimal's gaze that I hardly noticed Petra had followed him.

"So you work in mining?" I said. "You're scouting locations?"

He said the latter was true, but not the former. Then he spoke briefly with Amrita, who had been seated silently, fiddling with a teapot.

"She wants to know your opinion on these companies coming here," said Vimal. "I believe the term is 'compulsory purchase.' Or what you would call in the States 'eminent domain.' Here the law says the state government has authority to build on land it deems lucrative to the interests of the state. What is your opinion about this?"

I said I couldn't venture an informed opinion, but that it did seem to me that it was hard to make a living out there, that Amrita's co-op therefore seemed a genuine life-line. He translated for Amrita, who snorted and started on a story that took two or three minutes to get out.

"Yes," said Vimal, nodding as she spoke. "She is talking about kusha grass. You know this? She is saying it is meant to be used for many things, things which do not have an exchange value, in the capitalist sense. The Hindus believe this grass can purify objects, you can burn it in, in yajna. One can weave mats for meditation, spiritual mats, you understand, but the Europeans and Americans want kusha grass for table settings, so this is what they receive. For dinner parties."

I wasn't quite following the link between steel refineries and kusha grass, but I couldn't help but think of Simeon's declaration that grass was everything.

"Well, it's great that Amrita is supporting herself," I said.

"Supporting?" he said cryptically, not translating for Amrita. "And what is the *cost*?"

Suddenly I realized Petra was gone, and I stood up creakily, saying that I wanted to check in on her. He was gracious about it, but still gave off a vibe like something wasn't quite right.

He rose stiffly. "By all means check on your daughter."

He helped Amrita to her feet, and she began rounding up the remaining dishes as he lit a cigarette, smoke coiling around him like a deathly apparition.

I walked the yard, looking in on the chickens and garden, not urgently concerned about Petra, but somehow in the back of my mind interested in her whereabouts. Vimal was just sort of eyeing me as he smoked, this time I was sure of it, so I wandered out of his line of sight, bringing up my knees flagrantly, like I needed to stretch.

I caught Petra's voice through some trees on the edge of the yard, and I went over softly because I didn't want her to hear me approaching. I picked my way through the underbrush, in the unkempt field beyond the vegetable garden, to the edge of a primordial-looking banyan tree, whose branches hung roots like curtains to the earth. Through the screen of these roots I could see Petra and Pradeep, their backs to me, legs sticking out side by side—not, I noted, one on top of the other.

I could hear them talking, but not what they were saying, so I came around as close as I dared to see them through the roots. They were sitting close together, intimate, speaking in low tones, their hands seemingly clasped together. I stood as still as possible, insects ravenous around me, and after a minute I could make out Pradeep turning the page in a notebook on his lap. Then he recited some fourth-grader's sentence in halting English, and Petra corrected him, encouraging him to try again, and I realized that this was not a hot-mouthed tryst, as I had assumed, but a reading lesson.

I took a single step closer, aware of the ants trailing on the banyan tendrils but not the brittle twig underfoot, which broke with a deafening slasher flick snap at the most inopportune time, and they both jerked their heads like deer with predators upwind. When they saw me, Pradeep leapt to his feet, reflexively shamed, while Petra was instantly enraged, demanding to know what I thought I was doing.

"Why are you *spying* on me?" she screeched.

"No, no," I stuttered. "I'm sorry, I didn't know where you went."

She flung the notebook and stormed past me, crashing noisily, for effect, and shooting me a bitter look. Pradeep hung back guiltily, squinting to see where the notebook had landed.

"Petra!" I called after her. "I'm sorry!"

"Uh huh, sure," she said over her shoulder, stomping on the crunchiest leaves to emphasize her point.

She cooled off by tossing grain at the chickens for a while, clucking at them, laughing despite herself. Pradeep had materialized to shake my hand, and then left with his notebook for the clinic.

Finally she found me sipping tea under the tarp. Vimal had disappeared somewhere with Amrita.

"I accept your apology," said Petra solemnly.

"Thank you for that," I said. "I don't really know what I'm doing."

This she found amusing, and flashed me her toothy grin. "Forget it," she said. "It's forgotten. Come on!"

She wanted to show me around town, yelled into the house to thank Amrita, and we were off again, to tour her other favorite spots: the stall from which she purchased soap and licorice chewing gum she had never seen in any city; the wide creek where boys fished with nets and funnel baskets made from willow branches; and the "market," a walk-up counter staffed by a bored clerk blasting a transistor radio, and a wall of snugly stacked goods for sale, all pre-packaged: Taaza chai, Cif spray cleaner, Closeup toothpaste, Hamman soap, Kissan tomato sauce, brightly lettered and featuring light-skinned people on the wrappers ecstatic about the products inside.

Petra asked me for some bills to buy a Boost energy drink, and then indicated a tube of moisturizer near some shampoos and creams.

"Fair & Lovely," she said to me. "They're obsessed with protecting their 'natural fairness' here—you'll see that in every commercial, if you watch TV. But in the States everyone's into tanning. Ironic, Mom says. That's why she likes it here, because she's so pale." She laughed to herself.

"Does that Indulekha oil actually regrow hair?" I said, leaning across the counter.

She gave me a deadpan look of infinite pity. "Let's head home," she said.

On the way back to the big house, I asked her about what she had started to say earlier about her mother and how she wasn't really in the area merely to dispense microloans to hard-working local women.

It was now dusk, and we were walking on a raised footpath on the dike between two rice paddies, only slightly narrower than ones I had driven on mistakenly. Crickets had started up, a chorus echoing in an otherwise desolate part of the village, and she stared at me, considering.

"What were you talking about with Vimal and Amrita?" she asked.

"His job," I said. "Mining. Grass."

"Didn't you think it was weird that this character Vimal knew all about Mom?"

"I thought you said everyone knew one another?"

"Except that he's not from around here. I'd never seen him before." She shook off a bug that was feasting on her arm. "They were talking about you at first," she said. "I could understand a little when they were switching between Gondi and Hindi. He was asking if you worked for MK or Vedanta Steel, wanted to know if you worked with Mom."

"I thought *he* worked for the steel company?"

"No," she said, stopping on the edge of a paddy, the sun sunk lower beyond the trees to the west. "It's complicated."

She said that from what she understood, from what she had overheard from her mother's discussions with the men who visited the house, this Vimal Pottai was a known character, but that he went by a number of names. He worked in some capacity for the Communist Party of India—Maoist. In the old days they called themselves the PWG, People's War Group, making trouble for the government with guerilla stuff borrowed from Mao's assaults on the Nationalists and Ho Chi Minh's assaults on the Americans.

"How do you know so much?"

"Don't you ever read Arundhati Roy?"

"*The God of Small Things*? Sure."

"No," she said, "not *The God of Small Things*."

The hardcore Maoists, she said, southwest of there in the forested Dandakaranya region, down in Chhattisgarh, had set up like an alternative system of government that encompassed thousands of villages and probably millions of people. They had cadres, different wings and systems of administration, and were in a protracted battle with the national and state governments. People were being shot, tortured, and raped all the time—mostly, according to Pradeep, the Maoists, although they had scored some major victories against official forces in recent years. They had a rising guerilla army that slept in moveable camps, traveled by night far from roads, and were heavily armed.

Petra didn't say all this at the time, of course; I'm paraphrasing, filling in some things I learned later, but that was the gist of what's important to know.

There in the waning light that evening she was teasing and evasive, playing up the fact that she had information I didn't, even though it was clear she only knew these things in pieces, didn't understand the contexts and textures. A name here and there, the thrilling words "Maoist," forests, bombs—she deployed them with an affected knowingness, as though they were secrets only a true cosmopolitan could grasp.

"You haven't heard of any of this?" she said, amazed.

She went on to say "Maoists" again, to say "industrialization," "colonialism," and "tribal peoples," gave me snatches of narratives she had been told or had overheard.

Later, from Audra, I fit these pieces together: apparently the oldschool "Maoists" in the area had drawn their ranks from tribal peoples, those who had never quite been integrated into the modern Indian state. They had their own distinctive cultures and systems of rule, and at first it was easy enough for the state to ignore them, as they lived in relatively inaccessible forests and hills. But as India industrialized, native geologists and engineers confirmed British suspicions about the natural wealth in these areas, and regional power brokers began to strike deals with tribal leaders, deals that either enriched a very few or else cut out the local populations entirely. So as the state governments awarded contracts to corporations to build city-sized mining operations or hydroelectric dams, these tribal peoples were pushed out of what Petra called their "ancestral lands," and the Maoists subsequently grew more and more influential as they organized and represented not only the tribal peoples but anyone, Hindu, Buddhist, or otherwise, who felt they were being disenfranchised by the state. As a consequence, in the last twenty years they had been launching increasingly sophisticated guerilla attacks against the government. The prime minister called them India's number one security threat.

As far as Petra knew, this Vimal Pottai character was a Maoist. They'd been trying to build a mine around there and the Maoists had opposed it. Their very own Bokaro Steel City, the state had said—but ordinary people, they didn't want it and these guys in tinted SUVs kept coming around to survey things, and people were getting scared that they'd be run off their land, that they'd become indentured to MK Technologies or someone else.

Petra knew parts of this story from Pradeep, whose father was high up in the defense part of their Maoist "government" or whatever it was—this was "down in Chhattisgarh," she repeated—and she knew that Pradeep's dad had been riding him to join the cause, but for all his muscles, Pradeep just couldn't stomach it. According to Pradeep, Vimal Pottai was there to more or less poll the village, to test the waters and see if people were open to having the Maoists establish a real presence. Mainly the Maoists were in Chhattisgarh and Jharkhand, but people here were getting desperate too.

"What about your mother?"

"Probably," she shrugged, "from their point of view Mom is the enemy."

8.

OVER THE NEXT days I gradually found myself more at ease around Petra, figured out how to navigate her temper, and as we spent time together, the waifish stranger who talked like a forty-year-old seemed to be lowering her guard, revealing herself in greater complexity and contradiction.

She had a thousand interests, and spent those days showing them off to me. She was infatuated, for instance, with the plant life within walking or biking distance of the house, and had devoted several months to harvesting samples and then cataloguing them. This project had been inspired by another book she had discovered on some dusty shelf, *Flora of British India*, by J.D. Hooker. She took me to an otherwise unused bedroom, furnished only with an expansive table covered with pressed and drying leaves, stems, and petals.

"This book is so weird," she said, pointing to *Flora of British India* open on an inclined stand like a forbidding dictionary. "800 pages and not a single drawing. So it's hard to be sure if you have the right specimen. This is one I found the other day." She held out four leaves on a stem, dark green and brittle.

"I believe this is *Cryptocarya wightiana*," she went on, pronouncing the name slowly. Then she read from something she had copied on an index card: "The book says 'softly downy, leaves pinnate, sepals broadly ovate. A large woody climber, leaflets usually five, two inches, orbicular, or ovate-cordate, three to five lobed, densely villous and brown below, at length glabrate above.' OK, so first I looked up half those words, but who writes a book about identifying plants and doesn't include any drawings? Mom says it makes it more of a challenge. And it keeps me occupied and out of trouble. Anyway, I believe this is *Cryptocarya wightiana*, but I'm not positive. A lot of plants look alike."

She had dozens of "specimens" arranged across the table, each labeled with an index card on which she had neatly copied the scientific name and the identifying characteristics according to Hooker.

This seemed to me a deadly hobby, tedious and ultimately pointless, but I bent down to inspect the specimens anyway, doing my best to mimic her enthusiasm. She began pointing out all the minute aspects of the leaves or petals that she had used to identify them in Hooker's terms, and I wondered if it all wasn't evidence of some manic compulsion. The attention to detail was fierce—especially for a thirteen-year-old—but somehow misguided. And there was no way of knowing if the sorting and cataloguing was finally accurate.

Still, I tried to encourage her, said that she was a budding botanist (pun intended). "Who knows," I said, "you might discover a previously unknown flower, and you can name it after yourself."

"It's just something to pass the time," she said. "I'm thinking of getting into butterflies."

—

She took me around the back of the property, past some vines and elephant ears fanning over a bumpy brick path, to a falling-down gardener's shed, partly shaded by a coral tree in flame.

She stopped at the door as the birds in the tree chirped and whistled busily.

"You like cats," she said, half question, half statement.

"I have four, but no."

"I knew that," she said.

"Did you? Did I tell you that?"

She pushed open the door with a flourish. I had expected a shack full of cats hanging off ledges and bursting from baskets like in some children's picture book, but no life at all was apparent in the slice of light from the doorway.

"Welcome to my cat sanctuary," she said, like Richard Attenborough in *Jurassic Park*.

The cat sanctuary turned out to be damp and pungent, lined with wooden crates mounded with frayed blankets, water bowls, and cracked dishes with dried remnants of chicken or tuna.

"Quite an operation," I said. "But where are the cats?"

She shot me a conspiratorial smile and took a can of tuna from a shelf otherwise crowded with trowels and claw-like hand tillers. Plunging an old-fashioned opener into the top of the can, she made a clicking noise with her tongue, twisting the handle. Within seconds two scrawny tabbies poked their heads through a ragged hole cut in a back wall. Spotting me they froze, two heads and four huge eyes framed in shadow, but when Petra finished opening the tuna with a metallic snap, they decided I was an acceptable risk and squeezed themselves all the way inside, attacking the slippery pile she plopped onto a dish.

She stroked their spines as they wolfed down the tuna with sputter-breaths. "This is Elizabeth and Darcy," she said. "But they're siblings. There's eight or nine more around, not all related we think, but they won't come in when we're here. Or, they might with just me, but not with a stranger."

"At dawn," I said, "the homeless cat too … cries for love."

She looked up at me. "Huh?"

"An old Japanese haiku," I said, thinking of Angie.

"That's good," she said, "that's good," and it was unclear if she was talking to me or the cats, as she was now kneeling over them as they devoured the food, watching them intently as they purred and put their whole bodies into finishing the tuna, coating their noses and whiskers in oil.

—

When I had snooped in Petra's room in Lamu, her tastes had seemed to me oddly middle-aged, and she confirmed this sense again in those days in Bihar, making me question if it were a consequence of being sequestered with Audra, sequestered with Margit. Having moved on from her meltdown on my first night there, in the evenings she would insist on "calm" games of Scrabble or canasta. When Audra would come back from wherever she had gone, she would pour furtive vodka waters and take in Petra's detailed recounting of the day's events with bemusement, assenting to Scrabble if Petra agreed to "contain" herself.

In addition to Scrabble and canasta, Petra loved other old person games like cribbage and hearts; she adored artichokes, butter cookies, and wearing gloves in colder climates; she resented having to sew anything for herself, not because of "entitlement," she claimed, but because elbow holes and the like were marks of comfort that needn't be fixed; she loved vinyl records from the Seventies, Joni Mitchell and Leonard Cohen, which I already knew, and she would quiz me about them coyly.

"You know about The Original Caste?" she asked me. "They're from Alberta, Canada, like Joni. 'One Tin Soldier' and 'Mr. Monday'? So sad."

In some ways, she proved to be a study in contradictions: worldly but immature, open-hearted but mendacious, self-assured but hungry for approval. She ate with reckless gusto, spilling juice and slopping gravies onto the table, incensed when her mother insisted she wipe up after herself.

"It's not Rakesh's job to follow you around with a sponge," Audra would say.

"*Actually,*" Petra would mutter under her breath.

And yet she was meticulous with her index cards, had freaked out when I put one back in the wrong place according to her system. She had a neat wall of maps, stuck with green pins indicating places she'd been, blue pins places she wanted to go next, pink pins places she'd lived. Pennsylvania was inexplicably stuck with blue. To animals she was exceedingly tender, was constantly concerned about the welfare of the cats, and would shoo flies and other winged insects out windows instead of swatting them, would transport beetles out to the back patio before her mother could see them and have them exterminated.

—

Her heart would break over the syrupy anti-war fable "One Tin Soldier," and yet one morning she startled me by appearing in the kitchen with a rifle slung over her back.

I had just begun boiling water and she materialized behind me, nonchalantly taking out a box of muesli and waiting for me to comment on the gun. It was brown and ancient-looking, long enough that it hung down to the backs of her knees.

"You've got a little something on your back," I said, playing along.

She turned to eye me slyly. "Oh, this ole thaang?" she said in her Southern coquette drawl. "But seriously"—switching to normal register—"I thought maybe you might want to do some target shooting?"

"That's a legitimate working gun? Your mom lets you do this?" I was trying to not show that the rifle had rattled me, which is of course what she had intended.

"We don't like guns in this house," she said. "But my mom says they're an inevitable part of the modern world, so it's better to know how to use them, just in case."

"Audra said that?"

"Don't worry, we didn't buy this one or anything. I found it on the third floor and a friend of mom's cleaned it up and showed me how to use it. Supposedly it's pretty old but you can still get the cartridges for them. I have a box." She wiggled the rifle around to her front and hitched it off her shoulder to present it to me.

It had enough heft that I wondered how she could fire it at all, and who was this "friend"? It looked to me like how I pictured a Martini or Enfield or one of those other rifles Kipling describes in his India stories. I was nearly as surprised that you could still find ammunition for such a weapon as I was that Audra had apparently let her thirteen-year-old handle it unsupervised. It brought to mind some pictures Angie had once shown me by the Dutch photographer An-Sofie Kesteleyn, portraits of American five- and six-year-olds posing with their first "practice" rifles. These were girls half Petra's age, staring imperiously at the camera with pink kid-sized rifles in pink Disneyfied bedrooms, brandishing their guns like commandos, and Angie had pointed out the obvious: "This is so fucked up on so many levels."

Naturally, I had agreed with Angie, but at that moment thought fleetingly that perhaps there was more cause for gun knowledge out in remotest Bihar than there was in the suburbs of Texas and Kentucky. Or not.

Petra was matter of fact about it, rubbing the rifle's pock-marked stock and then easing the whole thing back over her shoulder. Maybe my shock was evident because she saw something on my face and explained that she was only allowed to shoot with an adult present. "You're an adult," she said. "You're present. So let's go."

The kettle wailed and I shook my head.

After breakfast I still went along as she took me down a new path behind the house, this one winding around to a small and thickly-shrubbed box canyon, at the end of which was set up a kind of scarecrow as target. An old oak desk, water-stained and warped, stood some yards out from the target, and Petra laid the rifle on it and began unloading various accouterments from her bag: the box of cartridges, yellow safety glasses, gray earmuffs looking like vintage hi-fi headphones.

She inspected the gun like she was born again hard in *Full Metal Jacket*, then loaded a round.

"Eyes and ears," she said, and put on the glasses and earmuffs.

I followed suit, and watched as she bent down over the desk, all elbows and concentration as she sighted the rifle, resting it on the wood because it must have indeed been too heavy to otherwise manage. She squinted and hunkered, adjusting her stance, pressing the butt against her shoulder, blowing a strand of hair out of her eyes. As the adult present, I looked on in a supervisory capacity, but didn't really know what to be watching for, in terms of safety.

There was a suspended moment, no breeze in the canyon, all birds and woodland things gone since we'd approached, and she counted down slowly from three, her attention focused utterly on the rifle and the distant bloated scarecrow—suddenly a crack and puff of smoke, and she was knocked back a little.

"Got it!" she cried, and indeed there was a tiny tendril of smoke wafting from the scarecrow's burlap chest.

It was a surreal scene, and I was unsure how I felt about it, how I was supposed to feel about it. I knew, abstractly, that it was advisable to encourage her interests, as the so-called grown-up, to ensure she wasn't pointing a loaded gun at people, that she had taken the appropriate safety precautions.

She was grinning at me, delighted by her marksmanship, even as I felt hollow and fraught.

"Wow," I said with as much enthusiasm as I could muster. "Annie Oakley."

"Your turn!" she said. She loaded the rifle again then patted the barrel. "Ever handle a gun before?"

"As a matter of fact, I have," I said, recalling Simeon and the way I had defended his grass reserves against the rustlers. That had been my first time holding a gun, of course, but I didn't let on because Americans, real men in particular, were assumed to be fluent in the language of firearms.

She gave me a basic lesson anyway, showing me how to center the bead on the end of the barrel between a fork closer in, explaining how I should breathe and exhale slowly as I pulled the trigger and I began to wonder who had coached her in these matters.

When I was ready she stood back and counted me down from three. I was hunched inelegantly, too tall for the desk, but not wanting to hold the rifle upright either, in case it somehow jumped from my hands when I fired. And so I was bent and contorted, my lower back wrenched as she got to one and I closed my eyes and pulled the trigger with a bang and a punch in the shoulder, a spasm throughout my torso. I opened my eyes and a burnt smoke haze hung over the desk.

"Oh man," she said, shielding her eyes with a hand at the forehead, scrutinizing the target. "Not even close!"

Usually there was time in the evenings for me to open the laptop and check back with my world. I couldn't wait to tell Angie about the rifle, the fact of my shooting a gun being the kind of news she would find horrifying but fascinating. She had sent me a lengthy email poetic in its attention to boring everyday details that I never would have noticed: she described cats perched side-by-side on the couch, "sleeping at the wall," a thunderstorm that had left "constellations" on the leaves and "subway maps" on her windshield, a matchstick on the sidewalk outside the coffeehouse, "defiant" in its persistence, even though it had been lit and discarded.

From such seemingly random observations, she went on, incongruously, to explain that there were four main holy sites in Buddhism: Lumbini, where Gautama was born; Bodh Gaya, where he became enlightened, Sarnath, where he "set the wheel in motion," and Kushinagar, where he passed into "pari-nirvana"—of these places, she wrote, Bodh Gaya was the most holy, the spot where he had figured out that what the Hindus thought of as consciousness, as a soul, was hardly the whole story.

The point of the lesson was that by Angie's reckoning Bodh Gaya was not far from where I was at that very moment. This was the place Mr. Kumar the rental car agent had mentioned, by far the main draw for foreigners flying into Patna.

"So you should find every excuse to go," Angie had written. "This is the most important pilgrimage site in Buddhism." Traveling there, she insisted, would help me "acquire merit"—and I was well aware that I needed all the merit I could get.

I wrote her back in a leisurely kind of way, trying to evoke the sights and smells of the house and its surroundings, telling her about the cat sanctuary and the botanical "specimens." I set the scene of Petra turning up in the kitchen with the farcical Danny Dravot rifle over her shoulder, wanting to show me what a crack shot she was, daring me to clutch my pearls in some pretentious meltdown. I mentioned the kettle and the muesli, because Angie appreciated details like that, and suddenly I was missing her presence acutely, missing her example. As I recounted how I had half-heartedly acknowledged the technical proficiency of Petra's shooting, I knew that probably Angie would wonder why I hadn't pointed out the travesty of the scene itself, a child with a gun, the fiction that such skills were necessary and normal, like the haunted children in those Kesteleyn photographs. I remembered that of those photographs she had also said something to the effect of, "We don't say: 'Welp, it's important to teach flame thrower safety early, so they can be responsible flame thrower owners later on. It's important to teach your kids real young proper bomb-handling etiquette, so that they learn to respect and appreciate bombs. Let's get cartoon Larry the Lark to help toddlers learn all about land mine safety, since definitely land mines will be around the house and we wouldn't want the kids experimenting with them without adults present.' Fucking demented." I sort of felt that way too, but for reasons not entirely clear to me, I hadn't said anything directly to Petra. I struggled to articulate my dereliction or cowardice to Angie, muddling my way through the last part of the letter.

Cubby had sent me a huge attachment that took a long time to load, and I was curious about what it could be; turned out it was a photograph of his kids lined up on a catamaran, wearing life preservers and chocolate smudges, and he had written something about my babysitting since I was now a pro with kids. Ignored it.

My sister assumed I was probably dead, "knowing me," or in jail, and demanded an update in a sarcastic sort of way that revealed the depth of her concern. I did quickly let her know I was among the living, mentioned Scrabble and cats but not guns, and asked how Chico was doing.

There was something from the Provost, a "friendly follow up" that I didn't click open. The heat of the computer was starting to burn in my lap, and I realized I couldn't bear to read anything from school, snapping the machine shut with a sigh.

—

Petra's less lethal interests included cooking, and one afternoon she banished Mrs. Krishnamurti, the house cook, from the kitchen, wanting to teach me how to make chapatti. The point seemed to be to show off her "native" knowledge, to prove that she had the skill-set to make the dish just as well as Mrs. Krishnamurti. Though this was unsettling in a different way than the gun, I felt it was better than target practice.

She rooted around in the pantry, knocking things over as she rummaged through boxes of Taj Mahal tea, bottles of Kissan tomato sauce, packets of Knorr soup mix and assorted other pre-packaged foods, eventually uncovering a tray-sized slab of marble, which she hauled out with histrionic huffing and puffing.

"Oof," she said, slamming it down on a butcher block. "That's the hardest part."

"I see that."

"Actually, it's very easy to make this, not that my mom ever learned."

She had torn into a paper container of gram flour, and I watched as she kneaded it into water on the marble, occasionally directing me to pour in a little oil or yogurt, and she took exquisite care, as though the universe and all its problems, cats, guns, taxonomies, Scrabble tournaments, had ceased to be important so that kneading was all there was, and she worked the blob slowly, saying that this was the key to making good chapatti, reminding me that her mother had never had the patience, that her mother was always "on the go."

She cocked her head in concentration, the tip of her tongue barely jutting out as she curled her unpainted lip, kneading as though meditating. She worked the dough, asking me to sprinkle a "smidge" more flour on the marble, and I wondered where she'd gotten that word.

Suddenly she turned to me, sensed me looking at her, and withdrew her tongue-tip reflexively, turning down her mouth and widening her eyes.

"What?" she said.

"Nothing."

"You're staring."

"Just studying your technique."

She looked down, a modest smile breaking across her face, one of those secret expressions only decipherable in nanoseconds. But I caught it before it flitted away.

"So what *is* your opinion about boarding schools," she asked, rolling the dough into little balls.

"I often wonder how I would've turned out had I gone to fancy private schools."

"Yeah, but what about *boarding* school? Mom just wants to ship me off to Switzerland and let me be raised by strangers. Don't you think that's just *wrong*? That she's like giving up her parental duties?"

"Think of the education you'll get. You'll probably hang out with princesses."

"That's my point," she said. "And I'm just supposed to move away to some whole other country? *By myself?* What if I hate it?"

From what I had observed, and it was a limited sample, she seemed like an independent person, and so could fit in anywhere. I told her this.

"But we've always been together," she said. "No matter what. Mom says she needs me to stay grounded. Now all of the sudden she's obsessed with sending me away to boarding school? Who's gonna keep her grounded?"

I knew I had to be careful. I watched her roll the dough and it dawned on me all at once, although it was obvious, that growing up, Petra had had no stable neighborhood, no bedroom or even constant bed, that every milestone like tonsillitis required flights to other smoggy cities, that to even have a friend like Cubby, who could name all my fads and crushes year by year, decade by decade, was for her an impossibility, that her mother had to be these things for her across time and space. She was, after all, a child, Audra's child, and it seemed to me that she needed to cling to that a while longer, even if she herself probably wouldn't admit it.

Whatever I said would have been insufficient, but I assured her, clichédly, that Audra would never abandon her, that her mother was only doing what she thought best.

"It's tricky," I said. "Put yourself in your mom's shoes."

"What about *my* shoes?"

I promised I would speak to Audra about it, try to get a better understanding of her reasoning.

Petra had flattened out her dough balls and arranged them on a smooth-planed board. She worked them in silence for several minutes, taking great care with each one.

"All right," she said finally. "You do that. You 'speak' to Mom, and let me know how it goes. Now come on, we're going to fry this chapatti over a real fire."

We cooked them on a brazier out back, and Rakesh kept the fire going until early evening, burning hunks of charcoal and raking them until they glowed orange and ashy. When she got home, Audra announced that she was going to grill some of her Halal steaks, that Rakesh had spent the afternoon maintaining the fire for this purpose, but at this announcement he retreated to the bowels of the house. Audra liked her steaks bloody while Petra demanded a well-done puck, was frustrated that her chapatti had no relationship to the slabs of meat and foiled potatoes her mother was preparing.

After the meal Petra seemed sullen, distracted, but suggested a game of cut-throat canasta, which seemed a kind of masochism on her part because if anybody but her racked up points, especially Audra, she would become flame-cheeked and even more withdrawn, her mother tense and ready to strike should any nasty remarks escape her lips. When Petra herself would score, she would gloat and Audra would raise an eyebrow and midway through, Petra couldn't contain her annoyance any longer, doodling graphite-dark storm clouds on the score pad.

"Let's finish this up tomorrow," Petra said. "There's a few things I need to take care of."

"Wise call, kiddo," Audra said, irritated.

Petra sulked upstairs, Audra left her largely untouched chapatti on a side plate, and beckoned me into the library, where she once again broke into the vodka.

"That child," she sighed, settling into a wing chair.

"Must be hard," I said.

"You have no idea."

She sipped her drink and went on to describe the first time she had brought Petra outside of Europe, when they had lived for three months in Anuradhapura, Sri Lanka.

This was late summer 2006, making Petra just six, and it was sweltering hot, much more humid than anything on this latitude, and on their second day they'd gone to the market in New Town to hunt down electric fans. It was Audra's first assignment in that part of the world and she didn't really know what she was doing, had allowed themselves to be booked at a third-rate hotel with weak air con, and poor Petra had tossed and baked all night, feverish and bug-bitten.

Audra recalled the human density of that market, crowded and closed-in, aisle after aisle of cinder block and rusting metal, people in stalls or selling things spread out on cast-off pallets or plastic sheets. She held Petra firmly, winding deep into the market, and finally after much searching located someone selling electric fans, and as they bargained, she suspected he was trying to swindle her, so made him demonstrate that each fan was in working order, which meant that he had to negotiate with the guy in the next stall over since his own outlet was broken. Audra had bent in to test the settings on the fans, and in that fraction of a second it took to do so, Petra had disappeared.

"You will never know the sheer panic a parent feels at that moment," Audra said.

She called Petra's name, twisting through the aisles, asking the women selling pot metal tableware had they seen a little girl, my daughter, and the women frowned, not really understanding, and Audra ran through the aisles and alleys, fearing Petra injured or kidnapped, sold into the sex trade; these are the thoughts, she said, that however irrational flash through your mind. She was screaming for Petra, terrified, accosting people who looked like they might speak English until she turned a corner, onto a slight open space, and there was Petra sitting on an edge of plastic used to display an array of carved wooden parrots, serenely eating a wedge of watermelon. She said hiya Mom, could she get one of those parrots? At moments like that, Audra said, she was overcome with relief, of course, but she also wanted to strangle her for doing that, and pulled her up by the wrist, breathing don't ever run off like that again and where did you get that watermelon, Petra saying ow, ow, that lady gave it to me.

"That was my experience in places like that," said Audra. "Being simultaneously terrified and enraged because she didn't know what she was doing, how to be careful."

I said I was surprised she'd brought Petra there in the first place.

"Anuradhapura? It's as safe as anywhere. I'm talking about wandering off and that terror that I'd lost her, that could happen in San Francisco."

"What were you doing in Sri Lanka?"

"Taking the temperature of foremen and plant managers. Rendering significant advice. I was there, essentially, because the month before in Kebithigollewa, the LTTE had set off a claymore underneath a bus, killing like sixty people on their way to a funeral. Only the latest in the campaign they were doing that year. Makes people nervous. Who's going to invest in infrastructure when you have these guys running around in suicide vests? They invented them, by the way."

"A great environment for a six-year-old," I said, almost to myself.

She looked at me steadily. "You're not questioning my judgment as a parent?"

"Who, me? Never."

"The feelings you have at a moment like that, they would be the same in Frankfurt or Athens or wherever. This is what I'm saying. The platitude is: what's more dangerous, south side Chicago or Anuradhapura? But it's true. Being in a market in a foreign place makes it more stressful, sure, but in a general, global sense, Sri Lanka was as safe as anywhere in the States. Statistically, I'm saying. I never brought her to truly unstable places. Sudan, for instance. I've been there many times, two week stretches, but that was back when we had a nanny."

"Who is the LTTE?" I asked.

"Was. The ole Tamil Tigers. They were one of these separatist groups made up of minority Tamils who were pissed off about Sinhalese exclusions. This is what happens in independent states after the old colonial masters leave. Then it becomes a proxy war between better powers."

"Was it like the Maoists here?" I asked. A couple of nights before, we had only briefly discussed the meal with Vimal Pottai, and Audra had been cagey about it; "Petra only *thinks* she knows everything," she had said.

"The Tigers," she said, "were no joke: they assassinated Rajiv Gandhi. They wanted to set up a completely new, Tamil-run country in northern Sri Lanka. And they almost did it, too. There were talks in the early 2000s, but by the time I was there, they had broken down, obviously, and the Sri Lankan military finally just blitzed the shit out of them."

"It's your job to know this?"

"It's my job to know that these guys are all full of shit, that they always claim to be about the oppressed minority masses, but in the end, they're all about money. Or money and power, same thing. And they bide their time, believe me. It was the same deal in Ayacucho in '09, when the SL killed a bunch of people way the fuck out in Huancavelica. For a decade the Peruvian government had been claiming the SL was dead and buried, I mean they were building TRC museums and everything in Lima. But the SL was just waiting, recruiting."

"Petra said something about Vimal thinking you were the enemy," I said.

"Look, I'm sure he thinks we're upsetting his apple cart by bringing industry to the region. The Naxals are just pissed because if it were up to them, they'd control the entire bauxite supply chain from here to China."

I realized she was buzzed, as was I, and her knowledge of guerilla factions was perversely turning me on. I wanted to press her. "Does he have a point? Vimal."

"A *point*? What do you mean *a point*? Al-Shabaab has a point. The Shining Path had a point. I'm sure if you asked him Osama bin Laden had a point. It doesn't mean they aren't batshit crazy. They don't engage rationally, these actors, with the world."

I reached for the vodka bottle, suddenly remembering that I'd promised Petra I would check in about the boarding school question. I topped off our drinks, and said that I understood what she was saying, but that there seemed to be a difference between fundamentalist ideology and people working for their fair share of capital.

"Ideology," she said. "It's all *ideology*. You think when the Naxals tricked seventy-plus military grunts—these are kids from the slums, by the way—into the woods in Chhattisgarh, only to gun them down, really slaughter them, you think that isn't ideology?"

"Sure, but."

"People are being brought opportunity, that's it. If they don't want to participate, that's up to them, isn't it? If they think they're better off bundling fucking tendu leaves from 5:00 in the morning and flipping them for nothing, only to do it all over again week after week, well, that's just because they're ignorant."

It was quiet for a moment, except for the clink of ice.

"Can I ask you something?" I said.

"Shoot."

I took another gulp and brought up boarding school.

She stared at the empty fireplace, changing gears in her mind, sipping.

"It's like being in that hotel in *The Shining* sometimes, the Overlook? Except that you know you're not hallucinating or being fucked with by ghosts. No, it's your own daughter who's decided to deliberately push all your buttons, just to see what will happen, like an experiment. But it's not like you can go to yoga or send her to a friend's house for a break. Oh no. You're snowed in together, circling the same hallways, and sometimes you sympathize not with Olive Oyl and the kid, but with Jack Nicholson, I mean you can sort of see where he's coming from with the axe."

As she was saying all this, speaking almost to herself, lost slightly in the vodka, I watched her, somewhat lost in the vodka myself, not really listening but unexpectedly fascinated with her anew. She tucked a strand of hair behind her ear, a simple stirring act that brought me back to the St. Francis and Guerneville, to conversations over plates at dimly-lit Aziza, Zombies at the Tonga Room. I drank loosely and observed parts of her body moving in the chair, the light fabric stretched over her thighs and breasts.

"The Overlook," I repeated.

She smirked at me ambiguously, crossing her legs again, the fabric whispering.

"I'm not saying literally," she went on. "I'm not quite at homicide, but I'm making a point. You only get to want to take out your own kid if you're the one who's been doing all the work day by day. *You* couldn't want to axe her, for instance. This boarding school thing, it's not a sudden interest. It's been my general plan that once she reached a certain age, she would go to a proper school. Some of the international schools are fine, but I certainly don't see any here or in Lamu, and who knows where I'll be in six months or a year. You're a professor, you know as well as anyone how important an education is. It makes you who you are. If I get a little breathing room in the bargain, I get a little breathing room."

I started to imagine quitting my job, fleeing Pennsylvania, moving to wherever Audra was and creating a family with her and Petra. She arched her back and it stretched the fabric tighter across her chest. What if I were in the picture, suddenly, magically, and Audra didn't feel the need to send Petra away because it would be like a proper nuclear family-type situation and we wouldn't have to worry about money and could buy a cottage in the Cotswolds where I could read and write and Petra would be near Oxbridge—or else an airy house on California Street, high on the hill, San Francisco at our feet, Petra could go to Stanford or Berkeley and Audra would be lithe and glamorous in a black shift and Cartier bangles and it would be 1999 until we died.

I forced myself up, somewhat abruptly, and refilled our drinks, brushing her hand as I did so. She ignored that or didn't notice, and I flopped back down in my chair.

"What if she thinks you abandoned her? What if it's better to stay together?"

"I wouldn't call a hundred grand a year abandonment," she said, drinking.

"Just imagine if you quit this life and had a normal house, a normal home, I mean. It's not like you need the money, I'm guessing."

She looked at me quizzically, amused, and I couldn't tell if the look was flirtatious. "But this is what I do," she said, as though puzzled by the suggestion.

I considered her eyes and her toenails and the milky expanse of her forearm and the graceful curve of her philtrum, which may or may not have had the slightest bead of perspiration on it, or it could have been vodka, and I swigged again and pushed myself up, taking two plodding steps over and then swung my face right near hers, our lips nearly touching, and I could feel my heart surging, felt her breath on my face.

She didn't lean away for seconds; I didn't lean away.

Finally she did touch my cheek, her fingers cool and wet from the sweating drink—like an electric shock, a bad one, I was back upright again.

She already seemed focused on something else. I fell back into the chair, and she stood. "Will, Will, Will," she sighed.

"Audra-"

"-look at this shit!" she said suddenly, waving a stiff hand over the binders and paperwork stacked on the desk. "It's never ending. I need to go to bed."

"Audra," I said.

She set her drink on the desk, shaking her head. "I need to go to bed," she said again, gave me one last look, and then left me to finish my own drink alone.

—

Sitting on the edge of my mattress in the morning, I was panicked and ashamed, letting my chin sink into my chest, breathing. Never had I been so glad about not sleeping with someone. I unfolded Angie's Valentine and examined it a while, thinking that I needed to get a handle on my drinking. Again I was dehydrated, felt destroyed, and started to the kitchen, where the water cooler was.

But as soon as I opened my door, I could hear turmoil downstairs, urgent male voices, Audra shouting.

This is the part where the story goes off the rails.

—

The commotion was coming from the library, and at the doorway there I saw Audra arguing with two identical-looking men: black mustaches, cheap synthetic blazers, walkies on belt clips. They seemed surprised to see me appear in the hall, touched their hips where holsters might have hung beneath their blazers, and Audra's face was red and puffy as though she'd been crying. When I went in to investigate, one of the men jerked defensively and demanded I identify myself.

"Oh," said Audra, her breathing labored and uneven. "Long story."

My temples were pulsating, I was slow to process, and waited to be introduced.

Instead Audra went around to the desk and found a packet of Kleenex in a drawer and blew her nose. Her glass from the night before stood unfinished near the binders.

One of the men approached me, extended his hand, and explained he was Nagur Garg and the other was his partner, Sunir Naik.

"We work together," said Audra from behind the desk, blowing again. "These are my local guys. Will," she said to them, "is Petra's ... father."

This information was the jigsaw piece that fit everything together for them, and they both let out exhales of recognition.

"You have our deepest sympathies," said Nagur.

"What sympathies?" I asked Audra. "And where *is* Petra?"

A wet pause and listless glance over her maps and binders. "Petra's gone," she said.

"Gone? What do you mean, *gone?* Gone where?" My head was cracking in half.

She looked like she was about to lose it again, and pulled a fresh tissue from her packet. "Nagur," she said, "show him."

Nagur braced solemnly, and fished a piece of paper from his breast pocket and handed it to me. In deeply pressed block lettering, it read:

> Ms. Wester. In retaliation for your incursion into this area, where you do not belong and about which you have no understanding, we have taken your daughter, Miss Petra, and her fate is now yours to decide. We will allow you one week to cease your exploratory operations and provide a notarized statement from MK Technologies guaranteeing that they will no longer pursue mining operations in this district. Once our legal team has approved the document and you and your gang have vacated the area, including Woodburn House, we will return your daughter to you.

I was prickly hot and confused. "This was the Maoists?"

"That would be the indication," Audra said. She picked up the letter opener and contemplated it for a moment. "It doesn't make sense, though. It's not their style."

But Nagur said it *was* their style, that they'd been kidnapping collectors in Odisha, Chhattisgarh, Jharkhand.

"These filth do not care for innocents," he said with disgust. "They are ruthless." As he said this last part, he caught himself and apologized.

"But do they ransom them?" said Audra, almost to herself. "Or just kill them, to make examples?"

Probably I was in a state of shock since I wasn't reacting with the outpouring of electric concern that I myself would have expected—instead I felt anesthetized or as though I'd come up from underwater and my ears were clogged, my eyes bleary, only slowly appreciating the full weight of what was being said.

Images of Petra's face flashed through my mind's eye: her big-toothed smile as she flung a dirt clod at me on the creek bank, her theatrically-narrowed eyes and pursed lips when she was winning in canasta, her outsized look of horror when she noticed the peeling sunburn on my neck. I pictured her, blindfolded and bound, in an airless hut somewhere, being spooned gruel, deprived of water and forced to sleep with rats scurrying around on their bellies.

How? Why? What was happening? I said something along these lines.

"There is no 'why' with these people," said Sunir. "They are fanatics."

"She was gone when I came down this morning," said Audra. "Rakesh thought to get eggs, but then a boy showed up with this note. God, you were right. I should never have put her in this position. This is my fault."

"This is not Dantewanda," said Nagur. "This isn't your doing. It is new tactics for these dogs."

I went over behind the desk and put my hand on her shoulder, and she seized it, for a moment in no sort of control at all.

She was babbling what anyone would have babbled, doubting her maternal fitness, blaming herself, regretting the remarks about axing Petra in a bathroom.

"Shall I make the call?" said Nagur to me.

I looked at him like: You're asking me?

"To the police commissioner," he said. "He can enlist the IPS, the NSG. We need swift action, a direct assault on any camps here."

"Do we know where the camps are?" asked Audra wearily. "If they are?"

"We must have full military presence in the district," Nagur went on. "Eradicate the infestation and ensure that they do not spread successfully into Bihar."

"Evidently that has already happened," she said.

I was reminded of Vimal Pottai, that he was purportedly a Maoist, that he was Amrita's cousin and so maybe we should go find her. I said this aloud.

"This is only one of many names," said Nagur.

"How much do you really know about this Amrita?" asked Sunir.

"This is an idea," said Audra, her features tightening. She instructed Nagur to hold off on contacting the authorities for the time being because she didn't want to spook them into doing something that couldn't be undone.

She was transforming into problem-solving mode, her specialty, and I knew she was resolving to handle the matter with cold sobriety. She looked at the photograph on her desk, then turned to me.

"Will," she said, crumpling a tissue, "let's you and I take Nagur and pay a visit to Amrita and see what we can see."

—

Within the half-hour we were at the Bela District Female Enterprise Co-Operative, where everything was just as it had been when I had visited there days before with Petra: children were chasing the ball she had gifted them, the sun burned on, unconcerned, and we found Amrita inside, half her face obscured by those huge glasses, bent over a mat.

Audra was remarkably calm as she paraphrased the note for Amrita, Nagur translating, her attitude of cool self-discipline familiar to me. Once Amrita understood what Audra was asking, that Petra, who had hung around the workshop flipping bottle caps into metal trays more mornings than Amrita could count, had been taken, disappeared, she broke down utterly, speed-talking about something Nagur lagged in translating.

Nagur said finally that she didn't know anything, but he concluded that it must have been Vimal and his cadre, and it was unclear if Amrita had said this, or if it was Nagur's conjecture.

Amrita took Audra's hands in hers, kissing them wildly, frantic, saying something that came translated as: *How could they do this to a child they know?*

She had no other information, she swore.

Audra remained steady through this, and asked Amrita again if she had any information at all because she would prefer to leave the authorities out of it, that she just wanted her daughter back, without "provoking bloodshed."

Amrita reiterated that she didn't know anything specific, but that she would do whatever she could to help.

"She says," Nagur translated, "that if this is true, and if they discover she is helping you, they—well, it will not be very good for her."

—

Things developed erratically. Amrita had refused to be seen in town with us, but at her suggestion we went to speak with Pradeep, who was nowhere to be found, and none of the people who had shops and stalls in view of the clinic had seen him since the night before. Some women who had been in a remote part of the forest harvesting leaves just after sunrise thought they had seen three men, accompanied by what looked to be a white woman, walking off in the distance, on the way to the hills, but who could be sure?

Nagur advised caution, said that it was impossible to tell who might harbor secret "Naxal sympathies." We asked around anyway, but people were tight-lipped, wagging their fingers dismissively: who knew?

—

By the time we got back to the house, we discovered that Sunir had called the police commissioner despite Audra's instructions, and she had lurched to physically attack him, but Nagur and I managed to restrain her.

"If she dies," she screamed, momentarily wild-eyed, "her blood will be on your hands!"

"Nobody is going to die," Sunir said calmly. "Nothing will be done until we give him the word."

Audra settled down, had a glass of water in a wing chair, looked up at him and said she was beginning to seriously question his judgment.

After those first hours of investigatory flurry, there was a lull, a cloud over the house. Back at the co-op, Amrita had promised she would look into things in her own way, but that it would take time, so we waited. Audra made all the calls she could, then looked as if her soul had been sucked from her body. I slumped in a chair, useless as a vestigial organ, non-functioning but still somehow in the way. When nervous energy made sitting in a chair unbearable, I paced around the library, examining the spines of the few books left horizontal on the otherwise empty shelves, tracing my fingers through dust, shuttling to a window, then back to the chairs, where Audra had collapsed, and I noticed for the first time the bloom of gray in the part on the top of her head, visible as she rolled her shoulders and rubbed the bridge of her nose. Rakesh brought a light meal into the library at tea time, but only Sunir ate, oblivious to Audra's pale death stare.

At one point, Mrs. Krishnamurti, who had been crying all day, tapped softly on the door frame, came in ring-eyed and splotchy, embraced Audra, nodded at me, and floated away in silence.

Nagur and Sunir huddled in a far corner, debating something amongst themselves.

Audra remained in a wing chair for a long time, staring at the lifeless fireplace. The atmosphere was tensed like a war room as we all felt that there was something to do, but that the time had not yet come to do it. I imagined infantry felt the same way before an invasion: nauseated, tremulous, awake on canvas cots, knowing that in the morning they would be ordered to charge other men, to kill or be killed. This thought led me naturally to recall the target shooting, which seemed like it might be relevant under the circumstances.

"The rifle," I said aloud, surprised by the sound of my own voice.

Everyone turned to look at me. "What rifle?" said Audra.

"The one we shot the scarecrow with. Where is it?"

Audra seemed only mildly interested in the whereabouts of the rifle, but to placate me dispatched Rakesh to ensure that it was locked in the cabinet where it was supposed to be. I waited those minutes as though a clue would return with Rakesh, but he came back to report that the rifle was indeed secured in the cabinet.

"That relic won't do much anyway," said Audra vaguely.

Late, around midnight, Rakesh ushered in a small boy, I think the same one Pradeep had referred to as country text messaging, and positioned him before Audra as though she were a monarch receiving supplicants.

"Tell him not to be scared," Audra said to Rakesh as the quaking boy cast around the room with bulging eyeballs.

After some coaxing, the boy recited a memorized message and Nagur and Sunir looked at each other with pensive brows. It seemed, Nagur translated, that because the commissioner had been contacted and the villagers harassed, terms had changed. They wanted to speak, in person, with the new mister who was working for the company. Not, they stressed, the missus, who they were certain could not be trusted.

They all turned to me, although I was slow to appreciate what was being said.

I was the new mister working for the company.

"They are wanting you to travel to their encampment," said Nagur. "For negotiation."

"But I don't know anything about anything," I said automatically.

"I gather they believe you were not truthful, that you are here on company business."

"You're not going anywhere," said Audra.

"I'll do it," piped some voice that wasn't mine, even though it came from within me.

Arguments volleyed back and forth, Audra declaring that she couldn't allow me to take the risk, that it wasn't my problem or responsibility, Nagur reminding everyone again that they were barbarians, savages, dogs, I dismissing their points instinctively, saying it was indeed my responsibility, and I would accept the consequences. It was the idish, irrational part of my being taking over, directing my motor functions and ability to speak, and it was like watching myself becoming assertive from afar.

Suddenly I was sweeping, decisive, embracing Audra and telling her to leave it all to me, pressing Nagur for the details on "the meet." He explained that the boy had described a spot, a place where there used to be a well, thirty or forty kilometers outside the village where I was to present myself at dawn, totally alone.

"Not so fast," said Audra quietly, looking wasted, as though she'd just vomited. "What exactly are you planning on doing once you get to this meet?"

"Get Petra back."

"But how? Walk me through it."

I realized of course that I had no idea, that in my inept zeal to rescue I could very easily be making things worse, doing more damage.

"OK," said Audra. "Let's take a step back and strategize."

It was the middle of the night, we had only a few hours to prepare—"by design," said Nagur grimly—but it was finally decided that when I got wherever they would take me I should tell the person in charge that Audra would meet any demand, that I was to say: *Ms. Wester is prepared to leave the district if her daughter is returned unharmed.*

"Say it to me," she said, and I said it to her.

Nobody had really slept. I tried to force down soup and biscuits and Audra was saying that "rationally" they *had* to return her, that it would make no logical sense to harm her if they thought their demands were being met. This was basic game theory.

"You really will leave?" I said.

She said she was going to ensure they didn't touch a hair on Petra's head.

—

By 4:30 a.m. we were bumping in Nagur's SUV across a barren field. "I do not like this," he kept saying. "Two hostages instead of one. This isn't sound."

I was startlingly calm. I think the adrenaline was actually suppressing any sort of fight-or-flight panic, and I passively observed my reflection in the dark glass as they continued to debate the wisdom of the move. *Ms. Wester is prepared to leave the district if her daughter is returned unharmed.*

After an hour, two hours (time meant something different), we stopped and climbed out. Still remote from dawn, it was as black as the night I had spent in the Alto, which then seemed a thousand centuries before, although it had only been four days.

We conferred in the headlights, instantly awash with insect swarms, Audra wincing, pained, telling me one last time I didn't have to do it, and I assuring her I did. Paranoid Nagur was staring off into nothingness with the idea that we were being watched at that very moment, were being sighted in night vision scopes, that he needed to pull the vehicle out of there.

I looked at Audra in the diffused light, wondering if it would be the last time I would ever see her, or anyone. There we were, stripped of all degrees and sports cars, credit scores and expense accounts being so far from relevant as to be laughable, my years of studying and posturing all flaked away as mosquitoes buzzed my ears, her hair pulled back and unwashed, eyes bloodshot, wearing the same drawstring pants and linen shirt horribly wrinkled even in the humidity, I un-creamed and oily, feeling not exhausted but numb. She studied me with a kind of admiration I had never before elicited from her, even when we were dating, and I thought that she was impressed or grateful because I was doing something she herself could not do, a new and chilling feeling since if there was one thing I thought about Audra, it was that she was capable of absolutely anything, managing the most hostile of investors, driving a manual in San Francisco, recovering a missing child.

Yet I was the one handling the doomsday situation, she staying back to worry. She hugged me for a long time. "You take care of yourself, kiddo."

"Ms. Wester is prepared to leave the district if her daughter is returned unharmed," I said.

Nagur came over and insisted that they did need to get going, and Audra found a small backpack in the SUV and said she'd thrown some waters and protein bars in it.

"Be careful," was the last thing she said to me.

As the SUV circled and drove off, I was left alone, insects still needling into my ears, the stars beginning to fade as the barest suggestions of light shone from the east.

What a peculiar situation.

Was it really happening?

At that moment, my life in Pennsylvania was evaporated—I had flashes of Angie and the cats, wondered a second about what would happen to the rental car if I were held hostage indefinitely.

Probably Angie would be fearless in this spot, would assume, as she always did, that things would be "all right in the end"—though she was also sure that "the end" wasn't the end of this particular life, but of innumerable lifetimes hence.

And yet—

Despite my general terror, I found myself experiencing a single-minded focus on what I was internally referring to as "the mission," and felt pumping through my system, like a poor mantra, the thought that Petra would be OK no matter what else happened.

I couldn't say how long I waited, but the sun had come up and was already warming to hot when I detected a blur in the distance, and as it grew closer all I could think about was that scene in *Lawrence of Arabia* when Peter O'Toole is stealing water from Omar Sharif's well in the middle of a vast arid desertscape, and he sights a lone camelback rider coming in from the shimmering horizon, everything clean, in cobalt and khaki.

In my case it was a lone motorcyclist coming toward me, the sky a hazy gray, everything brown, the drone of the approaching motor dampening the morning calls of the birds starting their days. A billowing dust plume trailed behind it.

I watched and waited, dry-mouthed and unsteady on my feet.

The motorcycle bumped right up to me, stopped, and the rider, a helmet-less man of about twenty or so, began speaking in what didn't even sound like Hindi, pointing at the pack at my feet, agitated, and I deduced that he wanted to inspect it. He grabbed it roughly, then finding only the waters and protein bars, shoved it back at me and demanded that I tie a piece of cloth around my eyes as a blindfold. At first I tried to explain that I had no idea where I was, that one tree looked the same as the next, but it was impossible to communicate through dumbshow gestures and he was jumpy and impatient.

I didn't want to press it, so I let him tie the cloth around my head. He walked me by the wrist to the back of the motorcycle, guiding my hands behind me to hold on to a greasy handle. Once he was satisfied that I was clamped on, my elbows jutting out behind me like unusable wings, we set off, and rode for a long time without stopping— thirty minutes? two hours?—I taking refuge in my mantra: *Ms. Wester is prepared to leave the district if her daughter is returned unharmed.* There really wasn't much else to think about except holding on.

When finally we did stop, my body was half-paralyzed, my bones rattled, my face covered in a fine layer of dust, which also gummed up my nostrils. I stood unsteadily, the engine reeking of burned oil, the driver commanding me again in some way I couldn't comprehend. He whipped off the blindfold, and the light was a shock as I realized I was being handed over to another person, this one a wiry man in olive drab fatigues and a rifle slung over his shoulder. His rifle was newer and more powerful than Petra's.

They conferred as I blinked around. It seemed I was in the foothills near some higher hills or mountains, where the trees and underbrush became considerably more dense than the other topographies I had so far encountered in India. We were high enough that I could look out behind us to see a huge desolate plain lacking any distinguishing landmarks. It reminded me of the edge from which Simeon had shown us the Great Rift Valley: going on seemingly forever, the curve of the earth discernable, no human-built structures of any kind, no roads, no people.

After those two had conducted their business, mainly a low-level argument, ignoring me, the one with the rifle poked me in the chest with two fingers, then indicated that I should follow him onto a thin trail leading into a forested slope. I expected to be bound or roughed up, but he just took off, assuming, I guessed, that there was nowhere for me to flee, and I followed him as best I could while the motorcyclist kicked on his engine and sputtered away.

The wiry man moved with expert speed through the terrain, although the footpath seemed to disappear as frequently as it was perceptible, and it was hard to keep up as he powered deeper into the forest, higher into the hills, which became after a time steeper, scree-covered and tough-going, thick at times with massive tree ferns. We picked our way over streams and mossy boulders, around vines, through fragrant, wanton undergrowth. Up a series of switchbacks, I could tell we were ascending fairly high into the mountains. It was impossible for me to gauge how long we had been hiking, but even in the gloom of the knitted canopies, I went through most of my water and ate two protein bars. My energetic captor, though, never stopped to rest, in fact had nothing but his rifle and whatever was in his pockets, and didn't break stride to matchlight his beedis, whose smoke wafted back to me like the visible smell of banquet spreads in cartoon dreams.

In this way, after what seemed hours, we came to a tree-shaded level area breaking the mountainside. It was almost dark, I'd been trudging all day, and apparently we were at our destination.

I didn't quite realize we had arrived because I had expected an obvious encampment of some kind, with patrols and pup tents and cooking fires. Instead, we stopped in a flattish place with no one around. The guide lit another beedi and wandered off wordlessly, leaving me to wonder what I should do next, what the protocol was when being held prisoner in a Maoist guerilla camp.

Again I waited to be bound, smacked around, confined to a bamboo cage and ladled brackish water through the openings. But nobody appeared to do this. At that moment, in fact, after the tight-lipped rifleman crunched off into the woods, there was nothing to be heard but a few birds chirping above and monkeys nattering somewhere down the slope. I felt as stupidly incongruous as I ever had in my life. I thought I understood Audra's sense of helplessness that day in Sri Lanka when she had lost sight of Petra, and irrepressible images of her being tortured or killed ran through my mind the longer I stood there, wondering what to do. The silence closed in oppressively. Maybe he'd taken me to the wrong place?

I felt doubly dislocated because I was so far removed from any reaches of twenty-first century civilization, and had the acute sense of being abandoned by the rest of the world, with its built-in oversights and networks of professionals. Mere weeks before, on a laptop or even my phone, I was certain I could plug into anywhere in the world, could use Google Maps to home in on any two-meter-square patch of soil or ocean I chose. I knew what Audra had called the "better powers" maintained sophisticated spy satellites far out in geosynchronous orbit with the ability to capture quarter-sized images anywhere they pleased, had read that in 1985 the U.S. had tested kinetic energy weapons in space and destroyed an entire satellite, creating orbital debris, more than 3,000 pieces, and from some command center they still tracked the exact number of chunks larger than a centimeter because their velocities were such that they could damage other satellites, and it struck me as incredible that any person could know how many pieces of speck-like debris orbited 525 kilometers above the Earth, hurtling through nothingness, and the existence of such programs had given me the impression that everything on the planet was known by someone, that nothing was beyond the reach of radio signals or fiber optic cable.

There were people who specialized in all this, could access the data and interpret it correctly, yet there I was, incapable of surviving in those woods for more than a day, probably, despite countless hours watching worst-case-scenario shows on television. I couldn't even build a fire.

Audra was right: what *had* I expected to do?

My brain was shutting down, sapped of usable information. I couldn't remember how the hosts of those shows had constructed lean-tos or fashioned game traps using Native American wisdom, and I was hit with the realization that I had flown in commercial airliners through the stratosphere from the multi-tiered comfort of Pennsylvania, where complex invisible systems, governing bodies, and regulatory commissions functioned quietly in the background, to that spot in the mountains somewhere in Bihar or possibly Jharkhand, in a swath cut away from the laws and economic imperatives of the Republic of India, instead at the mercy not of any internationally-recognized sovereign state, but rather of a confederate affiliated only through terror, whose very reason for existence was a repudiation of the norms of semi-democratic late capitalism.

They had taken Petra, and who knew what norms were guiding them?

It was easy to feel defeated, dehydrated, unsure of what to do. I wilted at the base of a tree, if nothing else than to give my blistering feet a rest.

But then, as I sat leaning against the tree, running relaxation exercises in my head, I noticed busy ant trails around the root structures, and over what looked like a piece of Styrofoam. Odd. My line of sight rose up from the scrap to the middle distance, where I seemed to see suggestions of human occupation, what looked like a shirt hung from a far-off branch, but I couldn't be sure. Were those buff-colored sacks—the same color as the rock outcroppings—stacked near the mouth of a cave? Or were they stones? Was Styrofoam Styrofoam? Was I hallucinating?

As I became transfixed on what I was sure was a cave, trying to will myself to get up and walk the sixty yards over to it, I thought I detected some shadows moving in the darkness, and I stared harder, immobilized.

And as though my concentration had materialized it, a figure resolved itself, coming toward me, shadow on shadow at first, but as it drew closer I could see who it was, see that it was Vimal Pottai.

He had changed from his starched business look to the same crappy olive drab fatigues my wiry guide had worn, and like him he had a newer rifle slung over his shoulder. I stood and balled my fists reflexively.

"Ah," he said, approaching, "the professor has arrived. It is 'professor,' is it not?"

"Where is Petra?"

"And what is it you profess? Languages? Literatures?" He had come right up in my face.

"Where is Petra?" I said steadily, standing my ground, and he stepped back.

"And what is it you have for me?" he said.

"Ms. Wester is prepared to leave the district if her daughter is returned unharmed," I said.

"Ho! Is that right? This is good to know."

"Tell me where Petra is."

"And you are certain," he said, "that this doctorate of yours is not perhaps in geology or monetary policy or metallurgy?" He drew up to me again, his face mere inches from mine, his breath stinking of sour milk. He said I was pretending, dishonest, that they knew I was working with MK Technologies to finalize land deals.

I couldn't tell if this confusion was good or bad, in the circumstances.

"I'm just here for my daughter," I said. Audra—Ms. Wester—had agreed to vacate the area, this was not a problem.

"Unlikely," he said, then shouted back toward the cave.

More figures resolved themselves, and as I squinted through the dusk, with a surge of joy I saw Petra being brought over, little olive drab figures with identical haircuts holding her, one on each arm. I started toward her, but Vimal put his hand on my chest.

"Shh, professor," he said. "She is fine, she is fine."

I called to her and she said she was okay, that they weren't hurting her.

"You see?" said Vimal. "We did not want her here in the first place."

They brought her within ten or fifteen feet, close enough that I could see that she did indeed seem intact, was bucking in their grasp and crying "unhand me," as though she were a heroine in a pirate movie.

"She is perfectly unharmed," said Vimal.

"What do you mean you don't want her here?" I said. If that was the case, then why couldn't I take her back that minute?

"I think," he said, squinting at Petra, "you ought to have a talk with your daughter. We are not savages, and we do not bargain with children. You, on the other hand, might prove useful indeed."

"I don't understand what's happening," I said, and as I did so Petra managed to twist from the grasp of her captors and took off, running too close to the bluff, and Vimal sprung like a coiled snake to grab her, and I had a flash of him pushing her over the edge. I was between them and sprung faster, lunging and knocking Vimal away from her, and in slow motion I saw her still moving, running untouched as he absorbed the blow and tuck-and-rolled to the ground, while my momentum propelled me forward, there was nothing I could do, and I skidded over the chalky outcropping and pitched headfirst into the nothingness below.

9.

SOMETHING SHINING BEYOND my eyelids pulled me back to consciousness. Disoriented but immediately aware of new and untested plateaus of pain firing throughout my body, electrical pain surging into my very cells, I heard Petra's voice from behind the light saying hey, hey, are you there? She repositioned the beam so as not directly in my eyes, and after a moment I could see in its nimbus Petra bending over me, saying, "There he is!"

I realized I was prone in the dirt, but that my head had been cushioned by a bunched shirt. I felt truly paralyzed, achingly thirsty, relieved that she was before me, still apparently unharmed. I couldn't remember how I had wound up there.

"You took a header off that cliff," said Petra, pointing up into the darkness.

"Did I break anything?" I whispered. My body was racked with so much general pain, it was impossible to tell.

"I bet you it's a hundred feet to where you fell, luckily for you not straight down. Somehow it doesn't look like you broke anything. Definitely banged up, though. Cuts and bruises. You have a nasty gash on your forehead, but we bandaged it."

"We?" I said, straining to see.

Pradeep leaned over me. "Hello, sir," he said.

My processing abilities were sluggish, to say the least, and I was having a hard time figuring out what was going on.

"You tackled Vimal," Petra recounted. "But then just kept on going, accidentally. I thought you were dead. I was flipping out. I mean I lost

245

Steven Belletto

it, and Vimal was pissed but he just like waved it off and said whatever, go see if you and Pradeep can find him. He didn't care. They showed us how to get down here, but he said he wasn't risking any of his people so we came by ourselves. He gave us a first aid kit and a flashlight, though, and here we are. It took us forever. The ants were eating you alive."

"What?"

"Not literally but they were interested. I brushed most of them off."

"You saved me," I said.

"We found you. You must be made of rubber because I was positive we'd find you dead down here."

"I don't think I can move."

"It's fine," she said. "We'll stay right here."

She was squeezing my hand, and it seemed to me the one part of my body that wasn't throbbing. I was trying hard not to, but despite myself, I went out again.

—

When I opened my eyes next it was daytime, morning. People were talking, a couple of the olive drab persuasion were arguing with Pradeep, and he said to Petra that they wanted to bring me back up to camp.

She said absolutely not, that I was in no condition to walk. "Have them make a stretcher," she said, "and come back later."

"I can walk," I croaked, my throat dry and inflamed, but I wasn't sure I really could.

"No!" said Petra. "Tell them he's staying right here until I say it's safe for him to move. And leave the water."

I drifted out again.

—

"Dad?" Petra was saying. "Dad?" And her voice pulled me conscious again, everyone gone but Pradeep and her, and she was tipping a cup of water to my lips. It was better tasting than I could have ever imagined.

246

I managed to get myself sitting upright, testing different parts of my body and confirming her battlefield assessment was accurate: nothing seemed broken so far as I could tell. I noticed dried blood in splotches on my skin, a crusty layer over a landscape of bruises—amazing, I thought, as I examined myself tenderly, that a single body could have such a number of bruises. I felt like a mass of wounds, draped upon a heap of bones.

I asked for some more water.

"Back from the dead," she said, shaking her head in wonder. "Unbelievable."

It was suddenly urgently important for me to know what time it was, how long I'd been out, what had happened to her.

"Uh, afternoon sometime," she said. "You've been in and out all day. But some color's returned to your face. Looking good."

I saw then that there were pebbles and strings of grass lodged in the wider cuts and scrapes on my arms and legs, and I started to pick them out, which introduced a whole new theater of pain.

"Careful," she said. "Oh, that's disgusting."

"Oooof," I said.

Pradeep had made a fire and was boiling tea-colored broth in a pot apparently also left by the others. He asked me if I was hungry.

I was hungry, unexpectedly, and he scooped some broth into a cup. I sipped in tiny breaths, feeling better.

"Florence Nightingale," I said to Petra as she examined the bandage on my head.

"We better change this," she said, peeling it off delicately. "Ugh, gross. I really thought you were dead." She laughed a little. "You should of seen yourself rocket off that cliff."

I made a joke about the ground breaking my fall, laughing weakly. It hurt.

—

Later in the evening, as I regained my balance and got used to the aching and acute pains that had become part of how my body operated,

Petra remarked that she still couldn't figure out what I was doing there in the first place.

I told her, still foggy, that I had come to get her. The sharpest and most radial pain was in my forehead over my right eye, where I was gashed, which alternately throbbed and struck like a hot wire deep into my brain. I had been demanding to sniff things because I thought vaguely that the ability to smell was some measure of brain trauma, but when Pradeep handed me another cup of broth, this one with roots and berries boiled in, I could smell it just fine, and so concluded that likely I hadn't done any permanent damage.

"I know that you came to rescue me," said Petra. "It's just, I don't know what they would want with you."

Slowly, choosing to believe I didn't have a concussion but wondering what the symptoms of concussions were, I realized that something was off, that Petra didn't seem especially distressed by her apparent abduction. Where were the hysterics? Wouldn't she have lost it, at least a little? She was abnormally calm. I asked her what had happened, how they got her.

"I came with Pradeep," she said quietly.

Still I was confused, looking at Pradeep. "What do you mean? He's one of them?"

"No, I mean, I came on purpose. I wrote the note."

A hammering pounded through my brain, so swift and complete I could hardly concentrate on what she had told me. What? How? Why? My feeble questions once again.

She reminded me, casually, that Pradeep's father was a regional commander for the Maoists, and when Audra had insisted on the boarding school question, she and Pradeep figured that if they let Audra think she had been taken by them, she, Audra, would flinch and decide it wasn't worth being way out there, she would see a light, and they would move back to Europe and Petra would be spared boarding school. The bonus was that Pradeep would get points if Audra did leave, a win-win, and his father might even consider his duties to the cause fulfilled.

In my weakened state, I failed to understand what she was saying. Dumbfounded is probably the right word.

Her most spectacular lie yet: shooting an email out into cyberspace to see what stuck was one thing; orchestrating a fake kidnapping was quite another.

"Your mother," I said, "is ready to kill."

This seemed to give her pause, as though it hadn't occurred to her. "I knew this would get her attention."

"Imagine how you would feel if your mother was kidnapped and possibly dead."

"Well," she said, considering this, her voice cracking. "I mean I didn't mean to-" Then she began to cry, the onset immediate, saying that she had never meant to hurt her mom, only to "freak her out," and as though the severity of what she had done was just then sinking in, she concluded hollowly that she was a terrible person.

In thirty seconds her mood had plunged from sly triumph to horror. She sat hunched on log, thin arms bent outward, hands on her knees and smudged with charcoal dust, suddenly unsure, rings around her eyes lending her a haunted, feral look. Her lip wavered and she shook bloodlessly.

She exposed herself then—for all her studied sophistication and polyglot worldliness, she was still thirteen, and I remembered the malicious, ill-considered things I had done at thirteen, the stupid ways I had punished my own parents for all the trauma I had suffered, and I almost understood as she repeated I'm sorry, I'm sorry, I'm sorry, I just wanted to get her out of the business.

"And what if they want to keep you?" she sniffled to me. Then, motioning limply to Pradeep: "What will they do with him?"

Pradeep had been peeling the bark from a tuber or root, pretending not to listen. When he spoke, he did so haltingly, and it occurred to me that Petra had been the mastermind, that he had probably just followed along with the half-thought plan she had plotted.

"My uncle is like a politician," he said sadly, "traveling to the capital to speak at conferences. But in the past, in other states, his organization just kills people to make examples. Tax collectors and police officers, people like this. So I cannot say what will happen."

I pointed out that I was neither a tax collector nor a police officer, but Petra was not so sure about my safety, and turned in on herself all over again.

"We'll figure it out," I said, and she spluttered.

We drank the other batch of Pradeep's broth, and he built his fire up so it radiated just the right amount of warmth. We arranged ourselves around it and tried to distract ourselves with stories until well after dark, when you couldn't see where black space ended and the canyon walls began.

An enormous beetle with horns and red markings on its back lumbered over, attracted by the heat, and although it looked fearsome to me, Pradeep picked it up, humming even, trying to amuse Petra, saying that he used to play with them as a child, that you could loop a length of thread around its leg and it would fly in an arc around your fingers. Petra gasped, accusing him of cruelty, and he said no, it didn't harm them, that they would fly and you could feed them or free them when you were done. We didn't have any thread but he let it crawl over the back of his hand and his cord-like forearms, recalling his boyhood in the forests outside Korba, which in those days was still part of Madhya Pradesh, when these beetles would appear in droves at a certain point in the spring and he and his brother and cousins would look forward to it, would fly them and set them up in footraces.

The spring he was six, he said, they got some bad cooking oil and the entire family was sick for days, everything coming out both ends, as he put it, but they all eventually recovered, except his mother, who seemed to get sicker and sicker, and when after a week's time a doctor finally came to examine her, he said that it appeared she had had some sort of underlying condition, a virus or a cancer, Pradeep wasn't sure they ever knew exactly, and this condition had been inflamed by the food poisoning and she needed treatment in a city hospital. But his father could not afford transportation to a city hospital, let alone treatment there, and so the doctor had injected her with medicine the best he could, said he would check back in two weeks when he came around again. Pradeep remembered sitting by her bedside as her skin turned a sallow saffron and her eyes sunk in deep hollows in her skull.

He remained there for days on end with one of those horned beetles tied to a thread, and would try to make it perform tricks for her, and she would smile delicately, unable to move. Since that time, he had associated the beetles with his mother. His father, who couldn't stop working, would come in late in the evening and drink whole jars of whiskey his friends had distilled illegally, yelling at his sisters for some fault in their housekeeping, accusing Pradeep and his brother of lazing around doing nothing. I'm taking care of mama, Pradeep would say, and his father crashed around saying that was women's work, that he needed to learn how to be a man.

After his mother had died, Pradeep said, his father quit drinking and became more involved with the Maoists, who he increasingly viewed as the only recourse to the kind of systemic inequalities he was convinced had killed his wife. He took Pradeep and his brother to speeches and little plays that were always about how the Naxals cared about all the people, while the state only worshipped money. Eventually, Pradeep's father was spending more time criss-crossing the forested mountains in the south than he did at home, and when Pradeep was fifteen his father had wanted to induct him formally into the organization, but although Pradeep believed in the people, he felt his father had become unreasonable and indeed forbidding, not necessarily because of his mother's death but because of whatever he was doing in the forests, and Pradeep had told him no, defied him even in the face of a destructive rage, and after a vicious scene he left for Bihar to live with his auntie, Amrita. He had first learned about body building from a magazine he had found, and decided that if nothing else, he could defend himself, and thought it was perhaps a better route to manhood than his father's guerilla training in the forest.

When he finished telling this story, turning his arm gently so the beetle could walk along it, always upright, Petra contorted to hug him and he set the creature down carefully and it went off under a rock.

As the darkness intensified, we were accosted by thousands of gnats then mosquitoes, and Petra's empathy for insects did not extend to them, and she said she sure wished she had some bug spray, we all slapped them off our skin, and I said let the mosquitoes gorge themselves on me because I was a body-sized contusion and couldn't feel them anyhow.

Deep in the night, long after we'd dozed off, the insect-chirping air was broken by the crack of a rifle, a noise all the more shocking as it echoed through the canyon. We jerked, tensed like the monkeys who bounced unseen in the branches above, hysterical.

Instantly awake, we waited, not breathing, then all at once a barrage of fire erupted from somewhere on the slopes above us, and other pops reported back from directly overhead, from the encampment, and we scrambled as we realized there was an assault taking place, machine gun fire now deafening and the canyon lit up in garish oranges as small explosives went off, all of this happening above our heads, the smell of burnt cordite and electrical smoke rolling down and filling the air around us, shouting and screaming punctuating the shots. Pradeep and I used our bodies to form a tentlike shield over Petra, who crouched quaking in the dirt. It continued, relentless, and it was hard to tell where exactly everything was coming from, for a long time it went on, machine gun bursts, screaming, taunting, projectiles whirring, things exploding. Flames flickered above our heads, on the rise near our side where the cave was, and illuminated in that uneven light I could barely make out the shadows of figures moving erratically as the onslaught continued, tracer smoke visible in the firelight, voices still screaming. We were unseen, I thought, and gradually the exchange died down, only a few straggler pops from the far slope, then everything was eerily silent once more, even the insects gone, bitter smoke still slinking down the mountainside, fires now crackling above.

Then we heard voices, urgent, emanating from the far side, and points of light appeared like fairies from the wooded slopes. Someone was calling and Pradeep shouted back.

"It's the Black Cats," he said. "The police. We are saved."

The aftermath was ugly.

There was a dull moment in the acrid haze when our ears still rung with silence, and we waited to see if the calm was real, or if a bullet or bomb might come our way. The pinpoints of light bobbed through the trees in the distance then became orbs as they descended from the far side of the slope, diffusing as they approached us, Pradeep again calling to them, and finally they were upon us.

Men in night vision goggles and light body armor emerged cautiously from the trees, rifles drawn, scanning our tiny camp. Pradeep spoke to them desperately and I saw someone I recognized, Sunir, a helmet strapped to his head, step around a couple of the men, holstering a sidearm and striding over.

"You are all right," he declared, directing it at Petra.

"What the hell is going on?" I said.

He surveyed our area briefly, then asked if there was anyone else around.

I repeated my question.

"The Naxal infestation," he said with finality, "has been suppressed." He barked at the armored men, who looked like beetle-aliens in their night vision contraptions, and two of them grabbed Pradeep roughly by the shoulders and frog-marched him out.

Petra leapt after them and Sunir moved to stop her. I said don't you dare touch her and he put his hands up in a gesture of surrender while the men continued to drag off Pradeep.

"What are you doing?" Petra was shouting. "He's not one of them!"

"The circumstances," Sunir said calmly, "would appear to suggest otherwise. This man aided in the kidnapping of a U.S. citizen."

"There was no kidnapping!" she cried. "I went on my own."

"Please. There is no need to protect him," he said. "The truth will emerge." He turned to me. "Now, if I may, sir, I would like to get you two out of the area in case there are other snakes hiding in these woods. As we know, they do not hesitate to kill civilians."

Petra was crying wildly and arguing, but I realized Sunir was right, that it was probably best to get out of there. I put my hands on Petra's narrow shoulders and whispered to her that we would be okay, but that we should regroup elsewhere. Still she resisted and I had to hold her back from rushing Sunir.

"Your mother," he said to her, "is waiting for you, just at the base of the hills."

This calmed her slightly and she relented. We followed Sunir's men on the route they had blazed up the slope, my entire body feeling so stiff and bruised that I could hardly walk, but I clenched and coughed on, hacking and leading Petra by the hand through the darkness.

When we reached a certain spot where more men were gathered, Sunir said he wanted to show me something. "Leave the young miss a moment," he said.

Petra was being outfitted with a headlamp to make the walk out easier. I looked at her, cones of light cutting in angles across her face, and shuddered at the terror I had felt in those past days, upon learning she had disappeared, upon thinking some harm had come to her, and merely recalling them terrified me anew. She looked terrified herself, but was trying to put on a brave face, joking weakly with one of the soldiers.

Sunir was urging me over to a clearing that, I realized then, was near the cave I had seen earlier. He wanted to show me bodies. There were six or seven lain out side by side in the dirt, jackets or shirts covering their faces. They were already stiffening and contorted in obscene echoes of the instants they had been killed. Sunir was shaking his head as though profoundly troubled by what he was seeing, asking, to no one in particular, "Why do they do this?"

It was an embarrassing cliché, the implication that Sunir was exposing me to this because death was the truest reality one could know, that he assumed I'd been sheltered from such reality and so he was obliged to lay some ineffable wisdom on a man he took to be unaware of what actually went on in the world.

In fact, I only thought this out later, as I turned the scene over in my mind.

At the moment, in my stunned and broken state, I just watched in nausea as late gases escaped from the body nearest me, a travesty of the notion of a soul.

More men circled around, having come from sweeping the cave, and Sunir spoke with them quietly, then asked me to follow him. He led me to a copse where a couple of men were standing guard over a person slumped down at the base of a tree. It was Vimal Pottai. His shirt was open and he had been shot in the belly, was clutching a wadded bandana there, soaked through with blacked blood.

"Here!" said Sunir, kicking Vimal Pottai's leg with his heavy boot.

Vimal did not respond, instead remained slumped, eyes closed, but breathing shallowly, holding the bandana in place with one hand.

"Can you identify this man?" Sunir asked.

I said I had met him at Amrita's and later confronted him in that very camp.

"Yes!" said Sunir loudly, for Vimal's benefit, again kicking his leg. "This is the man trying to bring this cancer to Bihar. To my district! But he has been answered, has he not?"

"What will happen to him?"

"India is a modern state," he said, suddenly philosophical. "We exist in the twenty-first century. This means we cannot have insurgent groups challenging the state. Can you imagine one of your states going to war with another? No. You eradicated this possibility 150 years ago. Likewise, India has been unified. This is done, so why must we tolerate these radicals who wish to destroy us? How would you meet a break-away republic in the States? With action." He was working himself up, having gone from disturbingly calm to nearly shaking, fingering the weapon holstered at his thigh.

"What will happen to him?" I asked again.

He spat on Vimal, which appeared to pacify him. "What will happen?" he repeated. "What would happen in London or the Hague?"

"A trial?"

"A trial. So he will have his trial, and if convicted, he will be sentenced." He spat on him again. "Come. The others are waiting for us."

He strode off, two men still standing guard over Vimal Pottai, making no effort whatsoever to either move or bandage him, and it was clear by the finality and conviction with which Sunir walked away that he had no intention of bringing Vimal out of the forest at all.

We met back up with Petra, who was now wearing a headlamp strapped to her forehead and drinking from a bottle of water. "Supposedly it's four hours out of the mountains," she said. "Did they already move out the prisoners?"

She asked me this question with such open earnestness that it didn't strike me as absurd or naïve, her assumption that nobody had been killed, that she believed the corpses twisted in the distant leaves were merely prisoners. And although images of the dead still preyed upon my mind, her question expressed a kind of faith in the basic humanity of all people—even in the face of what she had witnessed over the past couple of days, even as she herself experienced the thunder of explosives and the crack of rifles, and even as she could at that very moment see the smaller fires still smoldering not a hundred yards off, still she asked.

So what was it all for her? A celluloid shoot-out in which bullets screamed but nobody was ever seriously injured? She seemed willfully ignorant that a man who had been in her house and was then taking a long drink from a canteen, that this man Sunir Naik had just led a deadly assault brought about by her own actions.

I couldn't see her face, as the headlamp was blinding me, but I said that yes, they had already moved out all the prisoners.

"Good," she said. "That's good."

Someone handed me a headlamp, and we began the trek out of the mountains, walking in single file, the men chatting and joking, lusty in their victory, but Petra was generally so quiet that I had to check in with her at intervals to make sure she was there. She said she was just tired—it was the middle of the night—and after what seemed much longer than four hours, we reached the edge of the forest or a clearing, lit up, a mobile command center with jeeps and SUVs circled like wagons and inundating the hub with floodlit pools where still more soldiers or police stood around smoking and drinking tea from tiny metal cups.

As soon as we descended into the encampment, Audra exploded from one of the vehicles, looking slightly crazed, shouting for her daughter.

Petra ran down into the light, into Audra's arms, and I stayed back to give them some space. Petra was sobbing, Audra shaking her head, taking Petra's face in her hands and saying something to her at close range.

I walked over after a few minutes to find Petra calmed, both mother and daughter red-faced and spent. Still Audra was checking Petra over, patting her down for broken limbs or cuts, seemingly unable to accept that physically she was unchanged. But when she saw me she was shocked, as though my obvious wounds reflected something she couldn't quite see in Petra. "Yikes!" she said. "What happened to you?"

"Nothing," I said, doing my best Gary Cooper.

"He saved me!" said Petra.

Audra let out a long outflow of breath as she examined the gash on my head, still more or less closed with the gauze and medical tape Petra had put on it. "We're going to need to have someone look at this," she said.

"He saved me!" said Petra again.

"How so?" asked Audra, peeling off the tape as though she knew what she was doing.

"Vimal Pottai was trying to hurt me," Petra said. "But Dad tackled him and fell off the cliff. Still, Vimal knew he meant business."

"Ow," said Audra. "This is going to need stitches."

"So where's Pradeep?" asked Petra.

Audra said she thought he was in one of the SUVs, and Petra said she'd be right back.

"Don't go far!" Audra called after her. Then, to me: "You look like shit."

"How did you find us?"

There was a GPS beacon sewn into that backpack she had given me, naturally. She explained how simple it was, that they merely waited until it pinged static, then went on in. After getting into position, Sunir's guys had watched the camp all day, knew that we three were way down at the bottom of the ravine, and so figured it would be relatively safe to launch a strike come nightfall. They had night vision and thermal imaging equipment, so the Naxals were like sitting ducks.

"Believe it or not," she said, "you did a good thing by getting her away from the camp, otherwise things would have been much trickier. Messier. But you two were never in any danger. And Sunir didn't lose a single one of his guys. The Naxals are shitty shots at the end of the day."

"I don't know," I said.

But Audra knew. "You've probably gathered that these are not nice people."

I told her that Petra had written the note, that she and Pradeep concocted a scheme to scare her, to get her to pack up and leave.

By the look on her face, I could see she hadn't known this. "Don't be ridiculous," she said.

I recounted the conversation that I had had with Petra, about her engineering the kidnapping, about the unintended consequences, about Vimal Pottai wanting to throw her back and keep me. As I was saying this, she took me over into the shadows, beyond the hearing of the men who were standing around, and asked me to explain everything again slowly, including every detail, however seemingly insignificant.

"You're sure about this?" she said when I was finished.

I said I was sure what Petra told me. And that Vimal Pottai had clearly wanted no part of having her there.

She was running a thousand calculations, evaluating what this new information meant for whatever scenarios and contingencies were in play in her head.

"It makes no difference," she said finally. "These guys were running around with guns and munitions openly making threats to the state. You saw yourself what they were setting up out here. It was inevitable that they'd do a car bomb or ambush a police convoy or something. So consider this a preemptive strike."

"What about Pradeep?"

"I think from the perspective of law enforcement, Pradeep is a non-state actor and therefore not subject to the protections of the Geneva Convention."

"Except," I said, "he had nothing to do with them. He was just following Petra."

"Not my call," she said. "What authority do I have? I'm merely an observer."

Suddenly it seemed very important to me that Pradeep get some clemency. I argued that they had their body count and looming media victory, asked her what possible justice could come of Pradeep rotting away in some dungeon on terrorist charges.

"You don't always know," she said, "who is or isn't friendly. But let's see what we can do, for Petra's sake."

Petra appeared in the light saying her ears were burning and I don't think it was clear to either Audra or me how much she had heard of our conversation.

"I found Pradeep over in the back of that SUV," she said. "Looks like he got punched in the face, but otherwise he's okay."

"I'm sure he'll survive," said Audra.

"Why *is* he in the back of that SUV, though?" she asked.

"We'll have to sort that out," said Audra, looking at me. "As well as your newfound love of theater."

It took her a few beats to pick up on what Audra was saying, but then she realized and called me a double-crosser.

"Did you really think I wouldn't find out?" said Audra. "I find out *everything*."

Petra's lip wobbled as though she were about to burst into tears again, but Audra leaned down to head off any significant outpouring, saying something to her I couldn't catch.

Petra eyed me from behind her mother's embrace, sucking in a wet breath, then pulled back to ask if we could all go home.

10.

THE DAYS IMMEDIATELY after are accessible to me mainly as blurred, isolated vignettes. It seemed that the pall of things that can't be undone had infiltrated my cells, was a contaminant in the stale air of every room I entered.

I remember in the early hours of that first morning, still before dawn after we had arrived back at the house. There were some minutes of burning excitement mixed with indifference: Sunir had decided to post a couple of his guys around the property just in case, but this clamor was tempered by the stone-faced leaf pickers who floated by, unconcerned with the utility vehicles peeling off into blackness. A contingent of men went off to get drunk and Sunir was loudly proclaiming that he would drink everything.

After all but the guards left, a strange calm settled over the house. I was in the library, where Petra had curled up in the sofa and passed out. For reasons still unknown to me, the electricity came on in fitful bursts, would sometimes flicker and brown out the lights, and at that moment was not working at all so somebody had lit candles and placed them around the room, adding to the cloistered mood. Drained for a moment of the will or ability to move, my body throbbing in global pain, I watched Petra sleep for several quiet minutes, until I realized Audra had materialized behind me.

She looked as wrung-out as I felt, her cheeks spider-veined and crimsoned, hair awry, and she sniffed and held out her hand, offering me what she called a "mutant Tylenol hybrid" so potent it was illegal in the West.

"For your general condition," she said.

I gulped some down with a tasteless wash of vodka and tepid water, and we watched Petra heave once then turn over, burrowing her face into tattered cushions.

Audra looked beyond the sleeping child with a thousand-yard stare.

"The horrible thing about being a parent," she said, "is that they pick up the worst in you. There's babyhood, then suddenly all you see are those parts of you you tried to pretend don't exist."

—

A compact, broad-shouldered man came to examine Petra and me. He informed us she was unharmed physically but wanted to know if Audra had any alprazolam on hand. When it was my turn, he ran a series of old-fashioned motor skills and basic memory tests. He was paid for, I assumed, by Audra's super-platinum health care plan, and as he probed me I wondered vaguely if he'd come in by helicopter.

He said I probably didn't have any brain damage, but that it would be worth my while to get X-rays and even a CAT scan when I was able to do so.

Petra watched the exam nervously, alternately crossing her arms and biting her nails, interjecting at the right time: "Wuddya mean *probably*?"

The doctor looked at her and said he was only human, and proceeded to give me twenty-something very fine stitches above my eye, the worst part of which was that he had to shave my hairline back inches in that spot. I said with the lidocaine I couldn't feel a thing, but Petra studied me anew, wincing because physically I looked terrible, pulpy and battered, latticed with cuts, and I knew she had to suppress the urge to ask me again how I was feeling, which she had already done a hundred times since we had returned from the forest.

I remember Petra slurping a cup of soup and saying she was worse than those ninety-year-old Nazi accountants who had intermittently been brought to trial in Germany when she was younger—worse because she might as well have pulled the trigger.

"No," said Audra, "no no, kiddo, you were merely caught in the middle of a complex and long-standing web of issues." Political, ethnic, and economic matters impossible to really understand. "You can admit you were stupid," Audra told her. "But what you can't do is blame yourself for the existence of terrorism."

Sunir had friends who had been tracking Vimal Pottai for years, they knew all about what was going on in Chhattisgarh and had intelligence indicating that he was planning to use the MK Technologies project as an excuse to stir up trouble in the area. These things would have played out eventually, she said, whether or not she and Petra had ever set foot on Indian soil.

"Yeah," said Petra, "but that's not what happened."

I remember Petra vanishing into her room, where she had shut up all the windows and retreated into a musty womb of sheets, listening to *New Skin for the Old Ceremony* and the Original Caste, over and over.

I remember being impressed that she had a portable record player.

—

An English-language paper, printed on cheap stock with smudgy ink, appeared in the house. It announced that the police, working with key special army forces and the NSG, had located a Naxal "training ground" deep in the forested borderlands between Jharkhand and Bihar. Acting on intelligence indicating imminent terrorist attacks, the authorities attempted to capture the insurgents, but were unfortunately met with gunfire and so had no choice but to return fire, resulting in eight dead terrorists, including their nefarious ringleader who went by the name of Vimal Pottai.

I remember looking through a front window at one of Sunir's skinny guards, a teenager probably, standing watch near the wrought iron fence, bored and absurd in his fatigues. He picked his nose and peed out by the cat shed. I had asked Audra if that would be it, just a handful of newspaper stories matter-of-factly reporting what wasn't quite true, and she said likely, but that the confrontation would get folded into campaign rhetoric as elections neared.

She was about to make coffee, she said, to see if she could entice Petra. The local politicians would either praise the swiftness of the government's response to terror, or else condemn another miscarriage of justice against the criminally-exploited Adivasi, depending on the crowd.

Did I want milk and sugar?

Petra sobbed in the night and Audra worked out some deal over the phone that resulted in Pradeep's release.

I took several trips to Petra's door, where I would knock and offer plates of food, and after a minute, a muffled voice would pipe from within to leave it, to leave her alone.

—

After two or three days in this state, one morning Petra emerged from her room, wrapped in a blanket and looking like a wounded bird.

"I think," she said, "I want to go to boarding school."

Audra took her up in a tangled hug and Petra pushed her back saying, "Ugh, wait, I really need to wash my hair."

She never explained why she had changed her mind, but Audra and I both thought she viewed it as a kind of atonement. I don't know how that logic worked in her adolescent mind, but later that night she brought down a stack of brochures, bearing them in front of her like a chalice, and then solemnly named to Audra the schools she wanted to visit, telling us it was time for her to enter "the mainstream."

"Maybe it'll be good for me," Petra said flatly.

Audra disregarded her lack of enthusiasm and lost no time in booking these visits, in fact seemed to have already been in contact with the admissions officers at several schools.

"No time like the present," Audra kept saying, a touch feverishly.

Within the week, efficient Audra had arranged tours of the four schools Petra had chosen, all mere hours apart from one another in Switzerland.

"The best in the world," she would assure me, and Petra would nod uncomfortably.

I was still swollen and bruised, my face looking purplish and tender, incapable of receiving even the lightest smear of creams or age-defying serums, and I settled again into the role of observer, the Phantom of the Opera watching the silent tensions between mother and daughter papered over with brochures for the most posh boarding schools in existence.

In fact, I was thinking about how to get myself back to the States, figuring that it was about time for me to pack up the Alto and get lost on my way to Patna.

But then Audra took an urgent phone call on the back patio, and Petra and I watched her through the kitchen window chopping the air to emphasize whatever point she was making.

"This won't be good," said Petra as her mother ended the call with a head shake.

"Bad news kiddo," said Audra, pushing through the door as though it had offended her. "We're going to have to hold off on the Switzerland trip. Just for a bit, but we need to go to Lamu soon. There's a crisis."

"There always is," sighed Petra.

"Sorry, Will," she said to me, and I shrugged like *apologize to your daughter.*

Audra seemed instantly absorbed in a new series of challenges, was opening one of her laptops and said to Petra that she might want to start getting her things together, because they would be leaving in the next day or two, if she could get flights.

Petra, though, was looking at her hands, examining her chipped and bitten-down nails, running some scenario through her mind, and then finally looked up and said quietly: "What if Dad took me?"

Audra was already clacking on the laptop but stopped mid-stroke, visibly tensed.

"What?" she said, and Petra repeated herself.

I, of course, had frozen, too.

"Well I don't think so," said Audra. "I'm sure he needs to get back to his school. Will, don't you need to get back to your school?"

I stammered something, imagining all the little ways I would fail Petra on a trip like that.

"Besides," Audra went on, taking my unintelligible mumbling as my saying I did indeed have to get back to the States, "I want to see what I'm getting for a hundred grand a year. The facilities."

My physical injuries were seeming to flair as I caught a look of complete dejection on Petra's face.

"I still have over a month until the semester starts," I said, startling myself.

At this Petra leapt up. "OK, then, he can," she said, bouncing over to Audra at her desk.

"I don't think so," said Audra wearily, and I was starting to feel slightly offended.

"Oh come *ooooonnnnnn,*" groaned Petra.

"Are you sure you even *want* to go to boarding school?" I asked her, immune to Audra's needling glare.

"Mom's right," said Petra. "This is necessary for my future. I need stability."

"You're saying you'd rather I not go with you?" said Audra, apparently stung by the stability remark.

"I need to be able to choose on my own," said Petra. "Plus it will be good bonding time for Dad and me."

Given recent events, Audra was understandably concerned about leaving Petra in my charge, but I just grimaced painfully.

"What's the worst that could happen in Switzerland?" I said.

"Yeah," said Petra, "what's the worst that could happen in Switzerland?"

—

After the sort of negotiations you might expect, finally Audra relented and said if that's what you want, fine, we'll make it happen. I said we would take lots of pictures and lots of notes. She booked us a flight from Patna through Dubai and finally Zurich, on Sunday evening, July 7th. I realized as she told me this I wasn't even aware of what day it was—Thursday, Audra assured me.

Petra's mood had improved markedly since we had all agreed on the particulars of the Switzerland trip, and yet still she seemed more morose than I had ever known.

As I watched her supine on the overstuffed sofa in the library, holding the brochures at arm's length and studying them languidly, Angie's recommendation suddenly occurred to me, and I thought it would be good for us both to acquire a little merit.

"Have you been to Bodh Gaya," I asked cautiously. "Where Buddha was enlightened? One of the four holy places in Buddhism? I think it's more or less on the way. Maybe we should stop over. We could even spend the night."

Petra looked intrigued.

"Tourist trap," Audra said sideways.

"We could get up early," I was saying to Petra, ignoring Audra for the moment. "Sunrise at the Mahabodhi Temple is supposed to be one of life's great experiences." (Angie had written this in her email.)

Petra was instantly sold on the idea. "Oohhh, yes!" she cried, scattering the brochures. "Mom? Huh? Can we? Wouldn't it be the right way to say goodbye to India?"

"I don't know," she said in a way that indicated she would eventually agree.

"I've been *wanting* to go there," Petra insisted. "But we've always been 'too busy.' How about it? Talk about an education? Where Buddha was enlightened. Hello?"

"All right," said Audra. "I've got to get back to Kenya anyway."

"Perfect," I said. We could poke around, have dinner, then maybe even get up at dawn to listen to the monks doing their thing. We'd be at the airport with time to spare.

"At *dawn?*" said Petra, who smiled for the first time in days.

—

The next morning I went with Petra so she could say goodbye to her friends "around town." She didn't think she'd return there before starting boarding school, or possibly ever again. Amrita wasn't working in the co-op, but we found her at home, sitting in a metal-tubed chair under her pergola, ruminating in a black mourning shroud. She looked like she hadn't slept in days. But she was relieved to see Petra, and took her hands and kissed her, saying desperately that Pradeep could not stay in the area, that he needed to get out of the district completely (Petra later paraphrased).

Amrita had some relatives near Patna, she said, and begged us to take him there. These relatives were on her husband's side, and were willing to help Pradeep get on his feet in the city, and maybe he could even join the Weight Lifting Association there, start a new life. Amrita looked at us with huge brown eyes, fuzzily distorted and magnified by her thick lenses. It would not be safe for her nephew to remain in town because people from the Raksha would be looking for him, she said, would assume he had been working with the authorities to attack the camp.

Petra translated the highlights for me, and I said of course we would take him, said that she should have him meet us at the house in the morning, and Amrita laughed as though she couldn't quite believe this turn of events, thanking me too profusely in her reedy voice.

That night, Mrs. Krishnamurti prepared an involved send-off meal of mutton stewed with butter and onions, great bowls of saffron and cardamom rice, various curries on a rotating tray (no steak); Petra insisted that she and Rakesh dine with us. Smaller side plates were produced for hours, during which everyone recounted stories about the creaky pleasures of the big house and the idiosyncrasies of town, and I could see Petra coming back to life, if not exactly self-absolved.

Rakesh was fascinated by the idea of Switzerland, thought it was about the most exotic place he could imagine, what with its chocolate fountains and mountains to heaven. He had never seen snow in person, he was saying, and wondered what it would be like to handle it—was it heavy? would it freeze your fingertips? was it dry?—and Petra promised to send him some pictures of her in snow, suggested that maybe he could even visit someday, something he considered an impossibility, like time travel.

As Audra and I watched her speaking authoritatively about Swiss snow, explaining why she thought it was ideal for skiing, we exchanged a look that said despite *The Shining*-like closeness of their circumstances, it would be awful indeed for Audra to be away from her daughter, much harder, actually, than it would be for Petra, who once settled in school would have a sudden crush of friends and classes and clubs and fieldtrips, while Audra would remain behind, there or in Kenya or some other humid place as yet unassigned, arranging whatever off-record deals she had spent her life arranging.

Later, after Petra had gone to bed, Audra was in a wistful mood. She had got a flight out the following evening, would be there to see us off, but was leaving herself right after. She offered to break into some expensive bottle of vodka an admiring official had given her. I told her just a splash, that I didn't feel much like drinking, but she poured them high anyway and we sat in front of the fireplace, a ritual we had stumbled into.

"Well," she said, "this probably isn't what you expected to do with your summer."

"I had it on my list," I said. "Any political developments?"

"All quiet. But it's probably a good idea for Petra's friend to lay low for a bit."

"He seems like a good guy."

She scrutinized her drink. "Yeah, sure. They all are until they're not."

"Is the mining plan they were talking about even happening?"

"After a while," she said, "these things take on a life of their own. They get larger and more complex than any single person could comprehend. So the future becomes difficult to predict."

"So all that was for nothing."

"Didn't dissuade any investors, if that's what you're saying. This vodka is not getting rid of my headache."

"Uh huh," I said, and we veered into small talk for long enough that she refilled her drink, I still nursing mine, and as she swirled the ice it was clear something had been on her mind since dinner.

Finally, winding around to what was bothering her, she said with my injuries I certainly had an Elephant Man vibe going on. I let that pass unremarked, and she asked me what was next.

"What'd you mean, next?"

"With Petra," she said, still swirling the drink. I had shown up from halfway around the world, announced myself as her father, and now was expecting to do "the flashy stuff" like school tours.

"I'm not expecting anything," I said. "She reached out to me."

She seemed exasperated, saying into her drink something about Mr. Man saving the day with John Wayne tackle maneuvers. "Was that literally the first time you've ever tackled someone? Another man. As an adult."

"What's the problem?"

"It's very male, is all," she said, suddenly sounding like my sister. "You roll in here assuming that with a heroic act or two you'll win her over, be her father. I don't know."

"I'm just doing my best. We'll call you every day if that's what you're worried about."

"I'm the one who's been there for thirteen years. I'm the one who did the million things she'll never remember—the 'little, nameless, unremembered acts.' That's Wordsworth, right professor?"

She was as hurt as I had ever seen her, still composed, and not exactly accusatory in her tone, but wounded, as though she were lamenting aloud an injustice that had been visited upon her by the universe. She drank without pleasure and I was unsure what to say, what my role in the play was, exactly.

"She's getting out of this shit," she went on. "That's for sure. Though I'm glad she thinks it's her choice, she's going, she's gone. What's the point of resources if you leave your own child exposed? What am I doing?"

"Audra."

"Just don't you dare let her down," she said soberly, resting the glass on her knee.

"Audra," I said. "All I can do is promise."

—

The next morning I felt invigorated, clear-headed despite my physical injuries, ready to face Bodh Gaya and Switzerland. Balancing a watery cup of coffee on the thin mattress, I perched on the edge of my bed and wrote to Angie, explaining the situation, that the cats would need a sitter for another week. I had written her as soon as we had come back from the forest, as soon as my brain could communicate with my fingertips—but I didn't tell her what had happened. I didn't tell my sister, either. Angie would have become a ball of worry, my sister would have been astonished, probably, by my general stupidity, so it seemed unnecessary or unkind to lay everything on them when there was nothing they could do from the States. So I hadn't said anything at all about "the events," as Audra called them, writing instead that the internet was spotty out there in the sticks, but otherwise everything was fine, status quo.

Composing what would certainly be my last dispatch from the big house, I decided to continue withholding "the events," and after the sad sack line about the cats, focused on Bodh Gaya, on letting Angie know that I was going there after all, bringing Petra to Mahabodhi Temple at sunrise, just as she had suggested, in the pale hope that we might both acquire some merit.

There was also another suggestion Angie had made, and it faced me then in black and white, demanding a response.

"You should see," she had written, "if Petra wants to come visit us in PA at some point. I'm sure you're dying to show her all your favorite haunts (see what I did there?). Seriously though, it must be wild getting to know your daughter after all this time, so you should keep it going. I know Pennsylvania is not your favorite but I'd be so excited to meet her."

The "us" seemed profound—the assumption that Petra would be visiting Angie and me together, as a unit, a couple, and this casual (?) use of the first-person plural made me wonder where her thinking was on "how a child in W.'s life would affect me," as she had scrawled on that pet LASER SURGERY pamphlet, centuries ago and on another planet.

I hadn't jumped at the idea, but it lingered like a recrimination. I was still anguished that I'd drunkenly made a move on Audra, and carefully I typed back to Angie that we would see how it went in Switzerland, but that I'd be open to the possibility if Petra were open, if her mother were amenable.

"Let's see what happens"—a promise or a cop out. "Miss you," I wrote in closing. "Love you and see you soon."

—

After lunch, we crammed the tiny Alto with luggage, and it had been washed and I think even waxed by Rakesh, who wanted us to be presentable in the big city. Petra hugged him and explained that she had created an email account just for him, so she could write him from school and send him pictures. Pradeep folded his bulk into the backseat as Audra pressed another wad of Euros in Petra's palm and said be careful and call me when you get there and I'll see you in one week, Petra saying yeah yeah yeah, I know.

Turning to me, Audra stuck her hand out as though she were only going to shake mine, businesslike, but then pulled me into a hug, saying into my ear, "If you write a novel about this, make me look good."

My last image of Audra was of her standing in the sun in drawstring linen pants and a tank top, again no shoes, toenails glinting defiantly, posture impeccable, shading her eyes with a hand, like a salute, almost crying as we drove away.

Petra twisted herself to keep waving as we bumped past the wrought iron and plaster lions, then down the hill, the house growing smaller in the distance. When Audra was a blur in the rearview mirror, Petra flopped forward and said to the car: "Hope she'll be all right."

"I think she's proud that you're so independent," I said.

"Yeah," she said. "But it doesn't mean she won't miss me."

She moved to take my hand, and I held it, and because she really seemed to want me to keep it there, when I needed to shift, I would steady the wheel with the top of my knee, a trick I had perfected long ago in my Tercel, and crossed over to use my right hand.

—

Since the rental GPS had proven worthless in that part of Bihar, we relied on human navigation, and together Petra and Pradeep directed us away from the village through a labyrinth of rutted roads and onto the highway, a task which seemed so simple with people who knew where they were going.

With impossible speed we were back on respectable macadam, heading north toward Patna. Once on the highway, Pradeep began pointing out features of the landscape, relieved to be outrunning what had happened, at least for now, and Petra was becoming gradually more buoyant, and as they talked, theorizing what Bodh Gaya would be like, she seemed excited, happy, and said she imagined that "pilgrims" from all over the world would be there, chanting and lighting incense.

"Perambulating," she informed us, "is when you walk around a stupa to pray. Sometimes people even crawl."

Despite living in a place his whole life, Pradeep was saying, he had never had the opportunity to go to this temple, even though he knew it to be famous.

After we turned off for the road to Bodh Gaya, the traffic was much denser, though no less swift: monster buses zoomed past the lumbering trucks and cautious motorcyclists, rickshaws puttered along the margins between pavement and compacted dirt, swerving around people walking, shouldering bags or babies, or just smoking and talking, people who were joined also by goats, sheep, chickens, an odd dog or cat, and cows wandering in loose packs, sometimes lazing, legs tucked under them on the side of the road, or else nosing lethargically through piles of garbage. A battered sign announced that this was the remnants of the old Grand Trunk Road.

We passed another sign for the back gate of Magadh University, and I thought briefly of what it might be like to teach in such a place, with its planted fields and shambolic homesteads, women bending to work in flooded rice paddies, men doing greasy moped repair, this interspersed the closer we got to Bodh Gaya with gleaming hotels, temple-white or fronted in green glass, and roadside stalls selling everything from prayer beads to onions to hot take-away meals. Aspects of it were not unlike Pennsylvania, in fact, although the stone monuments surrounding Bodh Gaya were dedicated to Buddha rather than the heroes of the Revolutionary or Civil Wars.

Where we were was pretty flat, and so soon I could make out the faintest suggestion of the temple complex in the distance. But the sun refracted through the windshield, catching me in the eye, a piercing that amplified the low-grade throbbing behind my forehead gash for a fraction of a second, and in that fraction the car ahead of us jerked then recovered, and kept going. I braked instinctively as a spotty afterimage floated in the aqueous part of my eyes, through which I could see a tiny cream-and-brown baby goat skidding on its side into the oncoming lane.

Petra saw it in the same instant and screamed for me to stop completely. I did, and before I could say anything she was unbelted and sprinting back down the road, flailing her long arms at vehicles that still kept coming. I jumped from the car as Pradeep unfolded himself from the back, and we hurled ourselves at the traffic, too.

By the time I got close, Petra was already kneeling over the goat, young enough to be indistinguishable from a lamb, pleading with people in the ragged crowd that had immediately and inevitably gathered. I thought of nothing but slowing down the traffic, and as Pradeep and I made ourselves known, a remarkable thing occurred: strangers who had been walking or conducting business nearby fanned out to help divert vehicles around Petra and the goat, wordlessly this happened, and soon a whole choking line was routed around the lane where Petra knelt, everyone slowed, an impossibility in India, rubbernecking as bystanders waved them on with low hand gestures.

I jogged over to find Petra stroking the neck of the baby goat, who had left a streak smeared on the road, bleating a screeching cry as she soothed him. I pushed through the people encircling her, and she looked up at me.

"He broke his little leg," she sighed, as though broken herself. "But otherwise he seems okay."

People from the crowd were offering opinions to one another and to Petra, saying in English it was better to be off the road. But Petra didn't budge. She kept asking, over and over: whose goat is this? Nobody seemed to know the owner. It was a rogue goat, apparently, motherless and ownerless, something Petra refused to accept knowing as she did that even in the seeming chaos of the roadside flow everybody kept tabs on whose livestock was whose; but as she kept insisting, the patience of the crowd wore thin, still nobody claiming any knowledge of this goat, and the impeded traffic was starting to honk more aggressively.

Finally two men elbowed in, shouting at her, and I made a conscious choice to spectate, to observe as she continued to handle what she had already been handling so well. They argued hotly for a few seconds, indignant or outraged, and she gave it right back to them, ending the conversation, in English, with "Absolutely not."

Her self-possession was something to note, and even those men who probably wanted to flame-broil the lamed goat were taken aback, in fact physically edged backward into the crowd, and Petra began saying things to the mass of people, pointing with one hand and still stroking the baby goat with the other. As she did so its bleating had calmed to a shallow pant, nestled in the crook of her arm and the road.

I've read enough novels to know it was one of those moments in which I should have experienced a flash of insight, as though witnessing this act of a girl who was part of myself and yet not myself at all would plug me into the vibrations of the cosmos. This didn't exactly happen, partly because I knew that the idea of the goat being nursed back to health and going on to live a bucolic life with a thousand grandgoats was girlish delusion. Beyond the realm of real possibility. But on the other hand, you never know, and sometimes it's okay to believe, so still I watched.

At her orders, someone handed Petra a couple of sticks of kindling, another a dirty rag, and she carefully made a splint around the goat's leg, cinching it tightly, then scooped him up as she might a human baby, I all the while immobile on the margins of the crowd. She nodded with her chin at a bearded man, saying to Pradeep and me that this man had agreed to take us to a veterinarian, and the people parted as she walked the goat to the Alto, where Pradeep held a door for her, and strangers still conducted traffic.

I was reminded of something from my childhood, realized viscerally that not only the goat but also I, Will Sorley, and even Petra would someday be gone, and felt that cold awareness of all living beings, the microbes pulsating unseen around my body, the palm trees swaying in view, the panicles of new grain just visible on the tips of rice stalks, bending for carbon dioxide and the ice crystals still suspended in the troposphere, all the elephants and cape buffalo I hadn't encountered in Africa, the uncatalogued creatures deep in the world's oceans and high in its remotest canopies. Would that all this and whatever else I didn't know were connected to that moment in time and space.

Instead, I watched Petra ease herself into the car, telling the shivering goat that everything was all right, finally looking up at me to say, "Hey, Dad, it's time to move."

VINE LEAVES PRESS

Enjoyed this book?
Go to *vineleavespress.com* to find more.
Subscribe to our newsletter:

Printed in the USA
CPSIA information can be obtained
at www.ICGtesting.com
LVHW032254081023
760534LV00010B/434